THE MOST UPDATED AIR FRYER COOKBOOK FOR BEGINNERS

3000 Days of Culinary Inspiration: Quick And Easy Recipes For Air Fryer. Become Low-Cost, Time Saving Cooking Expert

By
Harry Powers

© Copyright 2023 by - Harry Powers- All rights reserved.

This document is geared towards providing exact and reliable information in regards to the topic and issue covered. The publication is sold with the idea that the publisher is not required to render accounting, officially permitted, or otherwise, qualified services. If advice is necessary, legal or professional, a practiced individual in the profession should be ordered.

- From a Declaration of Principles which was accepted and approved equally by a Committee of the American Bar Association and a Committee of Publishers and Associations.

In no way is it legal to reproduce, duplicate, or transmit any part of this document in either electronic means or in printed format. Recording of this publication is strictly prohibited and any storage of this document is not allowed unless with written permission from the publisher. All rights reserved.

The information provided herein is stated to be truthful and consistent, in that any liability, in terms of inattention or otherwise, by any usage or abuse of any policies, processes, or directions contained within is the solitary and utter responsibility of the recipient reader. Under no circumstances will any legal responsibility or blame be held against the publisher for any reparation, damages, or monetary loss due to the information herein, either directly or indirectly.

Respective authors own all copyrights not held by the publisher.

The information herein is offered for informational purposes solely, and is universal as so. The presentation of the information is without contract or any type of guarantee assurance.

The trademarks that are used are without any consent, and the publication of the trademark is without permission or backing by the trademark owner. All trademarks and brands within this book are for clarifying purposes only and are the owned by the owners themselves, not affiliated with this document.

Contents

Introduction 9

Chapter 1: Introduction To Cooking With An Air Fryer 10

   1.1 Benefits Of Using Air Fryer 10

   1.2 Tips For The Proper Use Of Air Fryer 11

   1.3 Tips For Optimal Results With Air Fryer 12

   1.4 Tips On How To Choose The Air Fryer According To Personal Needs And Budget ... 13

Chapter 2: Breakfast Recipes 14

   2.1 Fluffy Cheesy Omelet 14

   2.2 Crust-Less Quiche 14

   2.3 Milky Scrambled Eggs 15

   2.4 Toasties and Sausage in Egg Pond 15

   2.5 Banana Bread 16

   2.6 Bacon Cups 17

   2.7 Ham Omelet 17

   2.8 Healthy Tofu Omelet 18

   2.9 Peanut Butter Banana Bread 18

   2.10 Savory French Toasts 19

   2.11 Potato Hash 20

   2.12 Pumpkin and Yogurt Bread 21

   2.13 Breakfast Soufflé 21

   2.14 Creamy Breakfast Egg Bowls 22

   2.15 Chicken Omelet 22

   2.16 Plain Bread 23

   2.17 Potato Pancakes 23

   2.18 Herbed Sweet Potato Hash 24

   2.19 Eggs, Ham, And Spinach 25

   2.20 Avocado Egg 25

   2.21 Zucchini Egg Nests 26

   2.22 Spinach Frittata 26

   2.23 Asparagus And Bacon Spears 27

   2.24 Bacon Egg Muffins 27

   2.25 Cheesy Breakfast Soufflé 28

   2.26 Japanese Omelette 29

   2.27 Feta Breakfast 29

   2.28 Cinnamon Toast 30

   2.29 Salmon And Cheese Frittata 30

   2.30 Mushroom And Cheese Omelette 31

   2.31 Baked Cheesy Eggs 32

   2.32 English Style Breakfast 32

   2.33 Tapioca Cheesy Bread 33

   2.34 Breakfast Potatoes 34

   2.35 Polenta Bites 34

   2.36 Eggs And Ham Muffins 35

   2.37 Eggs In A Bowl Of Bread 36

   2.38 Breakfast Muffin Sandwich 36

   2.39 Chipolatas With Eggs 37

   2.40 Breakfast Omelet 37

   2.41 Breakfast Tortilla Wraps 38

   2.42 Banana And Chocolate Chip Muffins .. 39

   2.43 Savory Breakfast Muffins 39

   2.44 Blueberries Oats Muffin 40

   2.45 English Muffins Pizza 41

Chapter 3: Family Favorites 42

   3.1 Chicken Sausage And Broccoli Casserole 42

   3.2 Chicken Ham Casserole 42

   3.3 Corn And Bell Pepper Casserole 43

   3.4 Grits And Asparagus Casserole 44

   3.5 Hillbilly Broccoli Cheese Casserole 44

   3.6 Fried Fish Sandwich 45

   3.7 Grilled Tomato And Pimiento Cheese Sandwiches 46

   3.8 Raisin Bread Monte Cristo 46

   3.9 Fried Banana And Peanut Butter Sandwiches 47

   3.10 Saucy Garam Masala Fish 47

   3.11 Golden Cod Fish Nuggets 48

   3.12 Pork Belly Bites 49

   3.13 Glazed Pork Belly 49

3.14 Sweet Glazed Ham 50
3.15 Herbed Beef 50
3.16 Ribeye Steak 51
3.17 Chicken Nuggets 52
3.18 Alfredo Chicken 53
3.19 Tandoori Chicken Thighs 53
3.20 Chicken Meatballs 54
3.21 Fruit Pudding 55
3.22 Pecan Strawberry Rhubarb Cobbler ... 55
3.23 Lemon Biscuits 56
3.24 Red Velvet Cookies 57
3.25 Walnut Chocolate Cookies 58

Chapter 4: Fast And Easy Everyday Recipes 59

4.1 Air Fried Broccoli 59
4.2 Air Fried Green Tomatoes 59
4.3 Bacon And Green Beans 60
4.4 Bacon-Wrapped Beef Hot Dog ...60
4.5 Baked Cheese Sandwich 61
4.6 Baked Chorizo Scotch Eggs 61
4.7 Beef Bratwursts 62
4.8 Buttery Sweet Potatoes 62
4.9 Carrot And Celery Croquettes ...63
4.10 Cheesy Baked Grits 64
4.11 Serrano Chili Toast 64
4.12 Cheesy Potato Patties 65
4.13 Cheesy Sausage Balls 65
4.14 Garlicky Baked Cherry Tomatoes 66
4.15 Garlicky Knots 66
4.16 Garlicky Zoodles 67
4.17 Golden Salmon And Carrot Croquettes 68
4.18 Chicken Fingers 68
4.19 Salmon Fritters 69
4.20 Chicken Strips 69

Chapter 5: Poultry Recipes 71

5.1 Herbed Fried Chicken 71
5.2 BBQ Fried Chicken 71
5.3 Chicken Nuggets 72
5.4 Greek Garlic Chicken 73
5.5 Creamy Garlic Chicken Thighs ...74
5.6 Lemon Garlic Chicken Thighs ...74
5.7 Brussels and Garlic Chicken 75
5.8 Creamy Brussels And Garlic Chicken 76
5.9 Garlic Parmesan Chicken Thighs 77
5.10 Black Pepper Chicken Thighs ..77
5.11 Spicy Chicken Strips 78
5.12 Turkey Parmesan Meatballs 79
5.13 Thanksgiving Turkey 79
5.14 Cheesy Chicken Sausage Rolls ..80
5.15 Crumbed Chicken Schnitzel 81
5.16 Japanese Chicken Tenders 81
5.17 Chicken Enchiladas 82
5.18 Chicken Quesadilla 83
5.19 Cosmic Wings 83
5.20 Chicken Parmesan Meatballs ...84
5.21 BBQ Chicken Drumsticks 84
5.22 Crispy Chicken Tenders 85
5.23 Turkey Meatballs 86
5.24 Asian Chicken Wings 86
5.25 Greek Chicken Meatballs 87
5.26 Orange And Maple Glazed Chicken 88
5.27 Apple Chicken With Blue Cheese 88
5.28 Black Pepper Chicken Wings ..89
5.29 BBQ Chicken Thighs 89
5.30 Chicken Sticks 90
5.31 Tandoori Chicken Legs 91
5.32 Mustard Chicken Wings 91
5.33 Chicken With Beans And Chili 92
5.34 Black Pepper Chicken Legs 93
5.35 Chicken Pizza 93
5.36 Crispy Chicken Wings 94
5.37 Spicy Crunchy Chicken 95
5.38 Garlic Chicken 95

5.39 Almond Crusted Chicken 96
5.40 Turkey and Tomatoes Patties 97
5.41 Chicken Patties 97
5.42 Zesty And Spiced Chicken 98
5.43 Siracha-Honey Wings 99
5.44 Parmesan Chicken Tenders 99
5.45 Hot Buffalo Wings 100

Chapter 6: Beef, Pork And Lamb Recipes 101

6.1 Air-Fried Meatloaf 101
6.2 Ground Beef Wellington 102
6.3 Taco Twists 103
6.4 Southern Style Fried Pork Chops 103
6.5 Honey And Mustard Pork Meatballs ... 104
6.6 Pork Chops With Broccoli 105
6.7 Air Fryer Pork Tenderloin 105
6.8 Salt And Pepper Pork Chops 106
6.9 Jamaican Jerk Pork Chops 107
6.10 Juicy Pork Chops 108
6.11 Boneless Pork Chop 108
6.12 Gingery Pork Meatballs 109
6.13 Mustard Pork Chops 110
6.14 Pork Belly 110
6.15 Pork Satay 111
6.16 Beef Ribs 111
6.17 Steak Cubes 112
6.18 Teriyaki Beef 113
6.19 Tenderloin Filets 113
6.20 Beef Steak 114
6.21 Thai Style Beef 114
6.22 Garlic Butter Flank Steak 115
6.23 Paprika Beef 115
6.24 Broccoli And Beef 116
6.25 Pork Tenderloin 117
6.26 Soy Pork Ribs 117
6.27 Bacon Cauliflower With Cheddar Cheese 118
6.28 Pork Bacon And Eggs Pockets 119
6.29 Garlic Rosemary Pork Chops 119
6.30 Chinese Style Pork Chops 120
6.31 Herbed Lamb Chops 121
6.32 Sweet Pork Barbecue 121
6.33 Perfect Pork Ribs 122
6.34 Pork Meat And Cabbage Rolls 123
6.35 Asian Flavored Pork Chops 123
6.36 Steak Cubes 124
6.37 Stuffed Beef Rolls 125
6.38 Mayo Pork 125
6.39 Honey Garlic Chops 126
6.40 Teriyaki Lamb Chops 127
6.41 Lamb Meatballs 127
6.42 Black Pepper Beef 128
6.43 Pork And Peanuts Mix 128
6.44 Rubbed Steaks 129
6.45 Milky Lamb 130

Chapter 7: Fish And Seafood 131

7.1 Crispy Salmon 131
7.2 Spicy Crunchy Salmon 131
7.3 Cajun Salmon 132
7.4 Black Pepper Parmesan Salmon 132
7.5 Tuna Stuffed Mushrooms 133
7.6 Crispy Salmon 134
7.7 Tuna Cakes 134
7.8 Salmon Cakes 135
7.9 Red Hot Tuna Cakes 136
7.10 Cajun Tuna Cakes 136
7.11 Lemon Tuna Cakes 137
7.12 Cod Fish Sticks 138
7.13 Tuna Sticks 138
7.14 Crunchy Garlic Salmon 139
7.15 Pistachio Crusted Salmon 139
7.16 Creamy Salmon 140
7.17 Ham Tilapia 141

7.18 Salmon In Garlic Sauce 141
7.19 Rice Flour Coated Shrimp.................. 142
7.20 Cajun Fish Patties With Cheese.......... 142
7.21 Spicy Shrimps................................... 143
7.22 Mustard Salmon 143
7.23 Creamy Shrimps 144
7.24 Lemon Parmesan Tilapia 144
7.25 Lean And Green Salmon.................... 145
7.26 Fish Nuggets 146
7.27 Mahi Mahi With Brown Butter 147
7.28 Spicy Scallops 147
7.29 Classic French Mussels 148
7.30 Cheesy Baked Mussels 148
7.31 Herbed Mussels 149
7.32 Crispy Crab Claws............................. 149
7.33 Cajun Catfish 150
7.34 Spicy Shrimp Patties 151
7.35 Fish Burgers...................................... 151
7.36 Salmon Steaks................................... 152
7.37 Sweet Cod Fillets 153
7.38 Balsamic Cod 153
7.39 Buttery Garlic Shrimps 154
7.40 Tilapia Nuggets 155
7.41 Lemon Pepper Shrimps...................... 155
7.42 Shrimp Kabobs 156
7.43 Crab Croquettes 157
7.44 Cajun Cod.. 157
7.45 Italian Fish Sticks 158

Chapter 8: Snacks And Appetizers 159

8.1 Air-Fryer Pickles................................. 159
8.2 Siracha Spring Rolls 159
8.3 Buffalo Cauliflower Bites 160
8.4 Calzones.. 161
8.5 Sweet Potato Tots 162
8.6 Hot Jalapenos Nachos 162
8.7 Sweet Potato Chips 163

8.8 Rosemary And Garlic Brussels Sprouts 164
8.9 Loaded Potatoes..................................164
8.10 Crispy French Fries...........................165
8.11 Corn Dog Bites..................................165
8.12 Kale Chips..166
8.13 Avocado Fries 166
8.14 Cheese Sticks....................................167
8.15 Apple Chips......................................167
8.16 Pumpkin Fries 168
8.17 Pepper Poppers.................................169
8.18 Turkey Croquettes 169
8.19 Zucchini Croquettes..........................170
8.20 Balsamic Zucchini Slices.................. 171
8.21 Buttery Corn 171
8.22 Cheese Sticks....................................172
8.23 Garlic Bread......................................172
8.24 Herbed Crackers 173
8.25 Broccoli Bites...................................173
8.26 Turkey Nachos 174
8.27 Cauliflower Tots 174
8.28 Turmeric Carrots 175
8.29 Eggplant Chips..................................175
8.30 Cheddar Muffins 176
8.31 Tortilla Chips....................................177
8.32 Potato Nuggets..................................177
8.33 Cheese Bread....................................178
8.34 Balsamic Eggplant Chips...................178
8.35 Zucchini Muffins 179
8.36 Chicken Vegetable Croquettes 179
8.37 Garlic Corn 180
8.38 Spinach Chips................................... 180
8.39 Waffle Cheese Fries 181
8.40 Jicama Fries......................................182
8.41 Cornbread...182
8.42 Tortilla..183
8.43 Skinny Pumpkin Chips......................183

8.44 Palm Trees Holder 184
8.45 Air Fried Ripe Plantains 184

Chapter 9: Vegetables And Sides 186
9.1 Asparagus And Potatoes 186
9.2 Garlic Roasted Carrots 186
9.3 Eggplant Cutlets 187
9.4 Roasted Shishito Peppers 187
9.5 Roasted Cherry Tomatoes.................... 188
9.5 Creamy Potatoes 188
9.7 Roasted Onions 189
9.8 Garlic Roasted Potato Wedges 189
9.9 Radish Chips....................................... 189
9.10 Carrot Chips 190
9.11 Vegan Pasta Chips 190
9.12 Creamy Corns 191
9.13 Tofu Nuggets 191
9.14 Roasted Squash Grits 192
9.15 Zucchini Boats.................................. 193
9.16 Mexican Style Corn On The Cob 193
9.17 Onion Rings...................................... 194
9.18 Roasted Pineapple 194
9.19 Potato Wedges 195
9.20 Herbed Potatoes 195
9.21 Acorn Squash 196
9.22 Creamy Beets.................................... 196
9.23 Salsa Zucchini................................... 197
9.24 Spicy Avocado Mix 197
9.25 Spicy Black Beans............................. 198
9.26 Cajun Tomatoes And Peppers 198
9.27 Herbed Tomatoes 199
9.28 Lemon Tomatoes 199
9.29 Zucchini Sauté 200
9.30 Cumin Eggplant Mix.......................... 200

Chapter 10: Vegetarian Mains 201
10.1 Mixed Veggies Pancakes 201
10.2 Vegan Coconut French Toasts........... 201
10.3 Delicious Lemon Tofu........................ 202
10.4 Crispy Potato Nuggets 203
10.5 Herbed and Spiced Baked Tofu Fries 203
10.6 Mushroom Pizza................................ 204
10.7 Vegan Air Fryer Cold Soup 205
10.8 Rosemary And Garlic Sweet Potatoes Wedges 205
10.9 Vegetable Fries 206
10.10 Easy Rocket Pancakes 207
10.11 Classic Falafel................................. 207
10.12 Vegan Peanut Noodles..................... 208
10.13 Mustard Cabbage Rolls 209
10.14 Vegetable Fried Rice 210
10.15 Cauliflower Poppers 211
10.16 Vegetable Cheesy Pizza................... 211
10.17 Spinach Casserole 212
10.18 Vegetable Egg Casserole 213
10.19 Cheesy Broccoli Fritters 214
10.20 Cheesy Carrot Fritters 214
10.21 Stromboli 215
10.22 Potato Fritters................................ 216
10.23 Zucchini Lasagna 216
10.24 Extra Cheese Pizza 217
10.25 Broccoli And Grits 218

Chapter 11: Dessert Recipes................ 219
11.1 Carrot brownies 219
11.2 Yogurt cake 219
11.3 Chocolate ramekins 220
11.4 Grapes cake...................................... 220
11.5 Pear pudding.................................... 221
11.6 Lime Cake.. 221
11.7 Pear stew 222
11.8 Carrot Coffee Cake............................ 222
11.9 Strawberry Shortcake 223
11.10 Chocolate brownies......................... 224
11.11 Orange Cake 224
11.12 Peanut Butter Cupcake.................... 225

11.13 Orange Cornmeal Cake 225
11.14 Chocolate Cupcake 226
11.15 Cinnamon Puffs 227
11.16 Apple Cupcakes 227
11.17 Orange Cake 228
11.18 Egg Pudding 229
11.19 Pear Pudding 229
11.20 Lemon Shortbread 230
11.21 Chocolate Walnuts Brownies 230
11.22 Fudge Brownies 231
11.23 Strawberry And Cream Mug Cake 232
11.24 Quick Brownies 232
11.25 Coffee Cake 233
11.26 Apricot And Raisin Cake 234
11.27 Pineapple Cake 235
11.28 Three Ingredient Cake 235
11.29 Eggless Cake 236
11.30 Chocolate Oatmeal Cookies 237

Chapter 12: Guide To Cleaning And Maintenance Of Air Fryer 238

12.1 The Importance of Cleaning and Maintaining Your Air Fryer 238
12.2 Cleaning Tips for Your Air Fryer 238
12.3 Maintenance of Air Fryer 238

Chapter 13: Weekly Cooking Plan 239

13.1 Week 1 239
13.2 Week 2 240
13.3 Week 3 241
13.4 Week 4 242

Chapter 14: Food Storage 244

14.1 Containers And Packaging Recommendations: 244
14.2 Cooling Procedure Before Storage 244
14.3 Refrigerator Storage 244
14.4 Freezer Storage 245
14.5 Labelling And Dating 245
14.6 Reheating And Annealing 246

Chapter 15: Sauce Recipes 247

15.1 Jelly Chili Li'l Smokies 247
15.2 S'mores Dip 247
15.3 Fry Sauce 248
15.4 Bolognese Sauce 248
15.5 Roasted Hot Sauce 249

Chapter 16: Allergen Free Recipes 250

16.1 Buffalo Broccoli Bites 250
16.2 Bacon Avocado Fries 251
16.3 Cajun Cod 251
16.4 Lemon Pepper Cod 252
16.5 Chicken Fajitas 252

Conclusion 254

Introduction

Congratulations on starting your journey toward easy cooking with the most updated Air fryer cookbook. Now, all you have to do is press a button to make the food. Does all of this sound like a way to make money? Yes, it's 100% true. It's cool to be in style right now to air fry food.

It's hard for people who are new to cooking to make healthy meals at home that taste great.
Also, many of us find it hard to enjoy home-cooked food because our lives are so busy.
Since this is the case, most of us eat bad food and fast food, which can lead to health problems like diabetes, obesity, and high blood pressure.

Don't worry—this guide is good for everyone who wants to eat less fat food to stay healthy. If you have trouble making meals that are good for your fitness and health, the air fryer is a great appliance that will help you out.

The air fryer isn't like other kitchen appliances because it can easily do more than one type of cooking. Most of the nutrients in food are lost when it is deep-fried. The air fryer, on the other hand, keeps the nutrients in the food and keeps the fat content very low without changing the texture or taste.

We've talked about meals that are broken up into different groups in this amazing guide. We have covered almost all types of recipes in this amazing cookbook, which are divided into many categories. The recipes in this cookbook are not just for beginner cooks; they are also ideal for anyone who wishes to develop healthier eating habits, lose weight, cook less fussy food, and enjoy cooking without using their hands.

The recipes are categorized into chapters such as Breakfast, Vegetarian Meals, Snacks and Appetizers, Poultry, Fish and Seafood, Beef, Lamb and Pork, Allergen Free Recipes, Desserts, and more.

Chapter 1: Introduction To Cooking With An Air Fryer

The air fryer has gained significant popularity due to its numerous health advantages and impressive functionalities.

The air fryer is a unique appliance that utilizes hot air to cook food. If you want an alternative to frying, the air fryer is the sole answer that provides a tenderly cooked dish with a crispy outside. Air fryers utilize the efficient principle of Rapid Air Technology to cook meals to perfection. Most air fryers employ the Maillard effect by circulating hot air at temperatures above 400 degrees Fahrenheit over food coated with oil. With one single gadget, you can effortlessly cook crispy fries, wings, pastries, and steak.

Since the air fryer's sales reached their highest point, several studies and research have been undertaken asserting that air fryers are the optimal appliance for creating a healthier alternative to fries, as they use 80 percent less oil and fat.

An argument that has been researched is that air fryers are more appropriate for frying than traditional techniques, making them a good choice for preparing nutritious meals.

As beginners, individuals may be concerned that air frying might result in a reduction of texture or crispness due to the limited amount of oil coating on the food. A study emphasizes that reducing the amount of oil used in cooking does not necessarily result in a loss of texture in food.

The air fryer can effectively aid in achieving weight reduction objectives by facilitating the preparation of meals. Ariana Cucuzza, a registered dietician at the Center for Functional Medicine, states that utilizing an air fryer for cooking can result in a reduction of calorie consumption by as much as 80%.

Certain fryer models include additional functionalities beyond air frying, such as dehydrating, grilling, baking, broiling, roasting, and reheating. Upon acquiring this appliance, you will be astounded by its remarkable efficacy.

Now, let us look at its potential benefits.

1.1 Benefits Of Using Air Fryer

Healthier Cooking

The biggest health benefit of air fryers is that they use far less oil than deep fryers. Much of the oil drains away without being absorbed by the meal. You eat fewer fat and calories.

These fryers use convection to cause the Maillard reaction, which browns food. This makes the dish delicious while having less fat and improves its look.

Crispier Food

One of the best things about air fryers is that they make meals crispy without oil. They do this by convection-heating food in a rack with super-hot air on each side or perforated basket.

Air fryers are ideal for crispy onion rings, French fries, fish sticks, and other fried meals.

An air fryer crisps food better than a convection oven because it can cover all sides and the frying basket drains grease.

Faster Cooking

Air fryers cook quicker than most other techniques due to their design. The fryer circulates high heat, speeding up frying.

Many models don't need preheating or take a short period. Depending on the meal, cooking time might be 30-50% faster than in a standard oven.

Easy to clean

Air fryers are cleaner than deep fryers. The cooking technique requires little oil, which creates most of the mess.

Air fryers are simplest to clean with a soft bristle brush, dishwashing detergent, and water.

Safe to use

Air fryers are safer because they're self-contained and use less hot fat. To prevent food from burning, machines switch off after the timer.

More adaptable

Air fryers can cook most deep-fried items as well or better. There are various recipes to try. Amazingly, baked things, veggies, and steaks work.

Don't spread Odor and Heat

Air fryers retain heat, so they don't heat up your kitchen like ovens. This characteristic is handy in smaller homes and apartments. Low oil use means no harsh scents when deep frying.

Compacter

No larger than toasters, air fryers are little kitchen appliances. They work well in tiny kitchens. They may be used on a campground or in an RV or camper because they are portable.

Affordable

Air fryers are surprisingly affordable for their versatility. Online vendors sell them for $50–$150. It is recommended to choose quality over cheap models, even if it costs more.

Easy to Operate

Air fryers are easy to operate and require minimal supervision. Set the time and temperature, put the food in the basket, and let the fryer work.

1.2 Tips For The Proper Use Of Air Fryer

If you have never used an air fryer before, here are the ten best tips you should know to make cooking better.

- In the kitchen, put the air fryer on a flat surface. To let the hot air from the air fryer escape, the surface should be level with the air fryer and there should be a space of about 5 inches behind it.
- It is very important to heat up the device before you start cooking. You can quickly heat it up for two minutes before using it.
- It's important to coat and bread whatever you're cooking in an air fryer. The food needs to have egg, oil, flour or bread bits on it. The hard breading is very important because the air fryer fan blows away most of the food's top layers.
- The right parts should be used in the air fryer so that they fit properly in the air fryer pan.
- Alum foil bands should be used to get the food out of the basket. It also makes it safer and easy to lift food. It keeps you from getting burned by chance.
- You must load the drawer in the basket of air fryer while cooking the fatty foods so that the grease doesn't get too hot and turn into smoke.
- It's important to flip the food over while it's cooking so that it cooks everywhere.
- It's very important not to put too much food in the basket.

- Take the basket out of the drawer before you take out the food. It's important to do this because if you turn the basket over in the box, all the grease will fall into the serving plate with the food.
- After the food is done cooking, clean the box and the pan. Then, wash the air fryer when it's cool.

1.3 Tips For Optimal Results With Air Fryer

Less oil is better

When you air fry, you get the crispiness of deep-frying without all the extra oil. You will still need a little oil to get the best crispiness, but it's really a case of "less is more." Also, make sure you use oil with a greater smoke point. For the best results, stay away from olive oil and use veggie, canola, rice bran, or even peanut oil.

If you want your food to be extra crispy, you can lightly spray the food inside your air fryer about halfway through the cooking time.

Put some grease in your basket

No one wants to have to lift their food apart from the bottom of their air fryer basket, so it's very important to grease it, especially for foods that tend to stick.

Do not overcrowd

This one is very important if you want the signature crispiness. Avoid cramming food together because it stops hot air from moving around. Instead, try to leave a lot of space around the food so that the hot air can spread it out evenly and make it crispy and crunchy.

Give it a shake

One of the best things you can do to learn how to use an air fryer is to shake the basket every so often while it's cooking. It's nothing crazy; just give the food a few good shakes while it's cooking to really move it around and make sure that every bite has the same, crispy skin. Take the basket out of the machine before shaking it. Only shake the basket rather than the whole machine. You could also flip your food over halfway through cooking to help it brown more evenly.

Get it clean

Another great thing about these little miracles is that they are very simple to clean. Now, who doesn't love that? But to get the best effects, you should clean it every time you use it. It only takes a quick wipe to get rid of any extra oil and dirt in the basket. The long run, it will save you time and make your device last longer.

Different recipes have different cooking times

Cooking times are very different. In the air fryer, something that might take 15 to 20 minutes in the oven cooks in a lot less time. If you don't want to burn your food, you should always check on your things as soon as possible.

Taking out the basket doesn't change the flavor or the cooking time, so keep an eye on things to make sure they're cooked uniformly and not too quickly.

Spend money on a thermometer

If you're going to cook meat in your air fryer, you need to make sure the temperature inside is right. The air fryer works so fast that meat can look perfectly golden on the outside but still be raw on the inside. Get a meat thermometer so you don't have to cut into the meat every time you want to know if it's done.

1.4 Tips On How To Choose The Air Fryer According To Personal Needs And Budget

If you want to buy an amazing air fryer, it can be hard to find one that fits your needs and your price because there are so many brands on the market that make great goods.

Before you buy an air fryer, you should think about your own wants, the size, the features, and your budget. What works for you might not work for everyone else, so be smart about what you buy. Here is a list of the best air fryers for 2023:

Air fryers	Functions or Buttons	Capacity	List Price Comparison
Cuisinart Air fryer, Convection Toaster Air fryer, Silver	Dial Buttons	16 liter	$199.99 or above
Instant Vortex Pro 9-in-1 Air Fryer Air fryer	LED	10 Quarts	1$49 or above
Ninja Foodi Tender Crisp Pressure Cooker, OP300	Automatic		$117.8
Instant Pot 6-Qt	Buttons	6-qt. cap	$119.95 or above
Philips Air fryer, Advance Turbo Star, Digital, Black, HD9641/96	Buttons or LED	0.82 Liters	$219.95
Elite Gourmet EAF0201BG Personal	Dial Button	0.68 Liter	$47.99
COSORI Air Fryer Max XL	LED	5.8 QT	$99.98

Chapter 2: Breakfast Recipes

2.1 Fluffy Cheesy Omelet

Preparation time: 10 mins

Cooking time: 15 mins

Servings: 2

Level of difficulty: Easy

Ingredients:

- 4 eggs
- ¼ tsp. soy sauce
- 1/8 cup grated cheddar cheese
- 1 large onion, sliced
- Cooking spray
- 1/8 cup grated mozzarella cheese
- Black pepper, to taste

Instructions:

- Use a cooking spray to grease a pan and preheat the air fryer to 360°F.
- In a bowl, whisk together eggs, black pepper, and soy sauce.
- Add onions to the greased pan and cook for ten minutes in a preheated air fryer.
- Now evenly cover the cooked onion with egg mixture and top it with cheese.
- Cook the omelet for another 5 minutes and then serve.

Nutritional facts per serving: Calories: 216 Kcal; Carbs: 8 g; Fat: 14 g; Protein: 15 g.

2.2 Crust-Less Quiche

Preparation time: 5 mins

Cooking time: 30 mins

Servings: 2

Level of difficulty: Easy

Ingredients:

- 4 eggs
- Salt, to taste
- ½ cup tomatoes, chopped
- ¼ cup onion, chopped
- 1 cup Gouda cheese, shredded
- ½ cup milk

Instructions:

- Preheat the air fryer to 340°F and lightly grease two ramekins.
- In a dish, mix all the ingredients together and then pour the mixture into prepared ramekins.
- Put them in the air fryer and cook for 30 minutes.
- Serve warm and enjoy.

Nutritional facts per serving: Calories: 348 Kcal; Carbs: 8 g; Fat: 24 g; Protein: 26 g.

2.3 Milky Scrambled Eggs

Preparation time: 10 mins

Cooking time: 9 mins

Servings: 2

Level of difficulty: Easy

Ingredients:

- 4 eggs
- Salt and black pepper, to taste
- ¾ cup milk
- ½ cup grated Parmesan cheese
- 8 grape tomatoes, halved
- 1 tbsp. butter

Instructions:

- Preheat the air fryer to 360 ° F and grease an air fryer pan with butter.
- In a bowl, mix milk, eggs, black pepper and salt together using a whisk.
- Put the egg mixture in the pan and then put it in the air fryer.
- Cook the eggs for 6 minutes and then add the top them with cheese and grape tomatoes and stir them in.
- Cook for another 3 minutes and then serve.

Nutritional facts per serving: Calories: 351 Kcal; Carbs: 25 g; Fat: 22 g; Protein: 26 g.

2.4 Toasties and Sausage in Egg Pond

Preparation time: 10 mins

Cooking time: 22 mins

Servings: 2

Level of difficulty: Easy

Ingredients:

- 3 eggs
- 1/8 cup grated mozzarella cheese
- 1 bread slice, cut into sticks

- ¼ cup cream
- 2 cooked sausages, sliced
- 1/8 cup grated Parmesan cheese

Instructions:

- Preheat the air fryer to 365°F and lightly grease two ramekins.
- Mix the eggs and cream together in a bowl, and then pour the mixture into the ramekins.
- Add the sliced sausages and bread sticks to the egg mix, and then sprinkle cheese on top.
- Put the ramekins in the basket of the air fryer and cook for 22 minutes.
- Serve hot and enjoy.

Nutritional facts per serving: Calories: 261 Kcal; Carbs: 4 g; Fat: 18 g; Protein: 18 g.

2.5 Banana Bread

Preparation time: 10 mins

Cooking time: 20 mins

Servings: 8

Level of difficulty: Intermediate

Ingredients:

- 1 1/3 cups flour
- 1 tsp. baking powder
- 1 tsp. salt
- 1 tsp. baking soda
- 3 bananas, peeled and sliced
- ½ cup milk
- 1 tsp. ground cinnamon
- 2/3 cup sugar
- ½ cup olive oil

Instructions:

- Grease a loaf pan and preheat the Air fryer to 330°F.
- Combine dry and wet ingredients to form dough.
- Put the dough in the loaf pan and place it in the air fryer basket.
- Remove the pan from air fryer after 20 minutes.
- Slice the bread and serve warm.

Nutritional facts per serving: Calories: 295 Kcal; Carbs: 44 g; Fat: 13 g; Protein: 3 g.

2.6 Bacon Cups

Preparation time: 10 mins

Cooking time: 15 mins

Servings: 6

Level of difficulty: Intermediate

Ingredients:

- 6 bacon slices
- 1 scallion, chopped
- 6 bread slices
- 6 eggs
- 3 tbsp. chopped green bell pepper
- 2 tbsp. low-fat mayonnaise

Instructions:

- Pre-heat the Air fryer to 375°F and coat 6 muffin cups with cooking spray.
- Insert one bacon slice into each muffin cup.
- Cut bread pieces with a circular cookie cutter and layer over bacon slices.
- Evenly top the muffin cups with scallions, bell pepper, and mayonnaise, then break one egg in each muffin cup.
- Cook for 15 minutes in the Air Fryer.
- Serve warm.

Nutritional facts per serving: Calories: 260 Kcal; Carbs: 7 g; Fat: 18 g; Protein: 16 g.

2.7 Ham Omelet

Preparation time: 10 mins

Cooking time: 30 mins

Servings: 2

Level of difficulty: Intermediate

Ingredients:

- 4 eggs
- 4 small tomatoes, chopped
- 1 onion, chopped
- 2 tbsp. cheddar cheese
- 2 ham slices
- Salt and black pepper, to taste

Instructions:

- Grease an Air fryer pan and preheat the air fryer to 390°F.

- Cook tomatoes in the Air fryer for 10 minutes.
- Cook onion and ham in a nonstick pan over medium heat.
- Transfer the cooked ham and onions to the Air fryer pan after 5 minutes of stirring.
- In a dish, whisk eggs with black pepper and salt and pour them into the Air fryer pan.
- Cook for 15 minutes at 335°F in the air fryer.
- Serve warm.

Nutritional facts per serving: Calories: 255 Kcal; Carbs: 14 g; Fat: 14 g; Protein: 19 g.

2.8 Healthy Tofu Omelet

Preparation time: 10 mins

Cooking time: 30 mins

Servings: 2

Level of difficulty: Intermediate

Ingredients:

- 2 tsp. olive oil
- 3 eggs, beaten
- 12 oz. silken tofu, sliced
- ¼ onion, chopped
- 1 garlic clove, minced
- 1 tbsp. chives, chopped
- Salt and black pepper, to taste

Instructions:

- Use olive oil to coat the surface of an Air fryer pan and preheat the air fryer to 355 °F.
- Add garlic and onion to greased pan and cook for 4 minutes.
- Season mushrooms, tofu, and chives with salt and black pepper.
- Pour beaten eggs over tofu mixture and cook them for 25 minutes.
- Eggs should be poked twice in between 25 minutes.
- Serve warm.

Nutritional facts per serving: Calories: 248 Kcal; Carbs: 6 g; Fat: 15 g; Protein: 20 g.

2.9 Peanut Butter Banana Bread

Preparation time: 15 mins

Cooking time: 40 mins

Servings: 6

Level of difficulty: Expert

Ingredients:
- 1 cup + 1 tbsp. all-purpose flour
- 1¼ tsp. baking powder
- 2 tbsp. sour cream
- ¾ cup walnuts, chopped
- 2 ripe bananas, peeled and mashed
- 1 large egg
- 1/3 cup granulated sugar
- ¼ tsp. salt
- 2 tbsp. creamy peanut butter
- ¼ cup canola oil
- 1 tsp. vanilla extract

Instructions:
- Grease a non-stick baking pan and preheat the Air fryer to 330°F.
- Mix flour, salt and baking powder in a bowl.
- In a bowl, mix egg, canola oil, vanilla, sugar, peanut butter, and sour cream.
- Blend bananas in wet ingredients until fully mixed.
- Now add the flour mixture into wet ingredients then gently fold in the walnuts.
- After mixing, evenly distribute the mixture in the prepared baking dish.
- Place the dish in an Air fryer basket and bake for 40 minutes.
- Transfer the bread to a wire rack to cool from the Air fryer.
- Slice the bread and serve.

Nutritional facts per serving: Calories: 384 Kcal; Carbs: 39 g; Fat: 3 g; Protein: 9 g.

2.10 Savory French Toasts

Preparation time: 10 mins
Cooking time: 4 mins
Servings: 2
Level of difficulty: Intermediate

Ingredients:
- ¼ cup chickpea flour
- 4 bread slices
- 2 tsp. finely chopped green chili
- Salt, to taste
- Water, as required
- ¼ tsp. ground turmeric

- 3 tbsp. finely chopped onion
- ¼ tsp. ground cumin
- ½ tsp. red chili powder

Instructions:

- Preheat the Air fryer to 375°F and prepare an air fryer pan with foil paper.
- Combine all ingredients except for the bread pieces in a large bowl and mix.
- Spread the mixture on both sides of the bread pieces and place in the pan of Air fryer.
- Cook for the toasts for 4 minutes, and serve.

Nutritional facts per serving: Calories: 151 Kcal; Carbs: 26 g; Fat: 2 g; Protein: 6 g.

2.11 Potato Hash

Preparation time: 10 mins
Cooking time: 42 mins
Servings: 8
Level of difficulty: Expert
Ingredients:

- 2 tsp. butter, melted
- 1 medium onion, chopped
- 5 eggs, beaten
- 1½ lb. russet potatoes, cubed
- ½ green bell pepper, chopped
- ½ tsp. dried thyme, crushed
- Salt and black pepper, to taste

Instructions:

- Pre-heat the Air fryer to 390°F and grease the pan with melted butter.
- Cook bell pepper and onion in Air fryer for 5 minutes.
- Add potatoes, salt, thyme, salt, and black pepper in the pan and simmer for 30 minutes.
- Meanwhile over medium heat, heat a greased pan and add the beaten eggs.
- Remove from pan after 1 minute per side.
- Slice the prepared egg into pieces and place them in the Air fryer pan.
- Now cook for another 5 minutes and serve warm.

Nutritional facts per serving: Calories: 229 Kcal; Carbs: 30 g; Fat: 7 g; Protein: 10 g.

2.12 Pumpkin and Yogurt Bread

Preparation time: 10 mins

Cooking time: 15 mins

Servings: 4

Level of difficulty: Intermediate

Ingredients:

- 2 large eggs
- 6 tbsp. oats
- 4 tbsp. plain Greek yogurt
- 2 tbsp. vanilla essence
- 6 tbsp. banana flour
- 8 tbsp. pumpkin puree
- 4 tbsp. honey
- Pinch of ground nutmeg

Instructions:

- Preheat the Air fryer to 360°F and grease a loaf pan.
- Beat all ingredients except oats in a bowl with a hand mixer until smooth.
- Add oats and combine well.
- Put the mixture in the prepared loaf pan and place it in basket of air fryer.
- Cook for around 15 minutes and then remove from the Air fryer.
- Allow the bread to cool on a wire rack, and then slice it before serving.

Nutritional facts per serving: Calories: 212 Kcal; Carbs: 36 g; Fat: 3 g; Protein: 6 g.

2.13 Breakfast Soufflé

Preparation time: 10 mins

Cooking time: 8 mins

Servings: 4

Level of difficulty: Easy

Ingredients:

- 4 eggs, whisk
- 4 tbsp. heavy cream
- 2 tbsp. chives, minced
- pinch of crushed red pepper
- 2 tbsp. parsley, chopped
- Salt and black pepper, to taste

Instructions:

- Combine eggs, vinegar, oil, chili pepper, heavy cream, chives and parsley in a bowl. Mix well and divide the mixture into 4 soufflé bowls.
- Broil soufflés at 350°F for 8 minutes in the air fryer.
- Serve hot and enjoy.

Nutritional facts per serving: Calories: 300 Kcal; Carbs: 15 g; Fat: 7 g; Protein: 6 g.

2.14 Creamy Breakfast Egg Bowls

Preparation time: 10 mins

Cooking time: 20 mins

Servings: 4

Level of difficulty: Intermediate

Ingredients:

- 4 dinner rolls, insides scooped out
- 4 eggs
- 4 tbsp. heavy cream
- Salt and black pepper to taste
- 4 tbsp. mixed parsley and chives
- 4 tbsp. grated parmesan

Instructions:

- Place the dinner rolls on a baking tray and crack an egg into each one.
- Add heavy cream and mixed herbs to each roll, and then sprinkle some salt and pepper.
- Top them with parmesan cheese and put the bread bowls in the air fryer and cook them at 350°F for 20 minutes.
- Serve the bread bowls for breakfast and enjoy.

Nutritional facts per serving: Calories: 238 Kcal; Carbs: 14 g; Fat: 4 g; Protein: 7 g.

2.15 Chicken Omelet

Preparation time: 15 mins

Cooking time: 16 mins

Servings: 8

Level of difficulty: Expert

Ingredients:

- 1 tsp. butter
- ½ jalapeño pepper, chopped
- 1 onion, chopped
- ¼ cup boiled chicken, shredded

- 3 eggs
- Salt and black pepper, to taste

Instructions:
- Grease an Air Fryer pan and preheat the air fryer to 355°F.
- Meanwhile melt butter in a pan over medium heat and add onions in it.
- Sauté the onions for 5 minutes and then add jalapeño pepper.
- Stir in chicken after 1 minute of cooking.
- Stop cooking and set aside.
- Meanwhile, mix eggs, black pepper and salt in a bowl.
- Add the chicken mixture to the greased pan and cover with the egg mixture.
- Cook the omelet for 10 minutes until done and serve hot.

Nutritional facts per serving: Calories: 161 Kcal; Carbs: 6 g; Fat: 3 g; Protein: 14 g.

2.16 Plain Bread

Preparation time: 10 mins

Cooking time: 15 mins

Servings: 19

Level of difficulty: Easy

Ingredients:
- 1 cup almond flour
- 4 eggs
- ¼ tsp. sea salt
- 1 tsp. baking powder
- ¼ cup butter

Instructions:
- Bring butter to room temperature. Beat the eggs. Make dough by mixing the two and adding the remaining ingredients.
- Knead the dough and wrap with a cling film for 10 minutes.
- Set the Air Fryer to 350°F and bake the bread for 15 minutes.
Remove the bread and cool it on a sturdy surface. Serve sliced with your preferred dish or individually.

Nutritional facts per serving: Calories: 40 Kcal; Carbs: 0.2 g; Fat: 4 g; Protein: 1 g.

2.17 Potato Pancakes

Preparation time: 10 mins

Cooking time: 10 mins

Servings: 4

Level of difficulty: Easy

Ingredients:
- 7 oz. potatoes
- 1 egg, beaten
- 1 chopped onion
- ½ tsp. garlic powder
- ¼ cup oat milk
- 3 tbsp. all-purpose flour
- ¼ tsp. kosher salt
- Pinch of ground black pepper

Instructions:
- Transfer shredded peeled potatoes to a dish of cold water to remove excess starch.
- Use paper towels to dry the potatoes after draining them.
- Mix egg, salt, garlic powder, flour and pepper in a bowl. Stir thoroughly. Add shredded potatoes.
- Preheat Air Fryer at 390°F.
- Start by adding ¼ cup of potato pancake batter to the Air Fryer cooking basket.
- Cook until golden brown, about 10 minutes.

Nutritional facts per serving: Calories: 40 Kcal; Carbs: 1 g; Fat: 0.2 g; Protein: 23 g.

2.18 Herbed Sweet Potato Hash

Preparation time: 10 mins
Cooking time: 25 mins
Servings: 5
Level of difficulty: Easy

Ingredients:
- 4 sweet potatoes, diced
- 1 chopped onion
- Salt and pepper, to taste
- 1 cup button mushrooms, sliced
- 2 tbsp. lemon juice
- ½ green bell pepper, chopped
- ½ tsp. thyme, dried
- 2 tbsp. olive oil
- ½ tsp. rosemary, dried

Instructions:
- Preheat Air Fryer at 360°F.
- Combine all of the ingredients in a bowl.

- Remove the Air Fryer basket and add the sweet potato mixture.
- Cook the hash for 25-30 minutes.
- Serve and enjoy!

Nutritional facts per serving: Calories: 203 Kcal; Carbs: 36 g; Fat: 6 g; Protein: 3 g.

2.19 Eggs, Ham, And Spinach

Preparation time: 10 mins
Cooking time: 22 mins
Servings: 4
Level of difficulty: Easy
Ingredients:

- 8 oz. sliced ham
- 4 tsp. cream milk
- 2¼ cup spinach
- 4 large eggs
- 1 tbsp. olive oil
- Salt and pepper, to taste

Instructions:

- Preheat air fryer to 356°F. Grease ramekins with cooking spray.
- Heat oil in a pan and sauté spinach until wilted. Drain.
- Divide the spinach and remaining ingredients into individual ramekins. Season with salt and pepper.
- Bake for 20 minutes until set and serve.

Nutritional facts per serving: Calories: 190 Kcal; Carbs: 2 g; Fat: 13 g; Protein: 5 g.

2.20 Avocado Egg

Preparation time: 5 mins
Cooking time: 6 mins
Servings: 4
Level of difficulty: Easy
Ingredients:

- 4 eggs
- chopped parsley
- 2 avocado
- chopped chives

Instructions:

- Preheat the fryer to 350°F.

- Remove avocado flesh with a help of spoon.
- Crack an egg into each half and air fry for 6 minutes in a preheated Air Fryer.
- Take out and garnish with parsley and chives.

Nutritional facts per serving: Calories: 288 Kcal; Carbs: 9 g; Fat: 26 g; Protein: 8 g.

2.21 Zucchini Egg Nests

Preparation time: 5 mins

Cooking time: 7 mins

Servings: 5

Level of difficulty: Easy

Ingredients:

- 10 oz. grated zucchini
- 5 oz. shredded cheddar cheese
- ¼ tsp. sea salt
- 2 tsp. olive oil
- ½ tsp. black pepper
- ¼ tsp onion powder
- 5 eggs
- ½ tsp. paprika

Instructions:

- Start by preheating the Air Fryer to 356°F.
- Grate zucchini. Pour olive oil into ramekins and nestle zucchini in them. Sprinkle with onion powder, paprika, pepper and salt.
- Mix eggs and add to the nest, then cover with cheese.
- Air-fry 7 minutes. After chilling for 3 minutes, serve in a ramekin.

Nutritional facts per serving: Calories: 221 Kcal; Carbs: 3 g; Fat: 18 g; Protein: 13 g.

2.22 Spinach Frittata

Preparation time: 10 mins

Cooking time: 15 mins

Servings: 4

Level of difficulty: Easy

Ingredients:

- 6 eggs
- 3 oz. grated cheddar
- 2 tbsp. olive oil
- 1 cup halved cherry tomatoes

- 8 oz. spinach leaves
- Salt and black pepper, to taste
- 1 chopped onion

Instructions:

- Preheat air fryer to 390°F.
- Mix 6 eggs in a bowl and season with salt and pepper to taste. Set aside.
- Set a skillet on medium-high heat and heat olive oil. After 2 minutes of stir-frying the onion, add the cherry tomatoes and spinach leaves. Cook for 3 minutes, tossing often.
- Place veggies in a small baking pan and add whisked eggs. Sprinkle with cheddar cheese.
- Place the baking pan in the Air Fryer basket and cook for approximately 10 minutes.

Nutritional facts per serving: Calories: 215 Kcal; Carbs: 8 g; Fat: 12 g; Protein: 14 g.

2.23 Asparagus And Bacon Spears

Preparation time: 5 mins

Cooking time: 8 mins

Servings: 4

Level of difficulty: Easy

Ingredients:

- 20 spears asparagus
- 1 garlic clove, crushed
- 1 tbsp. olive oil
- 4 bacon slices
- 1 tbsp. sesame oil

Instructions:

- Pre-heat your Air Fryer to 380°F.
- Combine oil, crushed garlic in a small bowl.
- Divide asparagus into 4 bunches and wrap with bacon.
- Coat asparagus and bacon wraps with garlic and oil mixture, then place in Air Fryer basket.
- Cook for 8 minutes. Serve and enjoy!

Nutritional facts per serving: Calories: 215 Kcal; Carbs: 8 g; Fat: 13 g; Protein: 14 g.

2.24 Bacon Egg Muffins

Preparation time: 5 mins

Cooking time: 7 mins

Servings: 2

Level of difficulty: Easy

Ingredients:
- 1 whole egg
- 1 English muffin
- 2 strips bacon
- salt and pepper, to taste

Instructions:
- Pre-heat your Air Fryer to 200°F.
- Crack an egg into an oven-safe dish.
- In the Air Fryer basket, place bacon, egg, and muffin.
- Cook 7 minutes. To assemble the muffin, place egg and bacon on top of the English muffin.

Nutritional facts per serving: Calories: 215 Kcal; Carbs: 8 g; Fat: 13 g; Protein: 14 g.

2.25 Cheesy Breakfast Soufflé

Preparation time: 10 mins
Cooking time: 8 mins
Servings: 4
Level of difficulty: Easy

Ingredients:
- 7 eggs
- ½ cup mozzarella cheese, shredded
- 1/3 cup milk
- ½ cup ham, chopped
- ½ tsp. garlic powder
- 1 tbsp. chopped parsley
- 1 tsp. black pepper
- 1 tsp. salt

Instructions:
- Grease 4 ramekins with cooking spray.
- Start by preheating your air fryer to 350°F.
  Combine all ingredients in a large bowl and whisk until well combined.
- Place the egg mixture in prepared ramekins in the air fryer.
  Cook for 8 minutes in an air fryer.
- Next, gently take the soufflé from the air fryer and let it cool.
- Serve and enjoy!

Nutritional facts per serving: Calories: 195 Kcal; Carbs: 4 g; Fat: 15 g; Protein: 7 g.

2.26 Japanese Omelette

Preparation time: 10 mins

Cooking time: 10 mins

Servings: 1

Level of difficulty: Easy

Ingredients:

- 1 cubed Japanese tofu
- Salt and pepper, to taste
- 1 chopped onion
- 3 whole eggs
- 1 tsp. cumin
- 2 tbsp. soy sauce
- 1 tsp. coriander
- 1 tsp. olive oil
- 2 tbsp. chopped green onion

Instructions:

- Start by preheating your Air Fryer to 400°F.
- Mix eggs, pepper, soy sauce, salt and oil in a medium bowl.
- Place cubed tofu in baking pan and cover with egg mixture. Place the baking pan in the air fryer basket and cook for 10 minutes.
- For garnish, add chopped green onion. Enjoy!

Nutritional facts per serving: Calories: 300 Kcal; Carbs: 19 g; Fat: 40 g; Protein: 72 g.

2.27 Feta Breakfast

Preparation time: 10 mins

Cooking time: 3 mins

Servings: 2

Level of difficulty: Easy

Ingredients:

- 3½ lbs. feta cheese
- 1 whole chopped onion
- Salt and pepper, to taste
- 5 filo pastry sheets
- 1 egg yolk
- 2 tbsp. chopped parsley
- 2 tsp. olive oil

Instructions:

- Pre-heat your Air Fryer to 400-degree F.
- Cut each sheet into three equal-sized strips and brush them with olive oil.
- In a bowl, combine onion, feta, pepper, egg yolk, salt, and parsley.
- Create triangles from cut strips and top with a little amount of feta mixture.
- Cook the triangles in the air fryer basket for 3 minutes.
- Add green onions to the side and enjoy.

Nutritional facts per serving: Calories: 217 Kcal; Carbs: 5 g; Fat: 12 g; Protein: 19 g.

2.28 Cinnamon Toast

Preparation time: 10 mins
Cooking time: 6 mins
Servings: 6
Level of difficulty: Easy
Ingredients:

- 12 slices bread
- 1½ tsp. cinnamon
- 1 stick butter
- ½ cup sugar
- 1½ tsp. vanilla essence
- Bananas, for garnish
- Berry sauce, for garnish

Instructions:

- Start by preheating your Air Fryer to 400°F.
- In a microwave-safe bowl, combine sugar, butter, and vanilla essence. Warm and whisk the mixture for 30 seconds to melt everything.
- Cover bread pieces with mixture.
- Place bread slices in air fryer basket and air fry for 5 minutes.
- Serve with berry sauce or fresh banana. Enjoy!

Nutritional facts per serving: Calories: 217 Kcal; Carbs: 5 g; Fat: 12 g; Protein: 19 g.

2.29 Salmon And Cheese Frittata

Preparation time: 10 mins
Cooking time: 15 mins
Servings: 4
Level of difficulty: Easy

Ingredients:

- 6 eggs
- 2 oz. grated cheddar
- 2 tbsp. olive oil
- Salt and black pepper, to taste
- 1 clove garlic, minced
- 1 chopped white onion
- 2 tbsp. dill weed, freshly chopped
- 8 oz. baked salmon
- 2 tbsp. chopped parsley

Instructions:

- Preheat air fryer to 390°F.
- Combine 6 eggs in a bowl and season with pepper and salt to taste.
- Heat olive oil in a pan over medium heat. Stir-fry garlic and onion for 3 minutes. Add dill and salmon; simmer for 2-3 minutes.
- Place mixture in a small baking dish and add beaten egg mixture. Sprinkle with cheddar cheese, set baking dish in Air Fryer basket, and air fry for 10 minutes.
- Garnish with chopped parsley and enjoy!

Nutritional facts per serving: Calories: 217 Kcal; Carbs: 5 g; Fat: 12 g; Protein: 19 g.

2.30 Mushroom And Cheese Omelette

Preparation time: 10 mins

Cooking time: 15 mins

Servings: 1

Level of difficulty: Easy

Ingredients:

- 2 eggs
- 1 tbsp. olive oil
- 1 small sliced onion
- 2 cup sliced mushrooms
- 1 tbsp. chopped Parsley
- ½ cup grated cheese

Instructions:

- Preheat the Air Fryer at 320°F.
- Add oil to a medium-heat skillet.
- Add mushrooms, onions and parsley and sauté for 5 minutes. Put the sautéed vegetables in Air Fryer.

- Add beaten eggs to the fryer on top of the vegetables. Sprinkle with cheese and air fry for 10 minutes and serve.

Nutritional facts per serving: Calories: 215 Kcal; Carbs: 9 g; Fat: 13 g; Protein: 14 g.

2.31 Baked Cheesy Eggs

Preparation time: 10 mins
Cooking time: 7 mins
Servings: 2
Level of difficulty: Easy
Ingredients:

- 1 tomato
- 2 eggs
- 1 tsp. parmesan cheese
- 2 tbsp. milk
- salt and pepper, to taste
- chopped parsley, for garnish

Instructions:

- Preheat oven to 180°F.
- Dice tomatoes and put in 2 ramekins.
- Add a spoonful of milk to each ramekin.
- Break an egg into each ramekin.
- Season the egg with pepper and salt.
- Add ½ teaspoon of parmesan to ramekins.
- Place ramekins in Air Fryer basket and cook for 7 minutes.
- Serve with parsley garnish and enjoy!

Nutritional facts per serving: Calories: 215 Kcal; Carbs: 9 g; Fat: 13 g; Protein: 14 g.

2.32 English Style Breakfast

Preparation time: 25 mins
Cooking time: 15 mins
Servings: 4
Level of difficulty: Intermediate
Ingredients:

- 4 breakfast sausages
- 4 slices bread
- 4 eggs
- 4 bacon strips, un-smoked

- oil spray, for greasing
- 2 cups of baked beans
- few slices of smoked tomatoes

Instructions:

- Preheat air fryer at 325°F.
- After greasing the air fryer basket with oil, add the sausages and bacon strips and cook for five minutes.
- After the bacon and sausage are cooked, remove and put aside.
- Grease two ramekins with cooking spray.
- Transfer the beans into the ramekins and use the air fryer basket to cook for approximately 8 minutes.
- Cook the egg in a frying pan in the meanwhile.
- After everything is cooked, place the smoked tomato slices and everything else on the platter and serve.

Nutritional facts per serving: Calories: 617 Kcal; Carbs: 42 g; Fat: 33 g; Protein: 35 g.

2.33 Tapioca Cheesy Bread

Preparation time: 12 mins

Cooking time: 18 mins

Servings: 4

Level of difficulty: Intermediate

Ingredients:

- ¼ cup heavy cream
- 6 oz. tapioca flour
- 6 oz. cheddar cheese
- 2 tsp. baking powder
- 2 eggs, whisked
- 6 oz. Swiss cheese

Instructions:

- In a large bowl, combine 5 ounces tapioca flour, cheddar and Swiss cheese, baking powder, heavy cream and whisked eggs.
- Mix into dough.
- Knead the dough on the flat surface with the remaining tapioca flour.
- Let it sit 30 minutes.
- Transfer it to a parchment-lined loaf pan.
- At 400°F, air fry loaf pan for 15-18 minutes.
- Remove when done. Let cool before slicing.

Nutritional facts per serving: Calories: 554 Kcal; Carbs: 43 g; Fat: 40 g; Protein: 25 g.

2.34 Breakfast Potatoes

Preparation time: 15 mins

Cooking time: 40 mins

Servings: 4

Level of difficulty: Expert

Ingredients:

- 3 russet potatoes, diced
- 2 tbsp. olive oil
- 2 tsp. onion powder
- 2 green pepper, diced
- 1 onion, diced
- Salt, to taste
- ½ tsp. paprika
- 1 tsp. garlic powder
- Water, as required

Instructions:

- Fill a bowl with water.
- Soak the potatoes for 20 minutes.
- Add the remaining ingredients to the mixing bowl.
- Spray air fryer basket with oil.
- Pat potatoes dry with a kitchen towel after draining.
- Pour potatoes into a bowl and toss thoroughly.
- Bake at 400°F for 40 minutes in the air fryer.

Nutritional facts per serving: Calories: 281 Kcal; Carbs: 50 g; Fat: 7 g; Protein: 5 g.

2.35 Polenta Bites

Preparation time: 15 mins

Cooking time: 16 mins

Servings: 4

Level of difficulty: Easy

Ingredients:

- 1 packet Polenta
- Cooking spray
- ½ cup potato starch
- Maple syrup, for topping

Instructions:

- Pre-heat the air fryer for a few minutes at 390°F.
- Sprinkle potato starch on polenta balls and place on an oil-sprayed cookie sheet.
- Spray oil on polenta balls.
- Add the basket to the air fryer with the cookie sheet inside.
- Cook Polenta Balls for 8 minutes from one side.
- Cook for 8 additional minutes after flipping.

Nutritional facts per serving: Calories: 429 Kcal; Carbs: 101 g; Fat: 1 g; Protein: 2 g.

2.36 Eggs And Ham Muffins

Preparation time: 20 mins
Cooking time: 15 mins
Servings: 4
Level of difficulty: Intermediate

Ingredients:

- 6 oz. Ham, sliced
- 6 eggs
- Handful baby spinach
- Cooking spray
- 1 tbsp. olive oil
- 6 tbsp. milk
- Salt and pepper, to taste

Instructions:

- Pre-heat the air fryer to 375°F.
- Use cooking spray to grease 6 ramekins.
- Stir cook baby spinach in pan oil for 1 minute.
- Divide ham among ramekins. Whisk thoroughly and add cooked spinach. Whisk milk, eggs, and olive oil.
- Pour the egg mixture evenly into the ramekins.
- Sprinkle black pepper and salt on it.
- Bake it for 15 minutes in an air fryer basket.

Nutritional facts per serving: Calories: 208 Kcal; Carbs: 4 g; Fat: 14 g; Protein: 16 g.

2.37 Eggs In A Bowl Of Bread

Preparation time: 15 mins

Cooking time: 22 mins

Servings: 3

Level of difficulty: Intermediate

Ingredients:

- 3 dinner rolls
- 2 tbsp. parsley
- 3 eggs
- 1 cup Parmesan cheese, grated
- Salt and pepper, to taste
- 1 tbsp. chives, chopped

Instructions:

- To make a central cavity, slice the top of three dinner rolls and remove some bread from the middle.
- The middle hole should be sufficient for eggs.
- Place rolls in oil-greased air fryer basket.
- Crack an egg in each hole.
- Sprinkle salt, parsley, chives, black pepper, and parmesan over eggs.
- Air fry the breakfast bowls for 18-22 minutes at 350°F.

Nutritional facts per serving: Calories: 519 Kcal; Carbs: 47 g; Fat: 22 g; Protein: 33 g.

2.38 Breakfast Muffin Sandwich

Preparation time: 15 mins

Cooking time: 12 mins

Servings: 2

Level of difficulty: Easy

Ingredients:

- 2 eggs
- 4 bacon slices
- 2 English muffins

Instructions:

- Use two heat-resistant soufflé cups.
- Crack one egg per cup and place in air fryer basket.
- Cook at 400°F for 6 minutes.
- Remove the basket, brush with oil, and add English muffins and bacon.
- Cook for 6 minutes.

- Cut the muffin in half and add bacon and eggs. Form a sandwich and serve.

Nutritional facts per serving: Calories: 332 Kcal; Carbs: 25 g; Fat: 17 g; Protein: 20 g.

2.39 Chipolatas With Eggs

Preparation time: 15 mins

Cooking time: 16 mins

Servings: 4

Level of difficulty: Intermediate

Ingredients:

- 6 chestnut mushrooms
- 6 cherry tomatoes, halved
- 4 chipolatas
- 4 smoked bacon
- Salt and pepper, to taste
- 4 eggs
- 2 cloves garlic, crushed
- Oil Spray

Instructions:

- Preheat the air fryer for 5 minutes at 400°F.
- Meanwhile, get an air fryer basket-compatible spherical tin.
- Spray with oil and leave aside.
- Add tomatoes, garlic, pepper, salt and mushroom to a bowl. Spray ingredients with oil.
- Add bacon and chipolatas to the tin and place in the air fryer basket. Place the basket in the machine and air fry for 12 minutes.
- Meanwhile, fry the egg in a cooking skillet.
- Serve eggs with bacon and chipotlas tin for a tasty breakfast.

Nutritional facts per serving: Calories: 275 Kcal; Carbs: 10 g; Fat: 18 g; Protein: 20 g.

2.40 Breakfast Omelet

Preparation time: 15 mins

Cooking time: 16 mins

Servings: 4

Level of difficulty: Intermediate

Ingredients:

- 4 eggs
- 1 small onion
- ¼ cup full-fat milk

- 1 tbsp. butter
- Salt and pepper, to taste
- ½ cup cheese, grated
- Oil Spray

Instructions:

- Pre-heat the air fryer for 5 minutes at 350°F.
- In a medium bowl, whisk milk, butter and eggs.
- Add grated cheese and stir thoroughly.
- Now add black pepper and salt.
- Now add chopped tomatoes and green onions.
- Pour the egg mixture into the oil-sprayed cake pan.
- Place cake pan in air fryer basket and cook for 8-10 minutes.
- When cooked, serve hot.

Nutritional facts per serving: Calories: 163 Kcal; Carbs: 3 g; Fat: 12 g; Protein: 10 g.

2.41 Breakfast Tortilla Wraps

Preparation time: 15 mins

Cooking time: 13 mins

Servings: 4

Level of difficulty: Intermediate

Ingredients:

- 4 tortillas wrap
- 4 chicken breast, cooked and sliced
- ½ avocado, chopped
- 8 eggs, whisked
- Salt and Pepper, to taste
- 1 cup mozzarella cheese, grated

Instructions:

- Pre-heat the air fryer for 5 minutes at 350°F.
- In a medium bowl, whisk eggs with pepper and salt.
- Put a small tin in the air fryer basket.
- Spray the tin with oil.
- Fill the tin with egg.
- Air-fry the egg for 8 minutes.
- Fill tortilla with chicken, egg, avocado and cheese after eggs are done.
- Put the tortilla wrap in an aluminum foil-lined air fryer basket and cook for 5 minutes.

Nutritional facts per serving: Calories: 511 Kcal; Carbs: 34 g; Fat: 22 g; Protein: 42 g.

2.42 Banana And Chocolate Chip Muffins

Preparation time: 10 mins
Cooking time: 16 mins
Servings: 4
Level of difficulty: Intermediate
Ingredients:

- Pinch of salt
- 2 tbsp. butter
- 2 eggs, whisked
- ½ tsp. baking powder
- 4 tbsp. almond milk
- 1 cup mashed bananas
- 1½ cup almond flour
- 4 tbsp. chocolate chip

Instructions:

- Pre-heat the air fryer for 2 minutes at 350°F.
- Combine baking powder, almond flour and salt in a large bowl.
- In another bowl, whisk butter, egg, and almond milk.
- Mix in chocolate chips and mashed bananas.
- Now combine wet and dry ingredients and divide this batter among 6 muffin-cup-lined ramekins.
- Add the ramekins to the air fryer basket.
- Cook for 16 minutes.
- After finishing, serve and enjoy.

Nutritional facts per serving: Calories: 249 Kcal; Carbs: 17 g; Fat: 18 g; Protein: 6 g.

2.43 Savory Breakfast Muffins

Preparation time: 16 mins
Cooking time: 15 mins
Servings: 4
Level of difficulty: Intermediate
Ingredients:

- 4 eggs, whisked
- 1/3 tsp. Worcestershire sauce
- 6 tbsp. full-fat milk

- 2 tbsp. olive oil
- 1 tbsp. baking powder
- 1½ cup all-purpose flour
- 6 oz. Parmesan, grated
- ¼ tsp. mustard powder
- Oil spray

Instructions:

- Pre-heat the air fryer for a few minutes at 350°F.
- Use oil spray to grease 6 ramekins.
- Whisk eggs in a small bowl, and then add milk and oil.
- Add baking powder, Worcestershire sauce, and mustard powder and parmesan cheese and mix well.
- Mix in flour and divide batter into ramekins.
- Put ramekins in the Air Fryer basket and bake for 5 minutes.
- Once done, serve.

Nutritional facts per serving: Calories: 342 Kcal; Carbs: 28 g; Fat: 20 g; Protein: 22 g.

2.44 Blueberries Oats Muffin

Preparation time: 12 mins

Cooking time: 15 mins

Servings: 4

Level of difficulty: Intermediate

Ingredients:

- 1 cup blueberries
- Salt, pinch
- 1/3 cup sugar
- 2 eggs
- 4 tbsp. almond milk
- 1/3 cup melted butter
- ¼ tsp. vanilla extract
- 1 tsp. lemon zest
- 1 cup all-purpose flour
- 1/3 cup oats
- ½ tsp. baking powder

Instructions:

- Use oil spray to grease 6 ramekins.
- Add eggs, milk, butter, vanilla essence and lemon zest to a bowl and stir.

- In another bowl, combine flour, salt, baking powder, sugar and oats.
- Mix well and add egg mixture to flour mixture.
- Finally, fold in blueberries.
- Put this mixture in 4 ramekins and bake in air fryer for 15 minutes at 375°F.

Nutritional facts per serving: Calories: 426 Kcal; Carbs: 50 g; Fat: 22 g; Protein: 7 g.

2.45 English Muffins Pizza

Preparation time: 15 mins
Cooking time: 18 mins
Servings: 3
Level of difficulty: Intermediate
Ingredients:

- 3 eggs, scrambled
- ½ cup shredded pepper jack cheese
- 3 sausages, cooked and crumbled
- Oil spray
- 3 English muffins, sliced

Instructions:

- Spray an air fryer basket with oil.
- Spray oil on ramekins.
- Cook half an English muffin in an oil-greased air fryer basket at 350°F for 4 minutes.
- Next batch, cook remaining half similarly.
- Add sausage and fried eggs to the muffin.
- Add cheese on top and air fry for 5 more minutes.
- Once done, serve.

Nutritional facts per serving: Calories: 255 Kcal; Carbs: 25 g; Fat: 10 g; Protein: 14 g.

Chapter 3: Family Favorites

3.1 Chicken Sausage And Broccoli Casserole

Preparation time: 10 mins

Cooking time: 20 mins

Servings: 8

Level of difficulty: Intermediate

Ingredients:

- 10 eggs
- ¾ cup heavy whipping cream
- ½ tbsp. salt
- 1 cup cheddar cheese, shredded
- 12 oz. cooked chicken sausage
- 2 cloves garlic, minced
- 1 cup broccoli, chopped
- ¼ tbsp. ground black pepper
- Cooking spray

Instructions:

- Preheat the air fryer at 400°F. Grease a baking pan. Whisk eggs, cheddar, and cream in a large bowl until well combined.
- In another bowl, mix broccoli, cooked sausage, salt, garlic, and ground black pepper. Stir thoroughly.
- After adding the sausage mixture to the baking pan, top it with the egg mixture.
- Put the baking pan in the basket of air fryer. Bake until eggs are set, about 20 minutes. Serve.

Nutritional facts per serving: Calories: 339 Kcal; Carbs: 13 g; Fat: 19 g; Protein: 28 g.

3.2 Chicken Ham Casserole

Preparation time: 10 mins

Cooking time: 15 mins

Servings: 4

Level of difficulty: Easy

Ingredients:

- 2 cups diced cooked chicken
- 6 slices Swiss cheese
- ¼ tsp. ground nutmeg
- 1 cup diced ham
- ½ tsp. ground black pepper

- ½ cup half-and-half
- Cooking spray

Instructions:

- Start the air fryer at 350°F. Cooking spray a baking pan. Mix ham, chicken, half-and-half, nutmeg, and ground black pepper in a large bowl. Stir thoroughly.
- Add half of the mixture to the baking sheet, top with 3 slices of Swiss cheese, and add the rest of the mixture and cover with remaining cheese slices.
- Place the baking pan in the basket of air fryer and bake for 15 minutes until the egg is set and cheese melts. Serve now.

Nutritional facts per serving: Calories: 320 Kcal; Carbs: 21 g; Fat: 18 g; Protein: 19 g.

3.3 Corn And Bell Pepper Casserole

Preparation time: 10 mins

Cooking time: 20 mins

Servings: 4

Level of difficulty: Intermediate

Ingredients:

- 1 cup corn kernels
- ½ cup low-fat milk
- ¼ cup bell pepper, chopped
- ½ cup yellow cornmeal
- 1 large egg, beaten
- ½ cup all-purpose flour
- ½ tsp. baking powder
- 1 tbsp. granulated sugar
- 2 tbsp. melted unsalted butter
- ¼ tsp. kosher salt
- Pinch of cayenne pepper
- Cooking spray

Instructions:

- Start the air fryer at 330°F. Grease a baking pan. Mix all ingredients in a big bowl. Stir thoroughly. Fill the baking pan with mixture.
- Preheat the air fryer and place the pan. Bake for 20 minutes until lightly browned and set. Remove the air-fried baking pan and serve immediately.

Nutritional facts per serving: Calories: 297 Kcal; Carbs: 29 g; Fat: 30 g; Protein: 26 g.

3.4 Grits And Asparagus Casserole

Preparation time: 10 mins

Cooking time: 30 mins

Servings: 4

Level of difficulty: Intermediate

Ingredients:

- 10 fresh asparagus spears, sliced
- 2 slices provolone cheese, crushed
- 2 tsp. Worcestershire sauce
- 2 cups cooked grits
- ½ tsp. garlic powder
- 1 egg, beaten
- ¼ tsp. salt
- Cooking spray

Instructions:

- Preheat the air fryer at 390°F. Grease a baking pan. Place the asparagus in the air fryer basket. Cover asparagus with cooking spray. Air-fry them for 5 minutes until crispy and lightly browned.
- Meanwhile, mix grits, egg, Worcestershire sauce, and salt and garlic powder in a bowl. Stir thoroughly.
- Place half of the grits mixture in the baking pan and top with fried asparagus.
- Add half the grits mixture to an air fryer pan and top with asparagus. Spread cheese on asparagus and top with remaining grits.
- Put the baking pan in the basket of air fryer. Bake for 25 minutes until the egg is firm and gently browned. Serve now.

Nutritional facts per serving: Calories: 370 Kcal; Carbs: 20 g; Fat: 26 g; Protein: 15 g.

3.5 Hillbilly Broccoli Cheese Casserole

Preparation time: 10 mins

Cooking time: 30 mins

Servings: 6

Level of difficulty: Easy

Ingredients:

- 4 cups broccoli florets
- salt and black pepper, to taste
- ½ cup cheddar cheese, shredded
- ¼ cup heavy whipping cream
- ¼ cup ranch dressing

Instructions:

- Preheat the air fryer up to 375°F. In a big bowl, mix all the ingredients together. Turn the broccoli around to coat it well.
- Put the mixture into a baking pan, and then put the pan into an air fryer that has already been heated up.
- Bake the broccoli for 30 minutes, or until it's soft.
- Take the baking pan out of the air fryer and serve right away.

Nutritional facts per serving: Calories: 375 Kcal; Carbs: 10 g; Fat: 33 g; Protein: 11 g.

3.6 Fried Fish Sandwich

Preparation time: 10 mins

Cooking time: 9 mins

Servings: 2

Level of difficulty: Easy

Ingredients:

- 1 large egg
- 2 tsp. lemon juice
- 1 tbsp. whole milk
- ¼ tsp. salt
- ½ cup plain breadcrumbs
- 2 hamburger buns
- 2 cod fillets
- 8 slices dill pickle
- 2 tbsp. Tartar Sauce
- 1/3 cup iceberg lettuce, shredded

Instructions:

- In a small bowl, mix the milk, egg, and lemon juice together with a whisk.
- Put breadcrumbs and salt in a small dish.
- First, dip the pieces in the egg mix. Then, coat all sides of the fish with the bread crumb mix. Warm up the air fryer for three minutes at 350°F.
- Put the fillets in an air fryer basket that has been lightly oiled. For 9 minutes, make sure the cod is opaque and can be easily flaked with a fork.
- Put the fish on the buns and top them with pickles, iceberg, and Tartar Sauce.

Nutritional facts per serving: Calories: 353 Kcal; Carbs: 38 g; Fat: 26 g; Protein: 9 g.

3.7 Grilled Tomato And Pimiento Cheese Sandwiches

Preparation time: 5 mins

Cooking time: 24 mins

Servings: 4

Level of difficulty: Intermediate

Ingredients:

- 8 oz. cheddar cheese, shredded
- 1/2 cup mayonnaise
- 4 oz. diced pimientos
- 8 slices whole-wheat bread
- ¼ tsp. salt
- ¼ tsp. black pepper
- 4 medium Campari tomatoes, sliced
- 4 tbsp. butter, melted

Instructions:

- In a medium bowl, mix together the cheese, pimientos, mayonnaise, and salt. Cover and chill for 30 minutes.
- Cover four pieces of bread with pimiento cheese mixture. Spread out the tomato pieces and add ground black pepper to them. Add the last few slices of bread on top. Preheat the air fryer for three minutes at 350°F.
- Spread a little warm butter on the outside of the top and bottom of a sandwich. In the air fryer basket, put the sandwich and cook it for three minutes.
- Turn it over and cook for three more minutes. Do it again for the rest of the sandwiches. Serve and enjoy.

Nutritional facts per serving: Calories: 685 Kcal; Carbs: 32 g; Fat: 48 g; Protein: 22 g.

3.8 Raisin Bread Monte Cristo

Preparation time: 10 mins

Cooking time: 12 mins

Servings: 2

Level of difficulty: Easy

Ingredients:

- ½ cup grated Gruyere cheese
- 2 tsp. Dijon mustard
- 2 tbsp. cream cheese
- Pinch of black pepper
- Pinch of salt

- 4 slices of raisin bread
- 1 large egg
- 2 thick slices of deli ham

Instructions:

- Put cream cheese, Gruyere cheese, salt, mustard, and pepper in a medium-sized bowl.
- Whisk the egg in a small bowl. Cover two pieces of bread with the cheese filling. Put in ham. Cover slices with the rest of the bread. Preheat the air fryer for three minutes at 350°F.
- Cover both sides of one sandwich with egg that has been mixed. Cook for three minutes in an air fryer basket that has been lightly oiled. Turn it over and cook for three more minutes. Serve and enjoy.

Nutritional facts per serving: Calories: 375 Kcal; Carbs: 30 g; Fat: 20 g; Protein: 20 g.

3.9 Fried Banana And Peanut Butter Sandwiches

Preparation time: 10 mins

Cooking time: 12 mins

Servings: 2

Level of difficulty: Easy

Ingredients:

- 2 tbsp. creamy peanut butter
- 2 tbsp. butter, melted
- 1 large banana, sliced
- 4 slices white sandwich bread
- 2 tsp. honey

Instructions:

- Put peanut butter on one side of each of the two pieces of bread. Put sliced bananas on top of each and drizzle honey over each. Layer the remaining pieces of the bread on top. Preheat the air fryer for three minutes at 350°F.
- Spread a little warm butter on the outside of the top and bottom of a sandwich. First put one at a time in the air fryer basket. Then cook for three minutes.
- Turn it over and cook for three more minutes. Do it again with another sandwich. Serve and enjoy.

Nutritional facts per serving: Calories: 412 Kcal; Carbs: 54 g; Fat: 20 g; Protein: 10 g.

3.10 Saucy Garam Masala Fish

Preparation time: 10 mins

Cooking time: 18 mins

Servings: 2

Level of difficulty: Intermediate

Ingredients:

- 2 catfish fillets

- 2 tsp. olive oil
- ½ tsp. cayenne pepper
- ¼ cup coconut milk
- ¼ tsp. black salt
- 1 tsp. Garam masala
- 1 garlic clove, minced
- ½ tsp. fresh ginger, grated
- ¼ cup coriander, roughly chopped

Instructions:

- Preheat Air Fryer to 390°F. Spray the baking dish with nonstick cooking spray.
- Mix milk, olive oil, Garam masala, cayenne pepper, ginger, black salt and garlic in a bowl.
- Cover catfish fillets with Garam masala. Cook catfish fillets in a preheated Air Fryer for 18 minutes, flipping halfway through.
- Garnish with fresh coriander and serve.

Nutritional facts per serving: Calories: 190 Kcal; Carbs: 10 g; Fat: 5 g; Protein: 26 g.

3.11 Golden Cod Fish Nuggets

Preparation time: 10 mins

Cooking time: 9 mins

Servings: 4

Level of difficulty: Intermediate

Ingredients:

- 1 lb. cod fillets, cubed
- 1 cup flour
- 2 eggs, beaten
- 2 tbsp. olive oil
- A pinch of salt
- 1 cup breadcrumbs

Instructions:

- Preheat air fryer to 390°F. Stir breadcrumbs, salt and olive oil in a bowl until mixed. Add eggs and flour to two separate bowls.
- Coat cod fillets with flour, then dip in eggs, and finally coat them in breadcrumbs.
- Place in frying basket and cook for 9 minutes. At 5 minutes, flip the cod nuggets once.
- Once cooked, transfer to a dish for serving.

Nutritional facts per serving: Calories: 198 Kcal; Carbs: 4 g; Fat: 7 g; Protein: 13 g.

3.12 Pork Belly Bites

Preparation time: 26 mins

Cooking time: 20 mins

Servings: 6

Level of difficulty: Easy

Ingredients:

- 2 lb. pork belly, patted dry
- 2 tbsp. brown sugar
- 4 tbsp. canola oil
- Salt and black pepper, to taste
- 1 tsp. garlic powder

Instructions:

- Take a few minutes to heat the air fryer up to 400°F.
- Cut the pork belly into pieces with a knife and pat them dry.
- Put oil, sugar, salt, garlic powder, and pepper in a big bowl and mix them together.
- Place the pork belly pieces in an air fryer basket so that they are all covered. Make sure the pieces are all in a single layer.
- Flip the food over halfway through the 20 minutes.
- When it's done, serve.

Nutritional facts per serving: Calories: 193 Kcal; Carbs: 4 g; Fat: 50 g; Protein: 60 g.

3.13 Glazed Pork Belly

Preparation time: 26 mins

Cooking time: 20 mins

Servings: 4

Level of difficulty: Easy

Ingredients:

- 2 lb. pork belly, patted dry
- 1 tsp. smoked paprika
- ½ tsp. cayenne powder
- ½ tsp. garlic powder
- 2 tbsp. dry sherry
- ½ cup maple syrup
- 1 tsp. cumin
- Salt and black pepper, to taste

Instructions:
- Take a few minutes to heat the air fryer up to 400°F.
- Cut the pork belly into 1-inch pieces with a knife and pat them dry.
- Whisk the rest of the ingredients together in a bowl.
- Cover the pork belly pieces well with the sauce.
- Put the pork belly in the air fryer. Cook for 20 minutes.
- Use the extra liquid in the bowl to baste the pork belly every five minutes.
- When it's done, serve.

Nutritional facts per serving: Calories: 184 Kcal; Carbs: 27 g; Fat: 60 g; Protein: 107 g.

3.14 Sweet Glazed Ham

Preparation time: 15 mins
Cooking time: 25 mins
Servings: 2
Level of difficulty: Easy
Ingredients:

- 1 lb. ham
- Pinch of cloves, powder
- 6 tbsp. maple syrup
- 1 cup orange juice
- ¼ tsp. salt

Instructions:
- In a bowl, mix the maple syrup, orange juice, salt and cloves together using a whisk.
- After that, put it on the ham.
- Place it in an air fryer basket that has been lined with parchment paper. Cook it at 400°F for 25 minutes.
- Every five minutes, baste the ham with marinade.
- When it's done, serve it when it's cool.

Nutritional facts per serving: Calories: 583 Kcal; Carbs: 19 g; Fat: 60 g; Protein: 40 g.

3.15 Herbed Beef

Preparation time: 10 mins
Cooking time: 45 mins
Servings: 4
Level of difficulty: Intermediate
Ingredients:

- 1½ lb. roast beef

- 1 tsp. cayenne pepper
- 1 tsp. fresh thyme, chopped
- 2 cloves garlic, minced
- 2 tbsp. olive oil, divided
- 1 tsp. fresh basil, chopped
- 1 tsp. fresh rosemary, chopped
- Kosher salt and black pepper, to taste

Instructions:
- Preheat the Air fryer to 375°F.
- Combine all the ingredients except for the beef in a mixing bowl.
- Dry the roast with a paper towel and marinate it.
- Now, use olive oil to grease the open pan in the air fryer oven.
- Put the beef in the air fryer and roast for 25 minutes.
- Flip the roast and cook for another 20 minutes.

Nutritional facts per serving: Calories: 325 Kcal; Carbs: 40 g; Fat: 6 g; Protein: 10 g.

3.16 Ribeye Steak

Preparation time: 10 mins
Cooking time: 18 mins
Servings: 4
Level of difficulty: Intermediate
Ingredients:
- 1 lb. ribeye steak, cut into cubes
- Sea salt and black pepper, to taste
- 2 tbsp. fresh cilantro, chopped
- 2 tbsp. fresh parsley, chopped
- 1 tsp. paprika
- 2 tbsp. apple cider vinegar
- 2 tbsp. olive oil
- 2 garlic cloves, minced
- 2 tbsp. fresh basil, chopped
- 2 tbsp. Worcestershire sauce

Instructions:
- Put all the ingredients in a bowl and marinate the meat for at least three hours.
- Preheat the Air fryer to 360°F.
- Put the beef in the air fryer and cook for 12 minutes.

- Baste the beef with the marinade you saved and cook for another 5 to 6 minutes.
- Serve right away, and have fun!

Nutritional facts per serving: Calories: 335 Kcal; Carbs: 4 g; Fat: 21 g; Protein: 2 g.

3.17 Chicken Nuggets

Preparation time: 12 mins

Cooking time: 10 mins

Servings: 4

Level of difficulty: Intermediate

Ingredients:

- 2 lb. chicken breasts, cubed
- 1/3 cup pickle juice
- 2 large eggs
- 1/3 cup milk
- 2 tbsp. powdered sugar
- 2 tsp. cayenne pepper
- 1 cup all-purpose flour
- ¼ tsp. chili powder
- 1/4 tsp. paprika
- 1/2 tsp. baking powder
- Salt and black pepper, to taste

Instructions:

- Add pickle juice to a large bowl and marinade chicken cubes in it.
- Let it sit 10 minutes.
- Mix flour, sugar, paprika, cayenne pepper, pepper, chile powder, salt, and baking powder in a bowl to make the coating.
- In another bowl, crack an egg and stir with milk.
- Preheat the air fryer to 370°F.
- Coat chicken cubes in egg wash and then coat in flour-batter.
- Remove extra flour.
- Place it in air fryer basket and spray with oil.
- Flip midway through 10 minutes at 400 degrees F.
- Once cooked, serve.

Nutritional facts per serving: Calories: 612 Kcal; Carbs: 30 g; Fat: 20 g; Protein: 72 g.

3.18 Alfredo Chicken

Preparation time: 10 mins

Cooking time: 8 mins

Servings: 2

Level of difficulty: Intermediate

Ingredients:

- ½ tbsp. lemon juice
- ½ tsp. garlic powder
- 2 slices provolone cheese
- 1 tsp. chicken seasoning
- 2 chicken breast, halved
- Salt and black pepper, to taste
- ½ cup Alfredo sauce
- ½ cup blue cheese, crumbled

Instructions:

- In a large bowl, combine chicken seasoning, lemon juice, pepper, and salt and garlic powder.
- Rub it on chicken breasts.
- Spray oil on the air fryer basket.
- Cook chicken in an air fryer basket at 400°F for 8 minutes per side.
- Meanwhile in a pan add blue cheese, provolone cheese and Alfredo sauce and mix it for 2 minutes on medium heat.
- Dip chicken in sauce and give it a good mix.
- Serve and enjoy.

Nutritional facts per serving: Calories: 458 Kcal; Carbs: 16 g; Fat: 25 g; Protein: 40 g.

3.19 Tandoori Chicken Thighs

Preparation time: 15 mins

Cooking time: 30 mins

Servings: 4

Level of difficulty: Easy

Ingredients:

- 2 lb. chicken thighs
- 2-inches ginger, crushed
- 1½ cup plain yogurt
- 1 tsp. red chili powder
- 6 garlic cloves, crushed

- ½ tsp. turmeric
- 1 tbsp. tandoori paste
- 2 tbsp. desi ghee
- ½ tsp. cumin powder
- ½ tsp. coriander powder
- Salt and black pepper, to taste
- 1 tsp. Garam Masala
- 2 tbsp. lemon juice

Instructions:

- Mix the ingredients in a large bowl and add the chicken thighs.
- Refrigerate the chicken for 30 minutes after coating it.
- Let it sit 30 minutes.
- Place chicken in an air fryer basket at 350°F and cook for 30 minutes.
- Flip midway through 30 minutes.
- Once done, serve and enjoy.

Nutritional facts per serving: Calories: 588 Kcal; Carbs: 7 g; Fat: 30 g; Protein: 70 g.

3.20 Chicken Meatballs

Preparation time: 12 mins

Cooking time: 12 mins

Servings: 2

Level of difficulty: Easy

Ingredients:

- 1 lb. chicken mince
- Black pepper, to taste
- 1 egg
- 1/2 cup Panko bread crumbs
- 1 tbsp. low sodium soy sauce
- 1/4 cup fresh parsley
- Oil spray

Instructions:

- Mix chicken mince, parsley, Panko bread crumbs, salt, egg, pepper, and soy sauce in a large bowl.
- Mix thoroughly and make meatballs.
- Spray meatballs with oil.
- Cook it for 12 minutes at 400°F in the air fryer basket.
- Rotate meatballs halfway through.

- Once cooked, serve.

Nutritional facts per serving: Calories: 450 Kcal; Carbs: 19 g; Fat: 27 g; Protein: 60 g.

3.21 Fruit Pudding

Preparation time: 20 mins

Cooking time: 25 mins

Servings: 3

Level of difficulty: Easy

Ingredients:

For topping:

- 3 oz. flour
- 1 egg
- 2 oz. sugar
- 2 oz. soft butter
- 2 tbsp. milk
- ½ tbsp. baking powder

For filling:

- 1 cup of fresh or canned fruit, sliced

Instructions:

- Mix the topping items together.
- Keep going for three minutes or until the mixture is soft and creamy.
- Put the filling ingredients into a baking dish. Then, spread the topping ingredients over the fruit and smooth the top.
- Set the air fryer to 320°F and bake for 25 to 30 minutes, or until golden brown.

Nutritional facts per serving: Calories: 492 Kcal; Carbs: 70 g; Fat: 20 g; Protein: 19 g.

3.22 Pecan Strawberry Rhubarb Cobbler

Preparation time: 20 mins

Cooking time: 30 mins

Servings: 3

Level of difficulty: Expert

Ingredients:

- 1 cup frozen or fresh rhubarb, sliced
- ¼ cup sugar
- 1 cup fresh strawberries, sliced
- 1 tsp. lemon juice
- 1 tbsp. quick-cooking tapioca

- A pinch of salt

Topping:

- 1/4 cup chopped pecans
- Dash salt
- 1/3 cup all-purpose flour
- 1/8 tsp. baking powder
- 3 tbsp. sugar
- 1 large egg
- 2 tbsp. cold butter

Sauce:

- 2¼ tsp. Marsala wine
- ½ cup vanilla ice cream

Instructions:

- Preheat the air fryer to 350°F.
- In two 8-ounce ramekins or custard cups that have been greased, mix the first six ingredients together. Wait 15 minutes.
- Mix the flour, sugar, pecans, salt and baking powder in a small bowl. Then, add the butter and mix until the mixture looks like coarse crumbs. Put the egg in. Add it little by little to the fruit mix and spread it out evenly.
- In the air fryer pan, put ramekins on a tray. Cook until the topping is golden and a toothpick stuck in the middle comes out clean. It may take thirty minutes to do this.
- Put the ice cream and wine in a bowl that can go in the microwave. Cover and heat on 50% power for one to two minutes, or until hot. Stir to mix.
- Serve the cobbler while it is still warm.

Nutritional facts per serving: Calories: 258 Kcal; Carbs: 27 g; Fat: 15 g; Protein: 5 g.

3.23 Lemon Biscuits

Preparation time: 20 mins

Cooking time: 8 mins

Servings: 4

Level of difficulty: Easy

Ingredients:

- ¼ cup melted butter
- Oil spray, for greasing
- 2 cups self-rising flour
- ½ cup caster sugar
- 2 organic eggs

- 1 small lemon, zest, and juice

Instructions:

- Preheat the air fryer to 350°F.
- Put all the dry ingredients in a bowl and mix them together.
- Mix the wet items together in a different bowl.
- Mix the wet and dry ingredients together and work the dough into a soft, nice ball.
- Cut the dough into cookie shapes after rolling it out.
- Place the biscuits in an air fryer basket that has been sprayed with oil to make it easier to use.
- Do not flip the food during the 8 minutes of cooking.
- When it's done, serve it.

Nutritional facts per serving: Calories: 456 Kcal; Carbs: 14 g; Fat: 72 g; Protein: 10 g.

3.24 Red Velvet Cookies

Preparation time: 24 mins

Cooking time: 22 mins

Servings: 3

Level of difficulty: Intermediate

Ingredients:

- 2½ cups all-purpose flour
- 2 tsp. baking soda
- 6 tbsp. unsweetened cocoa powder
- 1 cup softened butter
- Pinch of salt
- ½ cup granulated sugar
- ½ cup brown sugar
- 1 tbsp. cream cheese
- 3 whisked eggs
- 1 tsp. vanilla extract
- 2 tbsp. milk
- 8 oz. white chocolate chips
- 2 tbsp. red food coloring

Instructions:

- Put the baking soda, cocoa powder, flour and salt in a bowl and mix them together. Set the bowl away for now.
- In a separate bowl, mix the brown sugar and butter. Next, add the egg and use a hand mixer to beat it in.

- Put cream cheese, sugar, milk and food coloring in a bowl and mix them together.
- As soon as the dry ingredients are mixed in, the egg mixture will be ready.
- After that, add the white chocolate chips and mix them in.
- Arrange cookies on the air fryer pan.
- Before you bake the cookies, heat the air fryer to 350°F and then bake for 22 minutes.

Nutritional facts per serving: Calories: 304 Kcal; Carbs: 28 g; Fat: 42 g; Protein: 30 g.

3.25 Walnut Chocolate Cookies

Preparation time: 15 mins

Cooking time: 22 mins

Servings: 2

Level of difficulty: Intermediate

Ingredients:

- 2 cups all-purpose flour
- 2 tsp. baking soda
- 2 tsp. vanilla extract
- 6 tbsp. unsweetened cocoa powder
- 1 cup brown sugar
- 2/3 cup softened butter
- 5 tbsp. milk
- 3 eggs
- 8 oz. chopped walnuts

Instructions:

- Add flour, baking soda and cocoa powder and mix them together. In a different bowl, mix the butter, eggs, and sugar together.
- Add the milk and vanilla to the mix.
- Add the dry ingredient to the mix of eggs and milk.
- Put the walnuts into the mix.
- On the air fryer pan, arrange cookies.
- Before putting the pan in the air fryer, make sure it is heated up to 350°F.
- Bake for 22 minutes and serve.

Nutritional facts per serving: Calories: 92 Kcal; Carbs: 50 g; Fat: 10 g; Protein: 44 g.

Chapter 4: Fast And Easy Everyday Recipes

4.1 Air Fried Broccoli

Preparation time: 5 mins
Cooking time: 6 mins
Servings: 1
Level of difficulty: Easy
Ingredients:

- 2 cups broccoli florets
- 4 egg yolks
- 2 cups coconut flour
- ¼ cup butter, melted
- Salt and pepper, to taste

Instructions:

- Melt the butter and add the egg yolks to a bowl. Put in the salt, pepper, and coconut flour. Stir it in again to make sure it's well mixed.
- Coat each broccoli floret in the mix, and then put it in the air fryer pan. If you need to, you can air fry in batches at 400°F for 6 minutes. Be careful when you take them out of the air fryer, and serve them right away.

Nutritional facts per serving: Calories: 61 Kcal; Carbs: 6 g; Fat: 5 g; Protein: 3 g.

4.2 Air Fried Green Tomatoes

Preparation time: 5 mins
Cooking time: 6 mins
Servings: 4
Level of difficulty: Easy
Ingredients:

- 4 medium green tomatoes
- 2 egg whites
- 1 clove garlic, minced
- 1/3 cup all-purpose flour
- 1 cup ground almonds
- ¼ cup almond milk
- 2 tsp. olive oil
- ½ cup panko breadcrumbs
- 1 tsp. paprika

Instructions:

- Take off the thinner ends of the tomato slices and cut them into ½" pieces. Place the flour on your plate.
- In a small bowl, whisk the egg whites and almond milk together until they become foamy. Spread the garlic, nuts, breadcrumbs, olive oil, and paprika out on a different plate and mix them all together well.
- First, coat the tomato slices with flour. Then, dip them in the egg white mixture. Finally, coat them with almond butter.
- In the air fryer basket, put 4 of the tomato slices that have been covered. For 6 to 8 minutes, air fry at 400°F. Serve right away.

Nutritional facts per serving: Calories: 257 Kcal; Carbs: 15 g; Fat: 16 g; Protein: 4 g.

4.3 Bacon And Green Beans

Preparation time: 5 mins

Cooking time: 8 mins

Servings: 4

Level of difficulty: Easy

Ingredients:

- 28 oz. canned green beans, drained
- ¼ cup minced onion
- 4 bacon slices, diced
- 1 tsp. lemon juice, freshly squeezed
- 1 tbsp. distilled white vinegar
- ½ tsp. black pepper, freshly ground
- ½ tsp. salt
- Cooking spray

Instructions:

- Spray oil on a baking pan. Add the bacon, green beans, vinegar, onion, salt, lemon juice, and pepper to the pan and mix them together until they are well mixed. Put the pan on top of the air fryer basket.
- For 4 minutes, air fry at 370°F. Add more 4 to 6 minutes of air fry time and stir the green beans. Wait until they are soft. Serve right away.

Nutritional facts per serving: Calories: 45 Kcal; Carbs: 4 g; Fat: 3 g; Protein: 2 g.

4.4 Bacon-Wrapped Beef Hot Dog

Preparation time: 5 mins

Cooking time: 10 mins

Servings: 4

Level of difficulty: Easy

Ingredients:

- 4 beef hot dogs

- 4 slices bacon

Instructions:

- Put the toothpick through a slice of bacon and wrap it around the hot dog. Wrap the other hot dogs in bacon and do the same process again. Then, put each dog in the air fryer pan.
- Bake at 370°F and turn over once halfway through. The hot dogs are ready to serve when they are hot and crispy.

Nutritional facts per serving: Calories: 230 Kcal; Carbs: 5 g; Fat: 7 g; Protein: 13 g.

4.5 Baked Cheese Sandwich

Preparation time: 5 mins

Cooking time: 8 mins

Servings: 2

Level of difficulty: Easy

Ingredients:

- 8 slices hot capicola
- 2 tbsp. mayonnaise
- 4 slices Brie cheese
- 4 slices sourdough bread

Instructions:

- Spread some mayonnaise on one side of every bread slice. Mayo-side down put two slices of bread in the air fryer pan.
- Place the Brie and capicola slices on top of the bread. Top with the last two slices of bread, mayo side on top.
- Put it in the oven at 350°F for 8 minutes, or until the cheese melts. Serve right away.

Nutritional facts per serving: Calories: 250 Kcal; Carbs: 27 g; Fat: 30 g; Protein: 6 g.

4.6 Baked Chorizo Scotch Eggs

Preparation time: 5 mins

Cooking time: 15 mins

Servings: 4

Level of difficulty: Intermediate

Ingredients:

- 1 lb. Mexican chorizo
- 1 tbsp. water
- 4 soft-boiled eggs
- 1 egg
- 1 cup panko breadcrumbs
- ½ cup all-purpose flour

- Cooking spray

Instructions:

- Cut the chorizo into four equal pieces. For each, make a disc and place a soft-boiled egg in the middle of it.
- Take the egg and wrap it fully in chorizo.
- Add the raw egg and 1 tablespoon of water, and mix them together. Place the panko on one plate and the flour on the other.
- First, roll the egg in flour, and then dip it in the egg batter. After that, coat them in crumbs and set them on a plate. Do it again with all of the eggs that you have left.
- Spray oil on the eggs and put them in the air fryer basket. In 10 minutes, bake at 360°F.
- After 5 to 10 minutes, turn it over and bake it again. Serve right away.

Nutritional facts per serving: Calories: 409 Kcal; Carbs: 0 g; Fat: 20 g; Protein: 21 g.

4.7 Beef Bratwursts

Preparation time: 5 mins

Cooking time: 15 mins

Servings: 4

Level of difficulty: Easy

Ingredients:

- 4 beef bratwursts

Instructions:

- Place the beef bratwursts in the air fryer basket and for 15 minutes at 375°F, turning once halfway through. Serve and enjoy.

Nutritional facts per serving: Calories: 222 Kcal; Carbs: 7 g; Fat: 16 g; Protein: 11 g.

4.8 Buttery Sweet Potatoes

Preparation time: 5 mins

Cooking time: 10 mins

Servings: 4

Level of difficulty: Easy

Ingredients:

- 1 tbsp. light brown sugar
- 2 tbsp. butter, melted
- Cooking spray
- 2 sweet potatoes, cubed

Instructions:

- Use parchment paper to line the air fryer basket.

- In a medium bowl, mix the brown sugar and butter that has been melted together. Coat the sweet potatoes in the sugary butter mixture as a way to cover them.
- Arrange the sweet potatoes on the baking paper and spray them with oil.
- For 5 minutes, air fry at 400°F. Spray the sweet potatoes with oil and shake the pan. Air fry for another 5 minutes, or until they're sufficiently tender to cut with a fork. Serve right away.

Nutritional facts per serving: Calories: 126 Kcal; Carbs: 13 g; Fat: 8 g; Protein: 6 g.

4.9 Carrot And Celery Croquettes

Preparation time: 10 mins
Cooking time: 6 mins
Servings: 4
Level of difficulty: Intermediate
Ingredients:

- Cooking spray
- 2 carrots, grated
- ½ cup finely chopped leek
- 2 celery stalks, grated
- ¼ tsp. black pepper
- 1 tbsp. garlic paste
- 1 tbsp. finely chopped fresh dill
- 1 tsp. fine sea salt
- ¼ cup flour
- 1 egg, lightly whisked
- ½ cup breadcrumbs
- ¼ tsp. baking powder
- Chive mayo, for serving

Instructions:

- Place the celery and carrots on a paper towel to drain off any extra water.
- The veggies and all other ingredients except for the chive mayo and breadcrumbs should be mixed together.
- Shape one tablespoon of the veggie mix into a ball with your hands. Keep doing this until all the mix is gone.
- You can use a palette knife or your hand to press down on each ball. Cover the whole thing with breadcrumbs. Spray cooking spray on the croquettes.
- Put the croquettes in the air fryer basket so they are all in one layer. Cook for 6 minutes at 360°F. Put the chive mayo on the side and serve the croquettes warm.

Nutritional facts per serving: Calories: 25 Kcal; Carbs: 5 g; Fat: 0 g; Protein: 1 g.

4.10 Cheesy Baked Grits

Preparation time: 10 mins

Cooking time: 12 mins

Servings: 6

Level of difficulty: Easy

Ingredients:

- ¾ cup hot water
- 1 tsp. red pepper flakes
- 1 egg, large, beaten
- 2 oz. packages instant grits
- 2 cloves garlic, diced
- 1 tbsp. butter, melted
- 1 cup cheddar cheese, shredded

Instructions:

- Put the grits, butter, egg, red pepper flakes and garlic in a baking pan. Mix everything together well. Add the cheese shreds and mix well.
- Put the pan in the air fryer basket and cook at 400°F for 12 minutes, or until the grits are cooked all the way through and a knife stuck near the middle comes out clean.
- Give it five minutes to rest before you serve.

Nutritional facts per serving: Calories: 203 Kcal; Carbs: 20 g; Fat: 10 g; Protein: 9 g.

4.11 Serrano Chili Toast

Preparation time: 5 mins

Cooking time: 5 mins

Servings: 1

Level of difficulty: Easy

Ingredients:

- 2 tbsp. parmesan cheese, grated
- 2 tsp. salted butter
- 2 tbsp. mozzarella cheese. grated
- 2 slices sourdough bread
- 5 thin slices of serrano chili
- ½ tsp. black pepper

Instructions:

- In a small bowl, mix the mozzarella, parmesan, butter, and chilies.
- On one side of each slice of bread, spread half of the batter. Add pepper.

- Put the slices in the air fryer basket with the cheese side facing up.
- Put it in the oven at 325°F for 5 minutes, or until the cheese melts and starts to turn a little brown. Serve right away.

Nutritional facts per serving: Calories: 210 Kcal; Carbs: 28 g; Fat: 11 g; Protein: 2 g.

4.12 Cheesy Potato Patties

Preparation time: 5 mins

Cooking time: 10 mins

Servings: 8

Level of difficulty: Easy

Ingredients:

- 2 lb. white potatoes
- 1 cup crushed crackers
- black pepper to taste
- ½ cup scallions, finely chopped
- ½ tsp. hot paprika
- 1 tbsp. fine sea salt
- ¼ cup canola oil
- 2 cups shredded Colby cheese

Instructions:

- Let the potatoes boil until they're soft. After you dry and peel them, mash them well so there are no lumps.
- Add the cheese, pepper, scallion, paprika and salt to the boiled potatoes. With your hands, form the batter into balls. Then, press the balls down with your fingers to make burgers.
- Put the crushed crackers and olive oil in a small dish. Cover the patties with the crumbs.
- Put the patties in the oven at 360°F for about 10 minutes. If necessary, do this in several batches.

Nutritional facts per serving: Calories: 93 Kcal; Carbs: 7 g; Fat: 6 g; Protein: 5 g.

4.13 Cheesy Sausage Balls

Preparation time: 5 mins

Cooking time: 15 mins

Servings: 6

Level of difficulty: Easy

Ingredients:

- 6 oz. shredded cheddar cheese
- 12 oz. jimmy dean's sausage
- 10 mozzarella cubes

Instructions:
- Combine the shredded cheese and sausage. Split the mixture into 10 equal pieces that can be stuffed.
- Put a cheese cube in the middle of the sausage and shape it into a ball.
- For 15 minutes or until crisp, air fry at 375°F. Serve right away.

Nutritional facts per serving: Calories: 173 Kcal; Carbs: 1 g; Fat: 14 g; Protein: 10 g.

4.14 Garlicky Baked Cherry Tomatoes

Preparation time: 5 mins
Cooking time: 6 mins
Servings: 2
Level of difficulty: Easy
Ingredients:
- 2 cups cherry tomatoes
- 1 tsp. olive oil
- 1 clove garlic, thinly sliced
- 1 tbsp. basil, freshly chopped
- 1/8 tsp. kosher salt
- Cooking spray

Instructions:
- Spray cooking spray on the air fryer baking pan and set it away.
- In a big bowl, mix the sliced garlic, olive oil, cherry tomatoes, and kosher salt. Place the tomatoes in the pan in a single layer.
- Put the tomatoes in the air fryer and set it to 360°F. Bake for 6 minutes, or until they get soft and barely there.
- Put in a bowl and let it sit for 5 minutes. Add the chopped basil on top, and serve hot.

Nutritional facts per serving: Calories: 25 Kcal; Carbs: 1 g; Fat: 2 g; Protein: 1 g.

4.15 Garlicky Knots

Preparation time: 10 mins
Cooking time: 10 mins
Servings: 8
Level of difficulty: Easy
Ingredients:
- 11 oz. French bread dough, cut into 8 slices
- 1 tsp. dried parsley
- 2 tsp. garlic powder
- ¼ cup melted butter

Instructions:

- In a bowl, mix the butter, garlic powder, and parsley together. Mix well by stirring.
- Lay the slices of French bread dough out on a clean surface. Then, roll each slice into a rope that is 6 inches long. Put the ropes on a plate and tie them into knots. Use the butter mix to brush the knots.
- Place the knots in the air fryer.
- For 5 minutes, or until the knots are golden brown, air fry at 350°F. In the middle of cooking, flip the knots over. Serve right away.

Nutritional facts per serving: Calories: 90 Kcal; Carbs: 16 g; Fat: 3 g; Protein: 2 g.

4.16 Garlicky Zoodles

Preparation time: 10 mins

Cooking time: 10 mins

Servings: 4

Level of difficulty: Intermediate

Ingredients:

- 2 large zucchinis, spiralized
- 2 tbsp. fresh basil, chopped
- 1 tbsp. olive oil, divided
- 2 yellow summer squashes, spiralized
- 1 garlic clove, whole
- ½ tsp. kosher salt
- Cooking spray

Instructions:

- Spray cooking spray on the basket of your air fryer. Put the summer squash and zucchini in a big bowl. Add salt and 1 teaspoon of olive oil. Toss to cover well.
- Put the summer squash and zucchini in the air fryer and add the garlic.
- For 10 minutes, or until soft and smelling good, air fry at 360°F. Toss the summer squash and zucchini spirals in the middle of the cooking time.
- Put the summer squash and zucchini that have been cooked on a plate and set it away.
- Go ahead and take the garlic out of the air fryer. Let it cool down for a while. In a small bowl, mix the garlic and the rest of the olive oil that you have left over. Mix well by stirring.
- Spread garlic oil on the spiralized summer squash and zucchini, and then sprinkle basil on top.

Nutritional facts per serving: Calories: 80 Kcal; Carbs: 3 g; Fat: 7 g; Protein: 1 g.

4.17 Golden Salmon And Carrot Croquettes

Preparation time: 15 mins

Cooking time: 10 mins

Servings: 6

Level of difficulty: Intermediate

Ingredients:

- 2 egg whites
- 1 cup panko breadcrumbs
- 1 cup almond flour
- 2 tbsp. chopped chives
- 2/3 cup grated carrots
- 1 lb. chopped salmon fillet
- ½ cup chopped onion
- 2 tbsp. minced garlic cloves
- Cooking spray

Instructions:

- Spray cooking spray on the air fryer basket. In one bowl, whisk the egg whites. In a different bowl, put the flour. In a third bowl, put the bread crumbs. Put away.
- In a big bowl, mix the fish, garlic, carrots, chives and onion. Mix well by stirring.
- Use your hands to shape the batter into balls. Coat the balls well by dredging them in flour, then egg, and finally breadcrumbs.
- Put the fish balls in the air fryer and spray them with cooking spray.
- For 10 minutes at 350°F, or until golden and crispy. In the middle, shake the basket. Serve right away.

Nutritional facts per serving: Calories: 192 Kcal; Carbs: 0 g; Fat: 10 g; Protein: 25 g.

4.18 Chicken Fingers

Preparation time: 15 mins

Cooking time: 12 mins

Servings: 3

Level of difficulty: Easy

Ingredients:

- 2 lb. chicken breast fillet, striped
- 2 oz. ranch dressing seasoning mix
- 2 eggs, whisked
- 2 tbsp. olive oil
- 2 cups breadcrumbs

Instructions:
- Spray the chicken strips with oil first.
- Add ranch dressing and salt.
- Dump the pieces into bread crumbs after coating with egg.
- Cook it for 12 minutes at 400°F in the air fryer basket.
- Serve it with your preferred sauce.

Nutritional facts per serving: Calories: 981 Kcal; Carbs: 52 g; Fat: 38 g; Protein: 100 g.

4.19 Salmon Fritters

Preparation time: 15 mins
Cooking time: 15 mins
Servings: 4
Level of difficulty: Easy
Ingredients:
- 1 lb. minced salmon
- 1 tsp. fresh dill, minced
- 2 eggs
- ¼ cup all-purpose flour
- 7 oz. Halloumi cheese
- salt and black pepper, to taste

Instructions:
- Preheat the air fryer to 360°F.
- Grease a baking dish and in a big bowl, combine all the ingredients.
- From this mixture, form little fritters and arrange them on the basket f air fryer and cook for 15 minutes.

Nutritional facts per serving: Calories: 240 Kcal; Carbs: 15 g; Fat: 17 g; Protein: 35 g.

4.20 Chicken Strips

Preparation time: 10 mins
Cooking time: 15 mins
Servings: 4
Level of difficulty: Easy
Ingredients:
- 1 lb. chicken fillet
- 1 tbsp. butter
- 1 tsp. paprika
- Salt and pepper, to taste

- 1 tbsp. heavy whipping cream

Instructions:

- Cut the fillet into strips with a clean pair of scissors. Season each strip with salt and pepper to taste.
- Preheat your air fryer to 365°F. Put a bit of butter in the basket and wait for it to melt.
- Add the strips and air fry them for six minutes, then flip them and cook for another five minutes.
- Mix the heavy whipped cream and paprika together while you wait.
- Serve hot.

Nutritional facts per serving: Calories: 270 Kcal; Carbs: 15 g; Fat: 15 g; Protein: 20 g.

Chapter 5: Poultry Recipes

5.1 Herbed Fried Chicken

Preparation time: 15 mins

Cooking time: 15 mins

Servings: 4

Level of difficulty: Easy

Ingredients:

- 1 lb. chicken tenders
- 2 eggs
- 1 bay leaf
- ½ cup whole milk
- 2 tbsp. olive oil
- ½ cup grated parmesan
- ¼ tsp. salt
- ½ tsp. dried basil
- ½ tsp. dried parsley
- ¼ cup whey protein powder
- ¼ tsp. ground black pepper

Instructions:

- Preheat air fryer to 450°F and line tray or pan with foil.
- Combine chicken tenders, bay leaf, basil, parsley and whole milk in a large bowl. Marinate overnight covered in fridge.
- Mix parmesan, protein powder, salt, paprika and pepper in a small bowl.
- Whisk eggs in another bowl.
- Drain chicken from milk, dip into egg, and coat with protein powder mixture. Place chicken tenders on the prepared sheet tray and coat with olive oil.
- Bake tenders for 15 minutes in the air fryer until golden brown. Enjoy hot.

Nutritional facts per serving: Calories: 344 Kcal; Carbs: 3 g; Fat: 15 g; Protein: 48 g.

5.2 BBQ Fried Chicken

Preparation time: 10 mins

Cooking time: 15 mins

Servings: 4

Level of difficulty: Intermediate

Ingredients:

- 1 lb. chicken tenders
- 2 eggs
- ¼ cup whey protein powder
- ½ cup whole milk
- ¼ tsp. salt
- ½ cup BBQ sauce
- ½ cup grated parmesan
- ½ tsp. paprika
- ¼ tsp. ground black pepper
- 2 tbsp. olive oil

Instructions:

- Line the baking pan or air fryer tray with foil and preheat to 450 degrees F.
- Combine whole milk and chicken tenders in a large bowl. Marinate overnight in the fridge.
- Mix parmesan, protein powder, pepper, salt, and paprika in a small bowl.
- In another dish, whisk the egg.
- Coat the chicken in egg and protein powder. Place coated chicken tenders on the prepped sheet tray and drizzle with olive oil after dipping.
- Bake tenders for 15 minutes in the air fryer until golden brown.
- Enjoy hot with BBQ sauce on the side.

Nutritional facts per serving: Calories: 412 Kcal; Carbs: 4 g; Fat: 19 g; Protein: 48 g.

5.3 Chicken Nuggets

Preparation time: 10 mins

Cooking time: 15 mins

Servings: 4

Level of difficulty: Easy

Ingredients:

- 1 lb. chicken breast
- 1½ cups ground pork rinds
- 2 tbsp. mustard
- ¼ cup mayonnaise
- ½ tsp. ground black pepper
- ½ tsp. salt
- 2 tbsp. whole milk

Instructions:

- Set your air fryer to 400°F, line the tray with foil, and spray with cooking oil.
- Pat the chicken breast dry with a paper towel. Chicken strips should be 1 ½ inches thick and 2 inches long. You may slice it into any desired shape, but larger pieces will take longer to cook.
- Combine mayo, mustard, and milk in a small bowl and mix thoroughly.
- In another dish, mix salt, ground pork rinds, and pepper.
- Completely cover chicken nuggets by dipping them in the mayonnaise and pork rind mixtures. Once done, place on the tray and continue with remaining chicken pieces.
- Bake the nuggets for 8 minutes on the tray in the air fryer, then turn and bake for another 7 minutes. Serve hot!

Nutritional facts per serving: Calories: 278 Kcal; Carbs: 1 g; Fat: 18 g; Protein: 24 g.

5.4 Greek Garlic Chicken

Preparation time: 20 mins

Cooking time: 30 mins

Servings: 4

Level of difficulty: Intermediate

Ingredients:

- 1 lb. chicken thighs
- 3 tbsp. olive oil
- 1 zucchini, thinly sliced
- 3 tbsp. minced garlic
- 1 lemon, thinly sliced
- 3 tbsp. lemon juice
- ½ tsp. sea salt
- 1 tsp. oregano, dried
- ½ lb. asparagus
- ¼ tsp. ground black pepper

Instructions:

- Start by preheating your air fryer to 400°F and lining the tray with foil.
- Mix 2 tbsp. olive oil, dried oregano, lemon juice, and garlic in a large bowl.
- Toss chicken in the marinade and cover the bowl and refrigerate for two hours.
- Pour the remaining olive oil in a sauté pan and heat on high. To brown the marinated chicken, sear each side for 3 minutes.
- Pour the leftover marinade from the dish over the browned chicken on a foil-lined pan.
- Layer lemon slices, zucchini and asparagus around the chicken.
- Place tray in preheated air fryer and cook for 20 minutes. Serve hot.

Nutritional facts per serving: Calories: 244 Kcal; Carbs: 6 g; Fat: 15 g; Protein: 24 g.

5.5 Creamy Garlic Chicken Thighs

Preparation time: 20 mins

Cooking time: 30 mins

Servings: 4

Level of difficulty: Expert

Ingredients:

- 1 lb. chicken thighs
- 3 tbsp. olive oil
- ¼ cup heavy cream
- 1 zucchini, thinly sliced
- 3 tbsp. minced garlic
- 1 lemon, thinly sliced
- 3 tbsp. lemon juice
- ½ tsp. sea salt
- 1 tsp. oregano, dried
- ½ lb. asparagus
- ¼ tsp. ground black pepper

Instructions:

- Start by preheating your air fryer to 400°F and lining the tray with foil.
- Mix 2 tbsp. olive oil, dried oregano, lemon juice, and garlic in a large bowl.
- Toss chicken in the marinade and cover the bowl and refrigerate for two hours.
- Pour the remaining olive oil in a sauté pan and heat on high. To brown the marinated chicken, sear each side for 3 minutes.
- Pour the leftover marinade from the dish over the browned chicken on a foil-lined pan.
- Layer lemon slices, zucchini and asparagus around the chicken.
- Place tray in preheated air fryer and cook for 20 minutes. Add cream to the pan and simmer for 5 more minutes. Serve hot.

Nutritional facts per serving: Calories: 264 Kcal; Carbs: 10 g; Fat: 18 g; Protein: 24 g.

5.6 Lemon Garlic Chicken Thighs

Preparation time: 20 mins

Cooking time: 30 mins

Servings: 4

Level of difficulty: Easy

Ingredients:
- 3 tbsp. olive oil
- ¼ tsp. ground black pepper
- 3 tbsp. minced garlic
- 3 tbsp. lemon juice
- ½ tsp. sea salt
- 1 lb. chicken thighs
- 1 lemon, sliced thinly

Instructions:
- Start by preheating your air fryer to 400°F and lining the tray with foil.
- Mix 2 tbsp. olive oil, garlic and lemon juice in a large bowl.
- Toss chicken in the marinade. Cover the bowl and refrigerate for two hours.
- Place the last tablespoon of olive oil in a sauté pan and heat on high. Sear marinated chicken for 3 minutes per side to brown.
- Pour the leftover marinade from the dish over the browned chicken on a foil-lined pan.
- Layer lemon slices around the chicken and place tray in preheated air fryer and cook for 20 minutes. Serve hot.

Nutritional facts per serving: Calories: 201 Kcal; Carbs: 2 g; Fat: 14 g; Protein: 24 g.

5.7 Brussels and Garlic Chicken

Preparation time: 20 mins

Cooking time: 30 mins

Servings: 4

Level of difficulty: Intermediate

Ingredients:
- 1 lb. chicken thighs
- 3 tbsp. olive oil
- 1 tsp. oregano, dried
- 3 tbsp. minced garlic
- 3 tbsp. lemon juice
- ¼ tsp. ground black pepper
- ½ tsp. sea salt
- 1 lemon, sliced thinly
- 1 lb. Brussel sprouts, cut in half

Instructions:
- Start by preheating your air fryer to 400°F and lining the tray with foil.

- Mix 2 tbsp. olive oil, garlic and lemon juice in a large bowl.
- Toss chicken in the marinade. Cover the bowl and refrigerate for two hours.
- Place the last tablespoon of olive oil in a sauté pan and heat on high. Sear marinated chicken for 3 minutes per side to brown.
- Pour the leftover marinade from the dish over the browned chicken on a foil-lined pan.
- Layer Brussel sprouts and lemon slices around the chicken and place tray in preheated air fryer and cook for 20 minutes. Serve hot.

Nutritional facts per serving: Calories: 228 Kcal; Carbs: 4 g; Fat: 13 g; Protein: 24 g.

5.8 Creamy Brussels And Garlic Chicken

Preparation time: 20 mins

Cooking time: 30 mins

Servings: 4

Level of difficulty: Intermediate

Ingredients:

- 1 lb. chicken thighs
- ½ cup heavy cream
- 3 tbsp. olive oil
- 1 tsp. oregano, dried
- 3 tbsp. minced garlic
- 3 tbsp. lemon juice
- ¼ tsp. ground black pepper
- ½ tsp. sea salt
- 1 lb. Brussel sprouts, cut in half

Instructions:

- Start by preheating your air fryer to 400°F and lining the tray with foil.
- Mix 2 tbsp. olive oil, dried oregano, and garlic and lemon juice in a large bowl.
- Toss chicken in the marinade. Cover the bowl and refrigerate for two hours.
- Place the last tablespoon of olive oil in a sauté pan and heat on high. Sear marinated chicken for 3 minutes per side to brown.
- Pour the leftover marinade from the dish and cream over the browned chicken on a foil-lined pan.
- Arrange Brussel sprouts around the chicken and place tray in preheated air fryer and cook for 20 minutes. Serve hot.

Nutritional facts per serving: Calories: 265 Kcal; Carbs: 5 g; Fat: 15 g; Protein: 24 g.

5.9 Garlic Parmesan Chicken Thighs

Preparation time: 20 mins

Cooking time: 30 mins

Servings: 4

Level of difficulty: Intermediate

Ingredients:

- 1 lb. chicken thighs
- ½ cup parmesan cheese, grated
- 3 tbsp. olive oil
- 1 tsp. oregano, dried
- 3 tbsp. minced garlic
- 3 tbsp. lemon juice
- ¼ tsp. ground black pepper
- ½ tsp. sea salt

Instructions:

- Start by preheating your air fryer to 400°F and lining the tray with foil.
- Mix 2 tbsp. olive oil, dried oregano, lemon juice, and garlic in a large bowl.
- Toss chicken in marinade. Cover the bowl and refrigerate for two hours.
- Place the remaining tablespoon of olive oil in a sauté pan and heat on high. To brown the marinated chicken, sear each side for 3 minutes.
- Pour the leftover marinade from the dish over the browned chicken on a foil-lined pan.
- Place tray in preheated air fryer and cook for 20 minutes.
- Remove the pan from air fryer and sprinkle parmesan on chicken. Return to air fryer and cook for further 5 minutes. Serve hot.

Nutritional facts per serving: Calories: 289 Kcal; Carbs: 6 g; Fat: 17 g; Protein: 26 g.

5.10 Black Pepper Chicken Thighs

Preparation time: 20 mins

Cooking time: 30 mins

Servings: 4

Level of difficulty: Easy

Ingredients:

- 1 lb. chicken thighs
- 3 tbsp. olive oil
- ½ tsp. sea salt
- 3 tbsp. minced garlic

- 1 tsp. black pepper

Instructions:

- Start by preheating your air fryer to 400°F and lining the tray with foil.
- Mix 2 tbsp. olive oil, garlic, pepper and salt in a large bowl.
- Toss chicken in marinade. Cover the bowl and refrigerate for two hours.
- Put the remaining tablespoon of olive oil in a sauté pan and heat on high. Sear marinated chicken for 3 minutes per side to brown.
- Pour the leftover marinade from the dish over the browned chicken on a foil-lined pan.
- Place tray in preheated air fryer and cook for 20 minutes. Serve hot.

Nutritional facts per serving: Calories: 206 Kcal; Carbs: 1 g; Fat: 15 g; Protein: 24 g.

5.11 Spicy Chicken Strips

Preparation time: 5 mins

Cooking time: 12 mins

Servings: 5

Level of difficulty: Intermediate

Ingredients:

- 1 lb. boneless chicken strips
- 1 cup buttermilk
- 1 tsp. salt
- 1½ tbsp. hot pepper sauce
- 1 tbsp. olive oil
- ½ tsp. black pepper, divided
- ½ tsp. salt
- ¾ cup panko breadcrumbs
- ¼ tsp. hot pepper, or to taste

Instructions:

- Combine buttermilk, salt, hot sauce, and ¼ teaspoon black pepper in a small bowl. Add chicken strips in the marinade and keep it in fridge for two hours. Add and whisk oil to breadcrumbs, salt, hot pepper and the remaining black pepper in another dish.
- Discard the marinade from the chicken strips. Add a few strips at a time to the crumb mixture. Press the crumbs onto the strips for a firm, uniform coating.
- Put half the strips in the basket in a single layer. Cook at 350°F for 12 minutes. After cooking the first batch, cook the rest.

Nutritional facts per serving: Calories: 207 Kcal; Carbs: 5 g; Fat: 9 g; Protein: 25 g.

5.12 Turkey Parmesan Meatballs

Preparation time: 25 mins
Cooking time: 16 mins
Servings: 2
Level of difficulty: Intermediate
Ingredients:

- 1½ lb. ground turkey
- 1/3 cup shredded mozzarella cheese
- 1 egg
- 1 cup breadcrumbs
- Salt and black pepper, to taste
- 1 tbsp. Italian seasoning
- ½ cup marinara sauce
- ½ cup parmesan cheese

Instructions:

- In a large bowl, combine parmesan cheese, black pepper, salt, ground turkey, breadcrumbs, eggs, and Italian seasoning.
- Make meatballs of this mixture and spray meatballs with oil.
- Place chicken meatballs in air fryer basket and cook at 375°F for 12 minutes, turning halfway through.
- Then cover each turkey meatball with marinara.
- Finally, add mozzarella cheese and cook 4 more minutes.

Nutritional facts per serving: Calories: 384 Kcal; Carbs: 56 g; Fat: 36 g; Protein: 99 g.

5.13 Thanksgiving Turkey

Preparation time: 10 mins
Cooking time: 35 mins
Servings: 4
Level of difficulty: Intermediate
Ingredients:

- 2 lb. bone-in turkey breast
- Salt and black pepper, to taste
- 2 tsp. ground rosemary
- ½ tsp. dried thyme
- 1/3 tsp. garlic powder
- 1/3 tsp. dried sage
- 1 tsp. dark brown sugar

- 1/3 tsp. paprika
- Oil spray

Instructions:
- Spray an air fryer basket with oil.
- Add salt, thyme, black pepper, garlic powder, sage, paprika, and brown sugar to a large bowl and stir thoroughly.
- Rub it on turkey breast.
- Insert the turkey breast skin-side down into an air fryer basket.
- Cook at 400°F for 20 minutes.
- Flip the breast afterwards and cook another 15 minutes.
- After cooling, slice and serve.

Nutritional facts per serving: Calories: 393 Kcal; Carbs: 2 g; Fat: 16 g; Protein: 48 g.

5.14 Cheesy Chicken Sausage Rolls

Preparation time: 12 mins

Cooking time: 14 mins

Servings: 4

Level of difficulty: Intermediate

Ingredients:
- 4 cups chicken mince
- 1 cup zucchini, grated
- 1 cup corn kernels, roughly chopped
- 1 frozen puff pastry sheet, halved
- 2/3 cup cheddar cheese
- 2 small carrots, grated
- 1 egg, lightly beaten
- 2 tsp. Vegemite Squeeze
- 1 cup Panko breadcrumbs
- 2 garlic cloves, crushed
- 1 green onion, chopped
- Sweet chili sauce, for serving

Instructions:
- Mix minced chicken, carrots, corn, zucchini, cheese, and breadcrumbs in a large bowl.
- Stir in vegemite, green onions, and garlic.
- Season with black pepper and salt to taste.
- Finely mix.

- Next, place one half of puff pastry on a clean flat surface, add 1/3 cup of chopped mixture, and brush edges with egg, and roll up.
- Divide into 3 equal parts.
- Repeat with the other half of pastry.
- Cook it for 14 minutes at 400°F in an oil-greased air fryer basket.
- Serve with sweet chili sauce.

Nutritional facts per serving: Calories: 2127 Kcal; Carbs: 245 g; Fat: 57 g; Protein: 156 g.

5.15 Crumbed Chicken Schnitzel

Preparation time: 10 mins

Cooking time: 16 mins

Servings: 4

Level of difficulty: Intermediate

Ingredients:

- 2 eggs, lightly whisked
- 8 chicken thigh fillets
- 1 tsp. herb seasoning
- 1 cup Panko breadcrumbs
- 2 cups coleslaw
- 1/3 cup plain flour
- Salt and pepper, to taste

Instructions:

- Place chicken between two plastic wrap sheets and pound it using rolling pin.
- Mix herb seasoning and breadcrumbs in a small dish.
- Beat the egg in a medium dish.
- Sprinkle salt and pepper over flour on a dish.
- Dip chicken in egg and bread crumbs after flouring.
- Leave it in the fridge for 30 minutes.
- Air-fry the chicken for 16 minutes at 400°F and serve with coleslaw.

Nutritional facts per serving: Calories: 952 Kcal; Carbs: 41 g; Fat: 26 g; Protein: 41 g.

5.16 Japanese Chicken Tenders

Preparation time: 10 mins

Cooking time: 14 mins

Servings: 4

Level of difficulty: Intermediate

Ingredients:

Ingredient

- 2 tsp. pickled ginger
- 2 lb. chicken tenderloins
- Oil spray
- 2 tbsp. crumb seasoning
- 1/2 cup Japanese-style mayonnaise

Instructions:

- Season chicken with crumb seasoning.
- Spray oil on it.
- Pre-heat the air fryer for 3 minutes at 400°F.
- Cook chicken in air fryer basket for 14 minutes.
- Mix mayonnaise and pickled ginger in a bowl.
- Serve and enjoy cooked chicken with mayo sauce.

Nutritional facts per serving: Calories: 260 Kcal; Carbs: 2 g; Fat: 8 g; Protein: 45 g.

5.17 Chicken Enchiladas

Preparation time: 10 mins

Cooking time: 12 mins

Servings: 4

Level of difficulty: Intermediate

Ingredients:

- 1 cup Colby jack cheese, shredded
- 16 flour tortillas
- 2 onions chopped
- 2 lb. rotisserie chicken
- ¼ cup brown sugar
- 28 oz. enchilada sauce
- Chopped green onions, cherry tomatoes and sour cream for garnish

Instructions:

- Shred rotisseries chicken in a big bowl and add onions in it.
- Heat enchilada sauce in a pot over burner.
- Incorporate brown sugar and heat thoroughly. Allow to cool after turning off the flame.
- Spread sauce on tortillas, add onion and chicken mix, cheese, and fold.
- Add enchiladas to an oil-greased air fryer basket and cook for 12 minutes at 375°F.
- Serve with green onion, sour cream and cherry tomatoes and enjoy.

Nutritional facts per serving: Calories: 817 Kcal; Carbs: 61 g; Fat: 32 g; Protein: 73 g.

5.18 Chicken Quesadilla

Preparation time: 12 mins
Cooking time: 6 mins
Servings: 1
Level of difficulty: Easy
Ingredients:

- 6 oz. cooked chicken breast, cubed
- 2 corn tortillas
- 2 tbsp. grated cheddar cheese
- 2 tbsp. of guacamole

Instructions:

- Spray oil on the air fryer basket.
- Place tortilla in air fryer basket.
- Top with guacamole, chicken, cheese, and another tortilla.
- Cook 6 minutes at 350°F flipping halfway through.
- Serve and enjoy.

Nutritional facts per serving: Calories: 415 Kcal; Carbs: 11 g; Fat: 24 g; Protein: 35 g.

5.19 Cosmic Wings

Preparation time: 10 mins
Cooking time: 12 mins
Servings: 4
Level of difficulty: Easy
Ingredients:

- 1½ lb. chicken wings
- 8 oz. Tessemae's Cosmic Jerry Sauce
- ½ tbsp. onion powder
- 1 tbsp. garlic powder
- 1 tbsp. dried parsley
- ½ tbsp. paprika
- 1/3 tsp. rosemary
- 1/4 tsp. salt
- 1/4 tsp. pepper
- 1 tbsp. lemon juice

Instructions:

- In a bowl, combine garlic, paprika, onion, rosemary, parsley, salt, and pepper.
- Coat the chicken and toss.
- Place it in an oil-sprayed air fryer basket.
- Flip midway through 12 minutes at 375°F.
- Stir in cosmic jerry sauce once wings are done.
- Sprinkle lemon juice over top and serve.

Nutritional facts per serving: Calories: 337 Kcal; Carbs: 3 g; Fat: 12 g; Protein: 50 g.

5.20 Chicken Parmesan Meatballs

Preparation time: 25 mins

Cooking time: 16 mins

Servings: 2

Level of difficulty: Intermediate

Ingredients:

- 1½ lb. ground chicken breast
- 1/3 cup shredded mozzarella cheese
- 1 egg
- 1 cup breadcrumbs
- Salt and black pepper, to taste
- 1 tbsp. Italian seasoning
- ½ cup marinara sauce
- ½ cup parmesan cheese

Instructions:

- In a large bowl, combine parmesan cheese, black pepper, salt, chicken mince, breadcrumbs, eggs, and Italian seasoning.
- Make meatballs of this mixture and spray meatballs with oil.
- Place chicken meatballs in air fryer basket and cook at 375°F for 12 minutes, turning halfway through.
- Then cover each chicken meatball with marinara.
- Finally, add mozzarella cheese and cook 4 more minutes.

Nutritional facts per serving: Calories: 1384 Kcal; Carbs: 156 g; Fat: 36 g; Protein: 102 g.

5.21 BBQ Chicken Drumsticks

Preparation time: 15 mins

Cooking time: 25 mins

Servings: 2

Level of difficulty: Easy

Ingredients:
- 6 chicken drumsticks
- 4 tbsp. peach preserve
- 2 tbsp. Lemon Juice
- 1 cup coleslaw
- 1/2 cup barbecue sauce
- Salt and black pepper, to taste

Instructions:
- Mix BBQ sauce, lemon juice, peach preserve, black pepper and salt in a large bowl.
- Mix thoroughly, and then add drumsticks.
- Coat and layer thighs in an oil-sprayed air fryer basket.
- Cook at 375°F for 25 minutes, flipping midway.
- Serve with coleslaw and enjoy.

Nutritional facts per serving: Calories: 579 Kcal; Carbs: 55 g; Fat: 40 g; Protein: 60 g.

5.22 Crispy Chicken Tenders

Preparation time: 12 mins
Cooking time: 16 mins
Servings: 2
Level of difficulty: Intermediate

Ingredients:
- 1½ lb. chicken tender
- 1 tsp. Italian seasoning
- 1 cup Panko bread crumbs
- Salt and black pepper, to taste
- 1½ cup parmesan cheese
- 2 cups Italian bread crumbs
- Oil spray
- 2 eggs

Instructions:
- Season chicken tender with salt and pepper.
- In a bowl, combine Italian bread crumbs, Panko bread crumbs, Italian seasoning, and Parmesan cheese. In another bowl, whisk eggs.
- Coat chicken tender with eggs and then finally in crumbs.
- Place it in the air fryer basket and cook for 16 minutes at 400°F, turning halfway.
- After cooking, serve with ketchup.

Nutritional facts per serving: Calories: 821 Kcal; Carbs: 61 g; Fat: 28 g; Protein: 77 g.

5.23 Turkey Meatballs

Preparation time: 12 mins
Cooking time: 12 mins
Servings: 2
Level of difficulty: Easy
Ingredients:

- 1 lb. ground turkey
- Black pepper, to taste
- 1 egg
- 1/2 cup Panko bread crumbs
- 1 tbsp. low sodium soy sauce
- 1/4 cup fresh parsley
- Oil spray

Instructions:

- Mix turkey, parsley, Panko bread crumbs, salt, egg, pepper, and soy sauce in a large bowl.
- Mix thoroughly and make meatballs.
- Spray meatballs with oil.
- Cook it for 12 minutes at 400°F in the air fryer basket.
- Rotate meatballs halfway through.
- Once cooked, serve.

Nutritional facts per serving: Calories: 591 Kcal; Carbs: 20 g; Fat: 28 g; Protein: 70 g.

5.24 Asian Chicken Wings

Preparation time: 10 mins
Cooking time: 14 mins
Servings: 3
Level of difficulty: Intermediate
Ingredients:

- 12 chicken wings
- 4 garlic cloves
- Salt and black pepper, to taste
- 1/3 cup chicken broth
- Oil spray, for greasing
- 1 tbsp. soy sauce

- 1/3 tsp. garlic powder
- ¼ cup vinegar
- ¾ cup sugar
- 2 tbsp. cornstarch mixed in 3 tbsp. cold water

Instructions:
- Pre-heat the air fryer for a few minutes at 400°F.
- Sprinkle salt and pepper on wings and spritz with oil.
- Air-fry the wings at 400°F for 12 minutes.
- Meanwhile simmer broth in a pan for a few minutes.
- Continue cooking for 5 minutes with soy sauce, garlic cloves, vinegar and sugar.
- Add water-mixed cornstarch and then add wings in sauce for 2 minutes.

Nutritional facts per serving: Calories: 928 Kcal; Carbs: 83 g; Fat: 43 g; Protein: 51 g.

5.25 Greek Chicken Meatballs

Preparation time: 15 mins

Cooking time: 14 mins

Servings: 2

Level of difficulty: Intermediate

Ingredients:
- 1 lb. ground chicken
- 1½ tbsp. garlic paste
- ¼ tsp. fresh ground black pepper
- 1 large egg
- 1 tsp. lemon zest
- 1 tbsp. dried oregano
- ¾ tsp. kosher salt
- 1 tsp. dried onion powder
- Oil spray

Instructions:
- Add the ingredients in a big bowl and mix thoroughly and create meatballs.
- Spray meatballs with oil.
- Cook it for 14 minutes at 350°F in an oil-greased air fryer basket.
- Turn and flip meatballs halfway.
- Serve and enjoy.

Nutritional facts per serving: Calories: 535 Kcal; Carbs: 30 g; Fat: 20 g; Protein: 71 g.

5.26 Orange And Maple Glazed Chicken

Preparation time: 15 mins

Cooking time: 15 mins

Servings: 4

Level of difficulty: Intermediate

Ingredients:

- ½ cup maple syrup
- 2 garlic cloves, minced
- 2 tsp. onion powder
- ½ tsp. garlic powder
- 2 lb. chicken wings, bone-in
- ½ cup teriyaki sauce
- ¼ tsp. pepper
- 1/2 cup orange marmalade

Instructions:

- Pre-heat the air fryer for a few minutes at 400°F.
- Mix all ingredients in a large bowl, coat chicken wings, and marinate for 30 minutes in the fridge.
- After preheating, place wings in the oil-sprayed air fryer basket.
- Cook at 400°F for 15-20 minutes.
- Remember to flip midway.
- Once done, serve and enjoy.

Nutritional facts per serving: Calories: 672 Kcal; Carbs: 60 g; Fat: 16 g; Protein: 68 g.

5.27 Apple Chicken With Blue Cheese

Preparation time: 20 mins

Cooking time: 22 mins

Servings: 2

Level of difficulty: Intermediate

Ingredients:

- 1 tbsp. apple juice
- ¼ cup blue cheese, crumbled
- 4 chicken breast, halved
- 1 tbsp. lemon juice
- 4 tsp. chicken seasoning
- Salt and black pepper, to taste

Instructions:
- Preheat the air fryer for 5 minutes at 400°F.
- In a large bowl, combine chicken, apple juice, lemon juice, pepper, salt, and seasoning. Mix thoroughly.
- These ingredients should coat the chicken nicely.
- After heating, put chicken to the air fryer basket.
- Cook at 400°F for 15-22 minutes.
- When done, top with cheese and serve.

Nutritional facts per serving: Calories: 346 Kcal; Carbs: 14 g; Fat: 10 g; Protein: 46 g.

5.28 Black Pepper Chicken Wings

Preparation time: 20 mins

Cooking time: 30 mins

Servings: 4

Level of difficulty: Easy

Ingredients:
- 1 lb. chicken wings
- 3 tbsp. olive oil
- ½ tsp. sea salt
- 3 tbsp. minced garlic
- 1 tsp. black pepper

Instructions:
- Start by preheating your air fryer to 400°F and lining the tray with foil.
- Mix 2 tbsp. olive oil, garlic, pepper and salt in a large bowl.
- Toss chicken wings in marinade. Cover the bowl and refrigerate for two hours.
- Put the remaining tablespoon of olive oil in a sauté pan and heat on high. Sear marinated chicken wings for 3 minutes per side to brown.
- Pour the leftover marinade from the dish over the browned chicken wings on a foil-lined pan.
- Place tray in preheated air fryer and cook for 20 minutes. Serve hot.

Nutritional facts per serving: Calories: 260 Kcal; Carbs: 4 g; Fat: 15 g; Protein: 25 g.

5.29 BBQ Chicken Thighs

Preparation time: 15 mins

Cooking time: 25 mins

Servings: 2

Level of difficulty: Easy

Ingredients:
- 6 chicken thighs bone-in

- 4 tbsp. peach preserve
- 2 tbsp. Lemon Juice
- 1 cup coleslaw
- 1/2 cup barbecue sauce
- Salt and black pepper, to taste

Instructions:

- Mix BBQ sauce, lemon juice, peach preserve, black pepper and salt in a large bowl.
- Mix thoroughly, and then add thighs.
- Coat and layer thighs in an oil-sprayed air fryer basket.
- Cook at 375°F for 25 minutes, flipping midway.
- Serve with coleslaw and enjoy.

Nutritional facts per serving: Calories: 573 Kcal; Carbs: 50 g; Fat: 40 g; Protein: 60 g.

5.30 Chicken Sticks

Preparation time: 10 mins

Cooking time: 10 mins

Servings: 4

Level of difficulty: Intermediate

Ingredients:

- 1 lb. chicken strips
- 2 tbsp. mustard
- ¼ cup mayonnaise
- 2 tbsp. whole milk
- ½ tsp. ground black pepper
- ½ tsp. salt
- 1½ cups ground pork rinds

Instructions:

- Set your air fryer to 400°F, line the tray with foil, and spray with cooking oil.
- Pat dry chicken strips with paper towels.
- Combine mustard, milk and mayonnaise in a small bowl and mix thoroughly.
- In another dish, mix ground pork rinds, pepper and salt.
- Completely coat chicken strips by dipping them in the mayonnaise and pork rind mixtures.
- Bake the strips for 10 minutes in air fryer, turning once in between.

Nutritional facts per serving: Calories: 250 Kcal; Carbs: 2 g; Fat: 14 g; Protein: 27 g.

5.31 Tandoori Chicken Legs

Preparation time: 15 mins
Cooking time: 30 mins
Servings: 4
Level of difficulty: Easy
Ingredients:
- 2 lb. chicken legs
- 2-inches ginger, crushed
- 1½ cup plain yogurt
- 1 tsp. red chili powder
- 6 garlic cloves, crushed
- ½ tsp. turmeric
- 1 tbsp. tandoori paste
- 2 tbsp. desi ghee
- ½ tsp. cumin powder
- ½ tsp. coriander powder
- Salt and black pepper, to taste
- 1 tsp. Garam Masala
- 2 tbsp. lemon juice

Instructions:
- Mix the ingredients in a large bowl and add the chicken thighs.
- Refrigerate the chicken for 30 minutes after coating it.
- Let it sit 30 minutes.
- Place chicken in air fryer basket at 350°F and cook for 30 minutes.
- Flip midway through 30 minutes.
- Once done, serve and enjoy.

Nutritional facts per serving: Calories: 588 Kcal; Carbs: 7 g; Fat: 30 g; Protein: 70 g.

5.32 Mustard Chicken Wings

Preparation time: 10 mins
Cooking time: 10 mins
Servings: 4
Level of difficulty: Intermediate
Ingredients:
- 1 lb. chicken wings

- 2 tbsp. mustard
- ¼ cup mayonnaise
- 2 tbsp. whole milk
- ½ tsp. ground black pepper
- ½ tsp. salt
- 1½ cups ground pork rinds

Instructions:
- Set your air fryer to 400°F, line the tray with foil, and spray with cooking oil.
- Pat dry chicken wings with paper towels.
- Combine mustard, milk and mayonnaise in a small bowl and mix thoroughly.
- In another dish, mix ground pork rinds, pepper and salt.
- Completely coat chicken wings by dipping them in the mayonnaise and pork rind mixtures.
- Bake the wings for 10 minutes in air fryer, turning once in between.

Nutritional facts per serving: Calories: 257 Kcal; Carbs: 2 g; Fat: 14 g; Protein: 27 g.

5.33 Chicken With Beans And Chili

Preparation time: 15 mins
Cooking time: 25 mins
Servings: 2
Level of difficulty: Intermediate
Ingredients:
- 6 chicken breast, cubed
- ½ tsp. garlic powder
- 1 can corn kernels, drained
- 2 tbsp. olive oil
- Salt, to taste
- 1 cup black beans
- 1 tbsp. chili powder
- ½ tsp. garlic powder
- 1 bell pepper, finely chopped

Instructions:
- Pre-heat the air fryer for a few minutes at 400°F.
- Add all ingredients into a bowl and stir.
- Transfer it to an oil-sprayed air fryer basket.
- Cook at 390°F for 25 minutes.
- When done, serve and enjoy.

Nutritional facts per serving: Calories: 900 Kcal; Carbs: 82 g; Fat: 24 g; Protein: 88 g.

5.34 Black Pepper Chicken Legs

Preparation time: 20 mins

Cooking time: 30 mins

Servings: 4

Level of difficulty: Easy

Ingredients:

- 1 lb. chicken legs
- 3 tbsp. olive oil
- ½ tsp. sea salt
- 3 tbsp. minced garlic
- 1 tsp. black pepper

Instructions:

- Start by preheating your air fryer to 400°F and lining the tray with foil.
- Mix 2 tbsp. olive oil, garlic, pepper and salt in a large bowl.
- Toss chicken legs in marinade. Cover the bowl and refrigerate for two hours.
- Put the remaining tablespoon of olive oil in a sauté pan and heat on high. Sear marinated chicken legs for 3 minutes per side to brown.
- Pour the leftover marinade from the dish over the browned chicken legs on a foil-lined pan.
- Place tray in preheated air fryer and cook for 20 minutes. Serve hot.

Nutritional facts per serving: Calories: 256 Kcal; Carbs: 3 g; Fat: 15 g; Protein: 24 g.

5.35 Chicken Pizza

Preparation time: 12 mins

Cooking time: 12 mins

Servings: 1

Level of difficulty: Intermediate

Ingredients:

- 1 cup grilled chicken, cubed
- 2 tbsp. all-purpose flour,
- 1 tbsp. olive oil
- 6 oz. pizza dough
- 1 cup mozzarella cheese, shredded
- 1/2 cup pizza sauce
- 1/2 cup ricotta cheese

Instructions:

- Pre-heat the air fryer for a few minutes at 400°F.
- Roll out ready-made pizza dough to air fryer basket size on a level surface.
- Keep sprinkling flour into the dough to prevent sticking.
- Fork the dough after brushing half the oil over it.
- Place dough in basket and cook for 5 minutes.
- Remove it and put pizza sauce over it.
- Then add grilled chicken, ricotta and mozzarella cheese.
- Return it to the air fryer basket.
- Cook another 6 minutes.
- Serve and enjoy.

Nutritional facts per serving: Calories: 484 Kcal; Carbs: 18 g; Fat: 24 g; Protein: 4 g.

5.36 Crispy Chicken Wings

Preparation time: 15 mins

Cooking time: 15 mins

Servings: 2

Level of difficulty: Intermediate

Ingredients:

- 1½ lb. chicken wings
- 1 tsp. Italian seasoning
- 1 cup Panko bread crumbs
- Salt and black pepper, to taste
- 1½ cup parmesan cheese
- 2 cups Italian bread crumbs
- Oil spray
- 2 eggs

Instructions:

- Season chicken wings with salt and pepper.
- In a bowl, combine Italian bread crumbs, Panko bread crumbs, Italian seasoning, and Parmesan cheese. In another bowl, whisk eggs.
- Coat chicken wings with eggs and then finally in crumbs mixture.
- Place it in the air fryer basket and cook for 15 minutes at 400°F, turning halfway.
- After cooking, serve with ketchup.

Nutritional facts per serving: Calories: 500 Kcal; Carbs: 51 g; Fat: 28 g; Protein: 77 g.

5.37 Spicy Crunchy Chicken

Preparation time: 10 mins
Cooking time: 10 mins
Servings: 4
Level of difficulty: Easy
Ingredients:
- 1 lb. chicken strips
- ½ cup fresh grated parmesan
- 2 tbsp. dill, chopped
- ½ tsp. salt
- ½ tsp. cayenne pepper
- ¼ tsp. garlic powder
- ½ cup pork rinds, crushed
- ¼ tsp black pepper
- 2 tbsp. melted butter

Instructions:
- Pre-heat your air fryer to 450°F and line the tray with foil.
- Arrange chicken strips on the foil-lined tray.
- Combine remaining ingredients in a food processor or small bowl and blend thoroughly.
- Cover the chicken strips with the pork rind mixture, covering the top evenly and filling the crust.
- Bake the strips for 10 minutes in the preheated air fryer. The top crust should be nicely golden.

Nutritional facts per serving: Calories: 356 Kcal; Carbs: 3 g; Fat: 19 g; Protein: 40 g.

5.38 Garlic Chicken

Preparation time: 10 mins
Cooking time: 10 mins
Servings: 4
Level of difficulty: Easy
Ingredients:
- 1 lb. chicken tenders
- 2 tbsp. dill, chopped
- ¼ tsp. garlic powder
- ½ tsp. salt
- 2 tsp. fresh minced garlic
- ½ cup fresh grated parmesan

- ½ cup pork rinds, crushed
- ¼ tsp. black pepper
- 2 tbsp. melted butter

Instructions:

- Pre-heat your air fryer to 450°F and line the tray with foil.
- Arrange chicken on the foil-lined tray.
- Combine remaining ingredients in a food processor or small bowl and blend thoroughly.
- Cover the chicken tenders with the pork rind mixture, covering the top evenly and filling the crust.
- Bake the chicken tenders for 10 minutes in the preheated air fryer. The top crust should be nicely golden.

Nutritional facts per serving: Calories: 352 Kcal; Carbs: 2 g; Fat: 21 g; Protein: 40 g.

5.39 Almond Crusted Chicken

Preparation time: 10 mins

Cooking time: 15 mins

Servings: 1

Level of difficulty: Easy

Ingredients:

- 2 breast halves
- 1 tsp. olive oil
- pinch of garlic powder
- 3 tbsp. chopped almonds
- 1 tsp. mustard
- pinch of sea salt
- 1 tsp. lemon juice
- pinch of black pepper
- 1 tsp. grated Parmesan cheese

Instructions:

- Pre-heat the air fryer to 350°F and mix lemon juice, olive oil and mustard. Season chicken breast with pepper, salt, and garlic powder and apply mustard mixture to it.
- Mix finely chopped almonds with Parmesan cheese and sprinkle over chicken breasts. Chicken should be placed in the air fryer basket. Cook for 15 minutes or until desired.

Nutritional facts per serving: Calories: 255 Kcal; Carbs: 2 g; Fat: 3 g; Protein: 30 g.

5.40 Turkey and Tomatoes Patties

Preparation time: 12 mins

Cooking time: 16 mins

Servings: 2

Level of difficulty: Intermediate

Ingredients:

- 3 oz. almond flour, grounded
- Salt and black pepper, to taste
- 1½ lb. lean turkey, grounded
- 1 cup feta cheese, crumbled
- ½ cup tomatoes, chopped
- Oil spray
- 2 red onions, chopped

Instructions:

- Mix almond flour, ground turkey, tomatoes, salt, cheese, onions and pepper in a bowl.
- Make 1 inch thick patties from this mixture.
- Spray oil on both sides of patties.
- Place in air fryer basket.
- Cook each side for 8 minutes at 350°F.
- Serve with favorite sauce and enjoy.

Nutritional facts per serving: Calories: 712 Kcal; Carbs: 65 g; Fat: 30 g; Protein: 42 g.

5.41 Chicken Patties

Preparation time: 12 mins

Cooking time: 12 mins

Servings: 2

Level of difficulty: Intermediate

Ingredients:

- 3 oz. almond flour, grounded
- Salt and black pepper, to taste
- 1½ lb. chicken mince
- 1 cup feta cheese, crumbled
- Oil spray
- 2 red onions, chopped

Instructions:

- Mix almond flour, chicken mince, salt, cheese, onions and pepper in a bowl.

- Make 1 inch thick patties from this mixture.
- Spray oil on both sides of patties.
- Place in air fryer basket.
- Cook each side for 6 minutes at 350°F.
- Serve with favorite sauce and enjoy.

Nutritional facts per serving: Calories: 444 Kcal; Carbs: 23 g; Fat: 29 g; Protein: 42 g.

5.42 Zesty And Spiced Chicken

Preparation time: 15 mins
Cooking time: 25 mins
Servings: 2
Level of difficulty: Intermediate

Ingredients:
- 1½ lb. chicken breasts, boneless
- 1-inch ginger, paste
- 2 cloves of garlic, minced
- ¼ tsp. lemon zest
- 1½ tbsp. lemon juice
- 2 cups plain yogurt
- 2 tbsp. olive oil
- 1 tsp. red chili powder
- Salt and black pepper, to taste
- 1 tsp. thyme
- 1 tsp. turmeric powder
- 1 tsp. five-spice powder

Instructions:
- Combine all ingredients and coat chicken thoroughly.
- Marinate chicken for 2 hours in fridge.
- Put it in an oil-sprayed air fryer basket.
- Cook for 18-25 minutes at 400°F, flipping midway through.
- Serve and enjoy.

Nutritional facts per serving: Calories: 900 Kcal; Carbs: 20 g; Fat: 22 g; Protein: 100 g.

5.43 Siracha-Honey Wings

Preparation time: 15 mins
Cooking time: 20 mins
Servings: 2
Level of difficulty: Easy
Ingredients:

- 10 chicken wings
- 2 tsp. lemon juice
- 2 tbsp. Siracha sauce
- 1/3 cup honey
- 1 tbsp. soy sauce
- 4 tbsp. butter, melted
- Salt and black pepper, to taste
- Oil spray, for greasing

Instructions:

- Mix honey, soy sauce, Siracha sauce, salt, pepper, melted butter and lemon juice in a big bowl.
- Simmer it to half amount over low heat.
- Season the chicken wings with salt and pepper and spritz them with oil.
- Cook chicken wings in the air fryer at 400°F for 15–20 minutes, turning halfway.
- Coat cooked wings in the prepared sauce and enjoy.

Nutritional facts per serving: Calories: 800 Kcal; Carbs: 47 g; Fat: 31 g; Protein: 40 g.

5.44 Parmesan Chicken Tenders

Preparation time: 10 mins
Cooking time: 12 mins
Servings: 2
Level of difficulty: Easy
Ingredients:

- 1 lb. skinless chicken breast, sliced
- ½ cup Panko bread crumbs
- Salt and pepper, to taste
- 1 cup parmesan cheese, grated
- 2 eggs
- ¼ tsp. paprika
- ½ cup buttermilk

- Oil spray for greasing

Instructions:

- In a bowl, mix the eggs and buttermilk together.
- In a different bowl, mix the paprika, Panko bread crumbs, salt, pepper, and Parmesan cheese.
- Dip the strips first in the egg wash and then in the mix of cheeses.
- Spray oil on all sides of the chicken.
- At 400°F, cook for 12 minutes, turning over once.
- Serve when it's done.

Nutritional facts per serving: Calories: 495 Kcal; Carbs: 25 g; Fat: 41 g; Protein: 20 g.

5.45 Hot Buffalo Wings

Preparation time: 15 mins

Cooking time: 25 mins

Servings: 4

Level of difficulty: Easy

Ingredients:

- Oil spray, for greasing
- 1/3 cup hot sauce
- Salt and black pepper, to taste
- 2 lb. chicken wings
- 1 tbsp. olive oil
- 2 tbsp. butter

Instructions:

- Put oil, butter, hot sauce, salt, and pepper in a bowl.
- Marinate wings in the prepared marinade for 30 minutes.
- Put the wings in air fryer basket that has been lined with parchment paper.
- At 370° F, cook it for 25 minutes and flip it over halfway through.

Nutritional facts per serving: Calories: 148 Kcal; Carbs: 13 g; Fat: 23 g; Protein: 65 g.

Chapter 6: Beef, Pork And Lamb Recipes

6.1 Air-Fried Meatloaf

Preparation time: 1 day

Cooking time: 55 mins

Servings: 4

Level of difficulty: Expert

Ingredients:

- ½ lb. ground veal
- ½ lb. ground pork
- 1 egg
- 2 spring onions, chopped
- ¼ cup fresh cilantro, chopped
- ¼ cup breadcrumbs
- 2 tsp. chipotle chili sauce
- 1/2 tsp. siracha salt
- 1/2 tsp. black pepper
- 1/2 cup ketchup
- 1 tsp. molasses
- 1 tsp. olive oil

Instructions:

- Preheat the air fryer until 400°F.
- In a bake dish that can fit in an air fryer, mix the beef and pork together.
- Then add the spring onions, egg, parsley, bread crumbs, and half a teaspoon of Siracha salt.
- Use clean hands to shape it into a loaf.
- In a bowl, mix together ketchup, chili sauce, molasses, and olive oil.
- The meatloaf goes in the air fryer for 25 minutes.
- After 25 minutes, pour the ketchup mix over the meatloaf.
- For an extra seven minutes or until the inside is 160°F, air-fry the loaf.
- Leave the loaf in the air fryer for another five minutes after turning it off for five minutes.
- You can serve it after five more minutes of rest.

Nutritional facts per serving: Calories: 585 Kcal; Carbs: 30 g; Fat: 38 g; Protein: 29 g.

6.2 Ground Beef Wellington

Preparation time: 20 mins

Cooking time: 25 mins

Servings: 4

Level of difficulty: Expert

Ingredients:

- ½ lb. ground beef
- 1 tube of crescent rolls, refrigerated
- 2 tbsp. all-purpose flour
- 1 tbsp. butter
- ½ cup Half & half cream
- 1 tsp. dried parsley
- ½ cup chopped mushrooms
- ¼ tsp pepper
- 1 egg yolk
- ¼ tsp. salt
- 2 tbsp. chopped onion
- 1 egg, whisked

Instructions:

- Preheat the air fryer until 300°F.
- In a pan, cook the mushrooms in butter for 5 to 6 minutes, until they are soft.
- Add the pepper and flour and mix until everything is well mixed.
- Add some milk. After it comes to a boil, whisk it thoroughly for two minutes to make it thick.
- The mushroom and onion mix in a bowl should be seasoned with salt and pepper added to taste.
- It should be well mixed with the beef.
- Use the dough to make two loaves.
- Cut the dough in half, and then roll out each half into a square. After putting the loaves inside, seal the squares' sides. Put down a layer of egg that has been beaten.
- Let the Wellington sit in an air fryer for 18 to 22 minutes, or until it hits 160 degrees Fahrenheit on the inside.
- The beef Wellington should be served with a mushroom sauce that has parsley in it.

Nutritional facts per serving: Calories: 317 Kcal; Carbs: 24 g; Fat: 10 g; Protein: 29 g.

6.3 Taco Twists

Preparation time: 25 mins

Cooking time: 30 mins

Servings: 4

Level of difficulty: Intermediate

Ingredients:

- 1 tube crescent rolls
- 1/8 tsp. salt
- 2/3 cup cheddar cheese, shredded
- 1/3 lb. ground beef
- 3 tbsp. diced green chilies
- 1 diced onion
- 1/8 tsp. ground cumin
- ¼ tsp. garlic powder
- ¼ tsp. hot pepper sauce
- 1/3 cup salsa

Instructions:

- Preheat the air fryer to 300°F.
- Cook the beef and onions over medium-high heat until the meat is done.
- Add butter, hot pepper sauce, salt, cumin, chili powder, and cheese.
- You should have four squares of dough. Put a half-cup of the meat mixture in the middle of each one.
- When the four sides are joined, twist them together.
- In an oil-covered air fryer basket, cook for 18 to 22 minutes.
- Serve right away.

Nutritional facts per serving: Calories: 316 Kcal; Carbs: 30 g; Fat: 21 g; Protein: 16 g.

6.4 Southern Style Fried Pork Chops

Preparation time: 10 mins

Cooking time: 20 mins

Servings: 4

Level of difficulty: Intermediate

Ingredients:

- 4 Pork chops
- ¼ cup all-purpose flour
- 3 tbsp. Buttermilk

- Ziploc bag 1
- Seasoning salt and pepper, to taste
- Cooking oil spray

Instructions:

- Use a towel to dry the pork chops.
- Season the pork chops with salt and pepper before you serve them.
- Before cooking, pork chops should be soaked in buttermilk.
- Put the pork chops in a Ziploc bag after flouring them. Allow it to cover well by shaking it well.
- The pork chops should be cooked in an Air fryer.
- Before you cook the pork chops, spray them with the oil.
- In an air fryer set to 380°F for 15 minutes, cook your pork chops. Turn the pork chops over after 10 minutes.

Nutritional facts per serving: Calories: 376 Kcal; Carbs: 35 g; Fat: 47 g; Protein: 33 g.

6.5 Honey And Mustard Pork Meatballs

Preparation time: 10 mins

Cooking time: 10 mins

Servings: 4

Level of difficulty: Intermediate

Ingredients:

- 1 lb. minced pork
- salt and pepper, to taste
- 1 tsp. mustard
- 1 small red onion
- 1 tsp. garlic puree
- 2 tsp. honey
- 1 tsp. pork seasoning

Instructions:

- Mix them all together in a food processor to make a paste, and then form the meatballs from this mixture.
- In an air fryer, cook your pork meatballs for 10 minutes at 360°F.
- Serve right away.

Nutritional facts per serving: Calories: 327 Kcal; Carbs: 28 g; Fat: 35 g; Protein: 17 g.

6.6 Pork Chops With Broccoli

Preparation time: 10 mins

Cooking time: 10 mins

Servings: 2

Level of difficulty: Intermediate

Ingredients:

- 2½ oz. Bone-in pork chops
- ½ tsp. paprika
- 2 cloves of garlic, minced
- 2 tbsp. avocado oil, divided
- ½ tsp. garlic powder
- ½ tsp. onion Powder
- 2 cups broccoli florets
- 1 tsp. salt, divided

Instructions:

- Preheat the Air fryer to 350°F. Spray non-stick spray on the basket.
- Before cooking, put a tablespoon of oil on each side of the pork chops.
- Season each side of the pork chops with garlic powder, onion powder, paprika, and half a teaspoon of salt.
- In the air fryer basket, cook the pork chops for five minutes.
- You can add the garlic, broccoli, and the last 1/2 teaspoon of salt and 1 tablespoon of oil to the dish while the pork chops are cooking and then toss everything together.
- In your air fryer, turn the pork chops over.
- After putting the broccoli in a basket, put it back in the air fryer.
- In the middle of cooking, stir the broccoli.
- Serve the pork chops with broccoli after taking it out of the air fryer.

Nutritional facts per serving: Calories: 310 Kcal; Carbs: 31 g; Fat: 17 g; Protein: 40 g.

6.7 Air Fryer Pork Tenderloin

Preparation time: 10 mins

Cooking time: 18 mins

Servings: 4

Level of difficulty: Intermediate

Ingredients:

- 1½ lb. Pork tenderloin
- 1 tsp. Dried rosemary

- 1 tbsp. minced garlic
- ¼ tsp. salt
- ⅛ tsp. Black pepper, freshly cracked
- 1 tsp. Italian seasoning
- ¼ cup yellow mustard
- 3 tbsp. brown sugar

Instructions:

- Clean the pork tenderloin and pat it dry. Cut a cut in the top of the tenderloin with a sharp knife. In the cuts, put slices of garlic. Season the meat with salt and pepper.
- Bowl for small things: Mix the rosemary, Italian spice, and mustard brown sugar together in a bowl. Put the pork in the mustard mixture and heat it for a few minutes. Put it in the fridge for at least two hours to marinate.
- Place the pork tenderloin in the oiled air fryer pan. Put the meat in the Air fryer at 400°F for 18 to 20 minutes, or until a fast-read meat thermometer reads 145°F.
- Let it rest for five minutes after taking it out of the air fryer before cutting it.

Nutritional facts per serving: Calories: 312 Kcal; Carbs: 25 g; Fat: 15 g; Protein: 36 g.

6.8 Salt And Pepper Pork Chops

Preparation time: 10 mins

Cooking time: 15 mins

Servings: 2

Level of difficulty: Intermediate

Ingredients:

- 4 pork chops
- ½ tsp. sea salt
- 2 tbsp. canola oil
- 1 white egg
- 1 tsp. sea salt
- ¾ cup potato starch
- ¼ tsp. black pepper, freshly ground
- 2 scallions, sliced
- 2 jalapeño pepper, sliced

Instructions:

- Put a little oil on the basket of the air fryer. In a medium-sized bowl, whisk egg whites with pepper and salt until the mixture is foamy.
- Cut pork chops in half and dry them off with paper towels to make cutlets. Whisk the egg whites together and add them to the pork chops in a bowl. Wrap around completely. Wait at least 20 minutes before serving.

- In a big bowl, sprinkle pork chops with Potato Starch. Potato Starch should be used to coat pork chops. Get the pork out of its skin and put it in the Air Fryer Basket. Spray oil on the meat.
- Set the oven to 360°F and cook for nine minutes, shaking the basket every so often and adding oil between shakes. After six more minutes at 400 degrees, the pork should be crispy and golden.

Nutritional facts per serving: Calories: 237 Kcal; Carbs: 19 g; Fat: 15 g; Protein: 30 g.

6.9 Jamaican Jerk Pork Chops

Preparation time: 25 mins

Cooking time: 10 mins

Servings: 2

Level of difficulty: Intermediate

Ingredients:

- ¼ cup Peach preserves
- 4 thin-cut, boneless pork loin chops
- ¼ tsp. pepper
- ½ orange pepper
- ½ yellow pepper
- 3 tsp. Caribbean jerk seasoning
- 1 tbsp. softened butter
- ½ tsp. salt
- ½ red pepper

Instructions:

- Preheat the air fryer to 400°F.
- Set aside a bowl to mix the butter and peach preserve in.
- Herbs and spices should be used to season pork chops. Spray oil on the air fryer basket.
- In an air fryer, fry seasoned chops one at a time for two to three minutes on each side. Bring them outside to keep them warm.
- Slice the bell peppers very thinly.
- Air fry for 5 to 6 minutes, or until crisp and golden brown. Shake the bin a few times.
- Again, put the pork chops back in the air fryer and butter them again. Cook until they're done the way you like.
- Put it in the Air fryer for one and a half to two minutes.
- Serve it with peppers on the side.

Nutritional facts per serving: Calories: 368 Kcal; Carbs: 32 g; Fat: 14 g; Protein: 28 g.

6.10 Juicy Pork Chops

Preparation time: 25 mins

Cooking time: 20 mins

Servings: 4

Level of difficulty: Intermediate

Ingredients:

- 1 tbsp. Dijon mustard
- 1 egg
- ¼ cup parmesan cheese, grated
- 4 boneless pork chops
- ½ cup panko breadcrumbs
- ½ tsp. onion powder
- ¼ cup dry breadcrumbs
- ½ tsp. garlic powder
- 1 tsp. kosher salt

Instructions:

- Preheat the air fryer to 400°F.
- Use a little salt on the pork chops before cooking them.
- In a bowl, mix ketchup and egg.
- In a zip-top bag, you should mix onion powder, garlic powder, Parmesan cheese and breadcrumbs. Shake the bag.
- Spread the egg mix over the pork chops, and then cover them with breadcrumbs. To make sure that everything is covered, shake the bag.
- Put two chops in the basket of the air fryer and oil them.
- After six minutes of cooking, the temperature inside should be 145°F. Flip them over and cook for another six minutes.

Nutritional facts per serving: Calories: 569 Kcal; Carbs: 17 g; Fat: 40 g; Protein: 32 g.

6.11 Boneless Pork Chop

Preparation time: 20 mins

Cooking time: 15 mins

Servings: 2

Level of difficulty: Easy

Ingredients:

- 2 boneless pork chops
- Salt and black pepper, to taste
- 2 tsp. Pork Rub

Instructions:

- Preheat the air fryer to 400°F.
- Season the pork with salt and black pepper, along with pork rub.
- In the air fryer, cook the chops for six minutes.
- Make sure the chops are cooked all the way through, which should take about 5 to 8 minutes on the other side.
- Let the chops rest before you serve them.

Nutritional facts per serving: Calories: 255 Kcal; Carbs: 19 g; Fat: 11 g; Protein: 19 g.

6.12 Gingery Pork Meatballs

Preparation time: 15 mins

Cooking time: 30 mins

Servings: 4

Level of difficulty: Intermediate

Ingredients:

- 1 lb. of ground pork
- 2 tsp. grated lime zest
- 1½ tbsp. honey
- 1 egg
- 2 tbsp. lime juice
- 2 scallions, chopped
- 1 tsp. fish sauce
- 1 tbsp. grated ginger
- Salt, to taste
- ¼ cup chopped cilantro
- 1 minced clove of garlic
- 1 jalapeño, chopped
- ½ cup Panko

Instructions:

- Put fish sauce, salt, egg, zest, lime juice, honey, and panko in a bowl and mix well. Put the powdered sugar on top after letting the mixture sit for 60 seconds.
- Now add the onions, garlic, ginger, and jalapeño and mix the meat and herbs in well.
- Form the meatballs and put the meatballs in the basket and splash oil on top of them.
- At 400°F, cook for 8 to 12 minutes.

Nutritional facts per serving: Calories: 620 Kcal; Carbs: 60 g; Fat: 31 g; Protein: 22 g.

6.13 Mustard Pork Chops

Preparation time: 5 mins

Cooking time: 15 mins

Servings: 4

Level of difficulty: Easy

Ingredients:

- 3 garlic cloves, minced
- Salt and black pepper, to taste
- 4 tbsp. Dijon mustard
- 2 tbsp. chives, chopped
- 1½ lb. pork chops

Instructions:

- Put all the ingredients in a bowl and marinate the pork chops for at least three hours.
- Preheat Air fryer to 350°F.
- Put the pork chops in the air fryer basket.
- The chops should be cooked for about 15 minutes.
- Serve right away, and enjoy!

Nutritional facts per serving: Calories: 260 Kcal; Carbs: 20 g; Fat: 12 g; Protein: 19 g.

6.14 Pork Belly

Preparation time: 30 mins

Cooking time: 12 mins

Servings: 4

Level of difficulty: Intermediate

Ingredients:

- 1 lb. pork belly sliced, patted dry
- 1 tsp. onion powder
- ¼ cup tomato sauce
- 2 garlic cloves, pressed
- 1 tbsp. Worcestershire sauce
- 1 tsp. cayenne pepper Sea salt and black pepper, to taste

Instructions:

- Put all the ingredients in a bowl and marinate the meat for at least three hours.
- Preheat Air fryer to 360°F.
- Put the pork belly in the air fryer and cook for 12 minutes.
- Serve right away, and have fun!

Nutritional facts per serving: Calories: 600 Kcal; Carbs: 60 g; Fat: 7 g; Protein: 12 g.

6.15 Pork Satay

Preparation time: 15 mins

Cooking time: 15 mins

Servings: 4

Level of difficulty: Intermediate

Ingredients:

- 1 lb. pork tenderloin cubes
- 2 tbsp. coconut milk
- 2 tbsp. freshly squeezed lime juice
- 2 tbsp. unsalted peanut butter
- 2 garlic cloves, minced
- ¼ cup minced onion
- 1 tbsp. curry powder

Instructions:

- Preheat the Air fryer to 375°F.
- Mix the pork, jalapeno, peanut butter, garlic, onion, lime juice, coconut milk and curry powder together. Set aside at room temperature for 10 minutes.
- Take the pork out of the marinade and thread it on bamboo skewers. Air Fry the pork for 15 minutes or until a meat thermometer reads at least 145°F.
- Serve right away.

Nutritional facts per serving: Calories: 194 Kcal; Carbs: 10 g; Fat: 7 g; Protein: 25 g.

6.16 Beef Ribs

Preparation time: 20 mins

Cooking time: 15 mins

Servings: 4

Level of difficulty: Intermediate

Ingredients:

- 1½ lb. chuck short ribs
- 1 tsp. garlic powder
- 1 tbsp. Dijon mustard
- 4 tbsp. apple cider vinegar
- 2 tbsp. oil
- 2 tbsp. BBQ sauce
- 1 tsp. onion powder

- 1 tsp. smoked paprika
- 2 tbsp. brown sugar
- sea salt and black pepper, to taste

Instructions:
- Put all the ingredients in a bowl and marinate the meat for at least three hours.
- Preheat the Air fryer to 360°F.
- Put the meat ribs in the basket of air fryer.
- The meat should be cooked for about 15 minutes.
- Serve right away, and have fun!

Nutritional facts per serving: Calories: 365 Kcal; Carbs: 34 g; Fat: 6 g; Protein: 5 g.

6.17 Steak Cubes

Preparation time: 20 mins

Cooking time: 16 mins

Servings: 4

Level of difficulty: Intermediate

Ingredients:
- 1 lb. top round steak, cubes
- 1 medium onion, cut into wedges
- Sea salt and crushed red pepper, to taste
- ¼ cup brown sugar
- 2 bell peppers, sliced
- 2 tbsp. toasted sesame oil
- 2 tbsp. rice vinegar
- 2 tbsp. soy sauce
- 1 tsp. stone-ground mustard
- 1 tsp. ginger, peeled and minced
- 4 cloves garlic, crushed
- 1 lb. broccoli florets

Instructions:
- In a mixing bowl, put the steak, vinegar, mustard, oil, garlic, soy sauce, ginger, salt, sugar, and red pepper flakes.
- Preheat the Air fryer to 365°F. Put the steak and veggies in the basket of the air fryer. The steak cubes should be cooked for about 8 minutes, during which time they should be turned over twice.
- Turn the heat up to 400°F and keep cooking for another 8 minutes.

Nutritional facts per serving: Calories: 317 Kcal; Carbs: 18 g; Fat: 12 g; Protein: 32 g.

6.18 Teriyaki Beef

Preparation time: 10 mins

Cooking time: 25 mins

Servings: 4

Level of difficulty: Easy

Ingredients:

- 1½ lb. beef, boneless
- 2 garlic cloves, minced
- 1 tsp. chili powder
- 2 tbsp. agave nectar
- ¼ cup teriyaki sauce
- 1 tsp. mustard powder
- Sea salt and black pepper, to taste

Instructions:

- Preheat the Air fryer to 350°F.
- Mix the beef and the other ingredients together.
- Put the beef in the basket of the air fryer. Cook for about 25 minutes.
- Serve hot and have fun.

Nutritional facts per serving: Calories: 377 Kcal; Carbs: 6 g; Fat: 25 g; Protein: 26 g.

6.19 Tenderloin Filets

Preparation time: 10 mins

Cooking time: 18 mins

Servings: 4

Level of difficulty: Intermediate

Ingredients:

- 1 lb. beef tenderloin filets
- 1 tsp. mustard seeds
- 1 tsp. paprika
- Sea salt and black pepper, to taste
- 2 tbsp. soy sauce
- ¼ cup red wine
- 2 tbsp. butter, melted
- 1 tsp. garlic, minced

Instructions:

- Put all the ingredients in a bowl and marinate the meat for at least three hours.

- Preheat the Air fryer to 360°F. Put the beef in the air fryer basket and cook for 12 minutes.
- Baste the beef with the marinade you saved and cook for another 5 to 6 minutes.
- Serve right away, and have fun!

Nutritional facts per serving: Calories: 367 Kcal; Carbs: 4 g; Fat: 28 g; Protein: 24 g.

6.20 Beef Steak

Preparation time: 5 mins
Cooking time: 10 mins
Servings: 2
Level of difficulty: Easy
Ingredients:

- 1 lb. sirloin steak
- 2 tbsp. steak seasoning
- 2 tbsp. sour cream
- ¼ cup grated cheese
- Salt and pepper, to taste

Instructions:

- Put all the ingredients in a bowl and marinate the steak for at least three hours.
- Preheat the Air fryer to 360°F.
- Put the marinated steaks in the air fryer and cook for 9 minutes.
- Serve right away, and enjoy!

Nutritional facts per serving: Calories: 436 Kcal; Carbs: 22 g; Fat: 22 g; Protein: 9 g.

6.21 Thai Style Beef

Preparation time: 10 mins
Cooking time: 25 mins
Servings: 4
Level of difficulty: Medium
Ingredients:

- 2 lb. beef tenderloin roast
- 2 tbsp. soy sauce
- 1 thyme sprig, chopped
- 2 rosemary sprigs, chopped
- sea salt and black pepper, to taste
- 2 garlic cloves, minced
- 2 tbsp. olive oil

- 2 tbsp. Thai sweet chili sauce
- 1 tsp. red pepper flakes, crushed

Instructions:

- Preheat the Air fryer to 360°F. Pat the meat dry. Rub the round roast all over with the olive oil, soy sauce, garlic, Thai sauce, and spices.
- Put the beef in the air fryer and cook for 25 minutes.
- Serve with side of your choice and enjoy.

Nutritional facts per serving: Calories: 433 Kcal; Carbs: 5 g; Fat: 23 g; Protein: 50 g.

6.22 Garlic Butter Flank Steak

Preparation time: 10 mins

Cooking time: 15 mins

Servings: 4

Level of difficulty: Easy

Ingredients:

- 1½ lb. flank steak
- ½ stick butter
- 2 tbsp. fresh chives, chopped
- 2 tbsp. fresh basil, chopped
- 1 tbsp. Dijon mustard
- 1 cup tomato sauce
- 1 tsp. cayenne pepper
- sea salt and black pepper, to taste
- 2 tbsp. fresh parsley, chopped 2 garlic cloves, minced

Instructions:

- Marinate the beef with all the ingredients and cover it and leave it for at least an hour.
- Preheat Air fryer to 360°F.
- Now, spray the basket of Air fryer with a nonstick spray.
- Put the beef in the air fryer. Cook for 15 minutes in the air fryer turning it twice.

Nutritional facts per serving: Calories: 417 Kcal; Carbs: 16 g; Fat: 20 g; Protein: 40 g.

6.23 Paprika Beef

Preparation time: 5 mins

Cooking time: 25 mins

Servings: 4

Level of difficulty: Easy

Ingredients:

- 1½ lb. beef fillet
- 1 red onion, roughly chopped
- 1 tbsp. Worcestershire sauce
- 2 tbsp. olive oil
- 3 tsp. sweet paprika
- ½ cup beef stock
- 1 tbsp. tomato paste
- Salt and black pepper, to taste

Instructions:

- Preheat Air fryer to 350°F.
- Mix the beef and the other ingredients together. Put the beef in the basket of the air fryer. Cook for about 25 minutes.
- Serve hot and enjoy.

Nutritional facts per serving: Calories: 304 Kcal; Carbs: 22 g; Fat: 13 g; Protein: 18 g.

6.24 Broccoli And Beef

Preparation time: 10 mins

Cooking time: 15 mins

Servings: 4

Level of difficulty: Expert

Ingredients:

- 2 tbsp. olive oil
- 2 tsp. hot sauce
- 1 tbsp. low sodium soy sauce
- 2 cups broccoli, cut into florets
- 2 tsp. rice vinegar
- salt and black pepper, to taste
- 1 tbsp. fresh minced ginger
- 1 tsp. sesame seed oil
- ½ medium onion, roughly sliced
- 4 cups beef strips
- ½ tsp. garlic powder

Instructions:

- Preheat the Air fryer to 350°F.
- Add boneless beef strips, broccoli and onion to a bowl. Mix them up well.

- Mix the ginger, hot sauce, rice vinegar, sesame oil, olive oil, garlic powder, and soy sauce together in another bowl. Then put the beef, broccoli, and onions into the marinade.
- Use sauces to cover the beef well. And put it in the fridge for 15 minutes to chill.
- Put the beef mix in an even layer in the air fryer basket and cook for 16 to 20 minutes. At the halfway point, gently shake the basket to cook the beef equally.
- Serve hot, with wedges of lemon.

Nutritional facts per serving: Calories: 213 Kcal; Carbs: 6 g; Fat: 12 g; Protein: 25 g.

6.25 Pork Tenderloin

Preparation time: 12 mins

Cooking time: 22 mins

Servings: 2

Level of difficulty: Intermediate

Ingredients:

- 2 tbsp. olive oil
- ¼ cup cherries, peeled
- 1 lb. pork tenderloin
- ¼ cup brown sugar
- 1 large onion, peeled
- Salt and black pepper, to taste

Instructions:

- Add oil, sugar, salt, and pepper to the pork and rub it all over.
- Put cherries and onions in a bowl. Season with black pepper and salt.
- Cherry and onion slices should be added to the air fryer basket along with the pork tenderloin.
- At 400°F, cook it for 22 minutes.
- Serve and enjoy when it's done.

Nutritional facts per serving: Calories: 543 Kcal; Carbs: 24 g; Fat: 22 g; Protein: 60 g.

6.26 Soy Pork Ribs

Preparation time: 16 mins

Cooking time: 22 mins

Servings: 2

Level of difficulty: Easy

Ingredients:

- 1 lb. pork ribs
- ¼ cup soy sauce
- ¼ cup balsamic vinegar

- ¼ cup hoisin sauce
- ½ tsp. garlic powder
- Pinch of salt

Instructions:

- Put the salt, soy sauce, balsamic vinegar, hoisin sauce, garlic sauce, and mix them all together well in a bowl. Then, put the pork ribs in the bowl and let them marinate.
- After that, put the chops in the air fryer basket and cook them for 22 minutes at 400°F.
- Don't forget to flip through halfway through.
- Serve and enjoy once it's done.

Nutritional facts per serving: Calories: 715 Kcal; Carbs: 17 g; Fat: 41 g; Protein: 60 g.

6.27 Bacon Cauliflower With Cheddar Cheese

Preparation time: 15 mins

Cooking time: 6 mins

Servings: 4

Level of difficulty: Intermediate

Ingredients:

- 10 strips bacon
- ¼ tsp. paprika
- 1 cup water
- ½ cups cooked pork meat, grounded
- 6 oz. cream cheese
- 1/3 medium cauliflower, diced small
- ½ cup cheddar cheese, shredded
- ½ cup heavy cream
- ¼ tsp. cayenne pepper
- salt to taste

Instructions:

- Air fry the bacon at 400°F for about 4 minutes, or until it's crispy.
- Put the cauliflower in hot water and boil it for two minutes.
- Put it in the bowl with heavy cream, cream cheese, bacon, cheddar cheese, chili pepper, salt, meat, and pepper. Remove the skin and add it to the bowl.
- Place this mix in an air fryer basket and cook for 6 minutes.
- Serve and enjoy when it's done.

Nutritional facts per serving: Calories: 715 Kcal; Carbs: 4 g; Fat: 60 g; Protein: 40 g.

6.28 Pork Bacon And Eggs Pockets

Preparation time: 10 mins

Cooking time: 12 mins

Servings: 2

Level of difficulty: Intermediate

Ingredients:

- 6 pork bacon, large slices
- 4 oz. cream cheese, full fat
- 4 eggs, whisked
- 6-8 oz. pizza dough, whole-wheat
- 1 tbsp. chives, fresh and chopped
- Oil spray

Instructions:

- Preheat the air fryer at 400°F for three minutes.
- Burn the bacon in a big pan until it's crispy. Once it's cool, break it up into small pieces.
- In the same pan, cook the eggs until they are set.
- Put the bacon bits, onions, and cream cheese in a bowl with the cooked eggs.
- The next step is to flatten the pizza dough out and cut it into four equal pieces.
- Spread the ready-made filling out among the pizza doughs.
- Brush the sides of the pizza dough with water, then wrap it up and seal the ends.
- Put it in an oil-sprayed air fryer basket.
- Flip the food over halfway through the 12 minutes of cooking.
- When it's done, serve it hot and enjoy.

Nutritional facts per serving: Calories: 832 Kcal; Carbs: 40 g; Fat: 53 g; Protein: 45 g.

6.29 Garlic Rosemary Pork Chops

Preparation time: 20 mins

Cooking time: 18 mins

Servings: 2

Level of difficulty: Expert

Ingredients:

- 1 cup sour cream
- 4 tbsp. butter
- 6 pork chops
- Salt and pepper, to taste

- 3 tbsp. olive oil
- 1 tbsp. thyme
- ½ tbsp. rosemary
- 4 garlic cloves

Instructions:

- Mix the thyme, oil, salt, rosemary, and butter, black pepper, and garlic cloves into a paste in a high-speed blender.
- Put it in a bowl, and let the chops sit in it for an hour in the fridge.
- Next, put it in an air fryer basket that has been sprayed with oil. Cook it at 400°F for 18 minutes.
- Flip it over in the middle.
- Put some sour cream on top after its done cooking.

Nutritional facts per serving: Calories: 403 Kcal; Carbs: 6 g; Fat: 27 g; Protein: 58 g.

6.30 Chinese Style Pork Chops

Preparation time: 15 mins

Cooking time: 25 mins

Servings: 4

Level of difficulty: Easy

Ingredients:

- 2 lb. pork chops

For Marinade

- 4 tbsp. soy sauce
- 2 tsp. five-spice powder
- 4 tbsp. oyster sauce
- ¼ cup red wine
- 1/3 cup honey
- 4 tbsp. hoisin sauce
- 2 tsp. ginger garlic, paste
- ¼ cup dark brown sugar
- Salt and black pepper, to taste

Instructions:

- To make the sauce, put all of the seasoning ingredients in a bowl and mix them together well.
- Put the pork chops in the fridge for an hour while you marinate them.
- Put the pork chops in the air fryer basket that has been greased with oil.
- Flip the food over halfway through the 25 minutes at 400°F.
- Every 12 minutes, baste the chop with sauce.

- Serve and enjoy when it's done.

Nutritional facts per serving: Calories: 180 Kcal; Carbs: 82 g; Fat: 13 g; Protein: 15 g.

6.31 Herbed Lamb Chops

Preparation time: 20 mins

Cooking time: 18 mins

Servings: 2

Level of difficulty: Expert

Ingredients:

- 1 cup sour cream
- 1 tbsp. thyme
- ½ tsp. black pepper
- 3 cloves of garlic
- 1 tbsp. rosemary
- Salt to taste
- 4 tbsp. butter
- 6 lamb chops
- 3 tbsp. olive oil

Instructions:

- Mix the thyme, oil, salt, rosemary, and butter, black pepper, and garlic cloves into a paste in a high-speed blender.
- Put it in a bowl, and let the chops sit in it for an hour in the fridge.
- Next, put it in an air fryer basket that has been sprayed with oil. Cook it at 400°F for 18 minutes.
- Flip it over in the middle.
- Put some sour cream on top after its done cooking.

Nutritional facts per serving: Calories: 403 Kcal; Carbs: 6 g; Fat: 27 g; Protein: 58 g.

6.32 Sweet Pork Barbecue

Preparation time: 26 mins

Cooking time: 32 mins

Servings: 2

Level of difficulty: Easy

Ingredients:

- 1/3 tbsp. onion powder
- 2 tbsp. olive oil
- 1/3 cup packed brown sugar
- 6 boneless pork loin chops

- French salad dressing
- 1/3 cup barbecue sauce

Instructions:

- In a bowl, mix the BBQ sauce, oil, brown sugar and sweet onion.
- Put the pork cubes on a foil-covered baking sheet.
- Pour the marinade over the meat and seal it in a foil dinner form.
- Put it in the fridge overnight.
- The next day, grill the pork on sticks, put them on sticks, move them to the foil box, seal it, and put it in the air fryer.
- Take it out of the oven and let it cook for 32 minutes at 375°F. Serve it with a French dressing salad.

Nutritional facts per serving: Calories: 170 Kcal; Carbs: 40 g; Fat: 50 g; Protein: 26 g.

6.33 Perfect Pork Ribs

Preparation time: 10 mins

Cooking time: 22 mins

Servings: 2

Level of difficulty: Easy

Ingredients:

- 6 pork ribs
- ¼ tsp. dried marjoram
- 2 tbsp. coconut oil
- 2 tbsp. almond flour
- ¼ tsp. garlic powder
- ¼ tsp. dry mustard
- Salt and black pepper, to taste

Instructions:

- For two minutes, heat the air fryer up to 400°F.
- In a bowl, mix all of the items on the list.
- Then put the ribs in it and let them sit in the fridge for two hours.
- Place it in an air fryer basket that has been sprayed with oil. Cook for 22 minutes, flipping it over halfway through.
- Serve and enjoy when it's done.

Nutritional facts per serving: Calories: 205 Kcal; Carbs: 39 g; Fat: 1 g; Protein: 18 g.

6.34 Pork Meat And Cabbage Rolls

Preparation time: 20 mins

Cooking time: 12 mins

Servings: 2

Level of difficulty: Easy

Ingredients:

- 5 tbsp. of Spicy Mustard
- 6 egg roll wrappers
- ½ cups stewed cabbage
- 1 cup pork meat, shredded
- Oil spray

Instructions:

- Put the meat, mustard, and cabbage in a bowl and mix them together.
- Put egg rolls on a clean, flat surface one on top of the other.
- Start on one side of the rolls and add the bowl mixture in similar amounts to all of them.
- Seal the sides and roll it up.
- Now put oil on the rolls to make them smooth.
- To cook in an air fryer, set it to 400°F and flip it over halfway through the 12 minutes.
- Serve it after it's done.

Nutritional facts per serving: Calories: 62 Kcal; Carbs: 56 g; Fat: 28 g; Protein: 32 g.

6.35 Asian Flavored Pork Chops

Preparation time: 10 mins

Cooking time: 16 mins

Servings: 2

Level of difficulty: Easy

Ingredients:

- 1lb. pork spare ribs
- 1 cup hoisin sauce
- ¼ cup of soy sauce
- ¼ cup apple cider vinegar
- 1 tsp. garlic powder
- 2 tsp. onion powder
- Salt to taste

Instructions:

- In a large bowl, mix all of the ingredients mentioned.

- Cover the pork chops well.
- After that, put it in the fridge for two hours.
- After that, put the chop in an oil-sprayed air fryer basket and cook it at 400°F for 16 minutes, turning it over once.
- Serve when it's done.

Nutritional facts per serving: Calories: 90 Kcal; Carbs: 62 g; Fat: 53 g; Protein: 41 g.

6.36 Steak Cubes

Preparation time: 20 mins
Cooking time: 16 mins
Servings: 4
Level of difficulty: Intermediate
Ingredients:

- 1 lb. top round steak, cubes
- 4 cloves garlic, crushed
- 1 medium onion, cut into wedges
- Sea salt and crushed red pepper, to taste
- ¼ cup brown sugar
- 2 tbsp. toasted sesame oil
- 2 tbsp. rice vinegar
- 2 tbsp. soy sauce
- 1 tsp. stone-ground mustard
- 1 tsp. ginger, peeled and minced
- 2 bell peppers, sliced
- 1 lb. broccoli florets

Instructions:

- In a mixing bowl, put all the ingredients and marinate the steak cubes and veggies.
- Preheat the Air fryer to 365°F.
- Put the steak and veggies in the basket of the air fryer. The steak cubes should be cooked for about 8 minutes, during which time they should be shake twice.
- Turn the heat up to 400°F and keep cooking for another 8 minutes.

Nutritional facts per serving: Calories: 320 Kcal; Carbs: 18 g; Fat: 18 g; Protein: 33 g.

6.37 Stuffed Beef Rolls

Preparation time: 15 mins

Cooking time: 20 mins

Servings: 4

Level of difficulty: Expert

Ingredients:

- 1 lb. beef tenderloin, thinly sliced
- 2 tbsp. yellow mustard
- 4 tbsp. mayonnaise
- 2 tsp. olive oil
- 2 tbsp. Worcestershire sauce
- 1 tsp. dried oregano
- 1 tsp. onion powder
- 1 tsp. garlic powder
- 4 oz. Gruyere cheese, crumbled

Instructions:

- Put the Worcestershire sauce, beef, spices, mustard, and olive oil in a mixing bowl. Marinate the meat for at least three hours.
- Mayonnaise and Gruyere cheese should be spread on each slice of beef tenderloin. The pieces should then be rolled up and held together with toothpicks.
- Preheat Air fryer to 400°F.
- Put the beef in the basket of the air fryer. Save the sauce for later.
- Cook the beef rolls for 20 minutes, basting them every so often with the sauce.

Nutritional facts per serving: Calories: 480 Kcal; Carbs: 5 g; Fat: 35 g; Protein: 30 g.

6.38 Mayo Pork

Preparation time: 10 mins

Cooking time: 10 mins

Servings: 4

Level of difficulty: Easy

Ingredients:

- 1 lb. boneless pork
- ½ tsp. salt
- 1½ cups ground pork rinds
- 2 tbsp. mustard
- ¼ cup mayonnaise

- 1 tsp. Italian seasoning
- ½ tsp. ground black pepper
- 2 tbsp. whole milk

Instructions:
- Preheat your Air fryer to 400°F.
- With a paper towel, pat the pork cubes to dry them.
- Mix the mustard, mayonnaise, and milk together well in a small bowl.
- Mix the salt, and Italian seasoning in a separate bowl.
- Dip the pork cubes into the mayonnaise mixture and then into the pork rind mixture, making sure the pork is fully covered.
- Bake it for 5 minutes in the air fryer, then flip it and bake for another 5 minutes. Serve quickly!

Nutritional facts per serving: Calories: 232 Kcal; Carbs: 11 g; Fat: 17 g; Protein: 25 g.

6.39 Honey Garlic Chops

Preparation time: 5 mins

Cooking time: 15 mins

Servings: 4

Level of difficulty: Intermediate

Ingredients:
- 1½ lb. rib chops
- 2 tbsp. olive oil
- 2 cloves garlic, minced
- 1 tsp. sage, minced
- Kosher salt and ground black pepper, to taste
- 1 tsp. rosemary, minced
- 1 tsp. basil, minced
- 2 tbsp. honey

Instructions:
- Put all the ingredients in a bowl and marinate the pork chops for at least three hours.
- Preheat the Air fryer to 360°F.
- Put the pork chops in the pan and put them in the air fryer.
- The chops should be cooked for about 15 minutes.
- Serve right away, and have fun!

Nutritional facts per serving: Calories: 410 Kcal; Carbs: 9 g; Fat: 26 g; Protein: 35 g.

6.40 Teriyaki Lamb Chops

Preparation time: 10 mins

Cooking time: 25 mins

Servings: 4

Level of difficulty: Easy

Ingredients:

- 1½ lb. lamb chops
- ¼ cup teriyaki sauce
- 1 tsp. mustard powder
- 2 garlic cloves, minced
- 1 tsp. chili powder
- 2 tbsp. agave nectar
- Sea salt and black pepper, to taste

Instructions:

- Preheat the Air fryer to 350°F.
- Mix the lamb chops and the other ingredients.
- Put the chops in the basket of the air fryer. Cook for about 25 minutes.
- Serve hot and have fun.

Nutritional facts per serving: Calories: 377 Kcal; Carbs: 6 g; Fat: 25 g; Protein: 26 g.

6.41 Lamb Meatballs

Preparation time: 12 mins

Cooking time: 12 mins

Servings: 2

Level of difficulty: Easy

Ingredients:

- 1 lb. lamb meat
- Black pepper, to taste
- 1 egg
- 1/2 cup Panko bread crumbs
- 1 tbsp. low sodium soy sauce
- 1/4 cup fresh parsley
- Oil spray

Instructions:

- Mix lamb, parsley, Panko bread crumbs, salt, egg, pepper, and soy sauce in a large bowl.
- Mix thoroughly and make meatballs.

- Spray meatballs with oil.
- Cook it for 12 minutes at 400°F in the air fryer basket.
- Rotate meatballs halfway through.
- Once cooked, serve.

Nutritional facts per serving: Calories: 591 Kcal; Carbs: 20 g; Fat: 28 g; Protein: 70 g.

6.42 Black Pepper Beef

Preparation time: 20 mins
Cooking time: 30 mins
Servings: 4
Level of difficulty: Easy
Ingredients:

- 1 lb. Boneless beef
- 3 tbsp. olive oil
- ½ tsp. sea salt
- 3 tbsp. minced garlic
- 1 tsp. black pepper

Instructions:

- Start by preheating your air fryer to 400°F.
- Mix 2 tbsp. olive oil, garlic, pepper and salt in a large bowl.
- Toss beef in marinade. Cover the bowl and refrigerate for two hours.
- Put the remaining tablespoon of olive oil in a sauté pan and heat on high. Sear marinated beef for 3 minutes per side to brown.
- Pour the leftover marinade from the dish over the browned chicken legs on a foil-lined basket.
- Cook for 20 minutes. Serve hot.

Nutritional facts per serving: Calories: 256 Kcal; Carbs: 3 g; Fat: 15 g; Protein: 24 g.

6.43 Pork And Peanuts Mix

Preparation time: 5 mins
Cooking time: 15 mins
Servings: 4
Level of difficulty: Easy
Ingredients:

- 2 tsp. chili paste
- 14 oz. pork chops, cubed
- 3 oz. peanuts, chopped
- 2 garlic cloves, minced

- 1 tsp. coriander, ground
- 1 shallot, chopped
- 2 tbsp. olive oil
- 7 oz. coconut milk
- Salt and black pepper to taste

Instructions:

- Start by preheating your air fryer to 400°F.
- Combine all of the ingredients into a pan that fits in your Air fryer and mix well.
- Put the pan in Air fryer at cook at 400°F for 15 minutes.
- Serve hot.

Nutritional facts per serving: Calories: 283 Kcal; Carbs: 22 g; Fat: 11 g; Protein: 18 g.

6.44 Rubbed Steaks

Preparation time: 5 mins

Cooking time: 14 mins

Servings: 4

Level of difficulty: Easy

Ingredients:

- 4 flank steaks
- ¼ cup ancho chili powder
- 2 tbsp. sweet paprika
- 1 tbsp. dry mustard
- 2 tsp. ginger, grated
- Salt and black pepper to taste
- 1 tbsp. coriander, ground
- 1 tbsp. oregano, dried
- Cooking spray

Instructions:

- Start by preheating your air fryer to 370°F.
- Combine all the ingredients except for the steaks in a bowl and then rub the steaks well with the mixture.
- Put the steaks in your air fryer's basket, grease with cooking spray, and cook at 370°F for 7 minutes on each side.
- Serve the steaks with a side of your choice and enjoy.

Nutritional facts per serving: Calories: 290 Kcal; Carbs: 22 g; Fat: 12 g; Protein: 19 g.

6.45 Milky Lamb

Preparation time: 5 mins

Cooking time: 15 mins

Servings: 4

Level of difficulty: Easy

Ingredients:

- 1 lb. lamb chops
- Salt and black pepper to taste
- 1 tbsp. rosemary, chopped
- 2 tbsp. olive oil
- 1 tbsp. butter, melted
- 1 garlic clove, minced
- 1 cup coconut milk

Instructions:

- Season the lamb chops with salt and pepper then put them in a pan that fits your air fryer. Add the garlic, butter, oil, rosemary, and milk to the pan and mix well.
- Place the pan in the fryer and cook at 400°F for 15 minutes.

Nutritional facts per serving: Calories: 281 Kcal; Carbs: 22 g; Fat: 13 g; Protein: 19 g.

Chapter 7: Fish And Seafood

7.1 Crispy Salmon

Preparation time: 10 mins
Cooking time: 10 mins
Servings: 4
Level of difficulty: Easy
Ingredients:
- 1 lb. salmon filets
- ½ cup fresh grated parmesan
- ½ tsp. salt
- ½ cup pork rinds, crushed
- 2 tbsp. melted butter
- 2 tbsp. dill, chopped
- ¼ tsp. black pepper
- ¼ tsp. garlic powder

Instructions:
- Pre-heat your air fryer to 450°F and line the tray with foil.
- Arrange salmon on the foil-lined tray.
- Combine remaining ingredients in a food processor or small bowl and blend thoroughly.
- Cover the salmon filets with the pork rind mixture, covering the top evenly and filling the crust.
- Bake the filets for 10 minutes in the preheated air fryer. The top crust should be nicely golden.

Nutritional facts per serving: Calories: 346 Kcal; Carbs: 2 g; Fat: 21 g; Protein: 40 g.

7.2 Spicy Crunchy Salmon

Preparation time: 10 mins
Cooking time: 10 mins
Servings: 4
Level of difficulty: Easy
Ingredients:
- 1 lb. salmon filets
- ½ cup fresh grated parmesan
- ¼ tsp. garlic powder
- ½ cup pork rinds, crushed
- ¼ tsp black pepper
- 2 tbsp. dill, chopped

- ½ tsp. salt
- ½ tsp. cayenne pepper
- 2 tbsp. melted butter

Instructions:
- Pre-heat your air fryer to 450°F and line the tray with foil.
- Arrange salmon on the foil-lined tray.
- Combine remaining ingredients in a food processor or small bowl and blend thoroughly.
- Cover the salmon filets with the pork rind mixture, covering the top evenly and filling the crust.
- Bake the filets for 10 minutes in the preheated air fryer. The top crust should be nicely golden.

Nutritional facts per serving: Calories: 346 Kcal; Carbs: 3 g; Fat: 20 g; Protein: 40 g.

7.3 Cajun Salmon

Preparation time: 10 mins

Cooking time: 10 mins

Servings: 4

Level of difficulty: Easy

Ingredients:
- 1 lb. salmon filets
- 2 tsp. fresh minced garlic
- 1 tbsp. Cajun seasoning
- ½ cup pork rinds, crushed
- 2 tbsp. melted butter

Instructions:
- Pre-heat your air fryer to 450°F and line the tray with foil.
- Arrange salmon on the foil-lined tray.
- Combine remaining ingredients in a food processor or small bowl and blend thoroughly.
- Cover the salmon filets with the pork rind mixture, covering the top evenly and filling the crust.
- Bake the filets for 10 minutes in the preheated air fryer. The top crust should be nicely golden.

Nutritional facts per serving: Calories: 301 Kcal; Carbs: 2 g; Fat: 21 g; Protein: 40 g.

7.4 Black Pepper Parmesan Salmon

Preparation time: 10 mins

Cooking time: 10 mins

Servings: 4

Level of difficulty: Easy

Ingredients:
- 1 lb. salmon filets
- ½ cup fresh grated parmesan
- ½ cup pork rinds, crushed
- ½ tsp. salt
- 1 tsp. black pepper
- ¼ tsp. garlic powder

Instructions:
- Pre-heat your air fryer to 450°F and line the tray with foil.
- Arrange salmon on the foil-lined tray.
- Combine the remaining ingredients in a food processor or small bowl and blend thoroughly.
- Cover the salmon filets with the pork rind mixture, covering the top evenly and filling the crust.
- Bake the filets for 10 minutes in the preheated air fryer. The top crust should be nicely golden.

Nutritional facts per serving: Calories: 354 Kcal; Carbs: 2 g; Fat: 21 g; Protein: 40 g.

7.5 Tuna Stuffed Mushrooms

Preparation time: 20 mins
Cooking time: 50 mins
Servings: 5
Level of difficulty: Intermediate

Ingredients:
- 1 lb. cremini mushrooms, gills and stems removed
- ¾ cup cream cheese, softened
- ¾ lb. canned tuna
- ¼ tsp. ground black pepper
- ¼ cup sour cream
- ½ tsp. salt
- 1/3 cup grated cheddar cheese
- 1 tbsp. mustard
- 1 tbsp. minced garlic
- ½ cup grated parmesan

Instructions:
- Turn on your air fryer to 375°F and line the tray with foil or paper.
- Bake the mushroom caps for 10 minutes in the air fryer. Remove tray from air fryer and drain extra water.
- In a large bowl, mix all ingredients except parmesan cheese. Thoroughly mix everything.

- Fill mushroom caps with crab mixture and top with parmesan.
- Return the dish to the air fryer and bake for 10 minutes until the mushroom tops are golden brown.

Nutritional facts per serving: Calories: 320 Kcal; Carbs: 8 g; Fat: 13 g; Protein: 24 g.

7.6 Crispy Salmon

Preparation time: 10 mins

Cooking time: 8 mins

Servings: 4

Level of difficulty: Intermediate

Ingredients:

- 1 lb. salmon filets
- ½ cup fresh grated parmesan
- ½ tsp. salt
- ½ cup pork rinds, crushed
- ¼ tsp. black pepper
- ¼ tsp. garlic powder
- 2 tbsp. dill, chopped
- 2 tbsp. melted butter

Instructions:

- Pre-heat your air fryer to 450°F and line the tray with foil.
- Place flounder filets on foil-lined tray.
- Combine remaining ingredients in a food processor or small bowl and blend thoroughly.
- Apply pork rind mixture to flounder filets, evenly covering the top and filling the crust.
- Bake the filets for 10 minutes in the preheated oven. The top crust should be nicely browned.

Nutritional facts per serving: Calories: 227 Kcal; Carbs: 2 g; Fat: 15 g; Protein: 32 g.

7.7 Tuna Cakes

Preparation time: 10 mins

Cooking time: 7 mins

Servings: 8

Level of difficulty: Intermediate

Ingredients:

- 10 oz. canned, drained tuna
- 3 tbsp. water
- 1 cup mozzarella cheese, grated
- 4 oz. pork rinds, crushed

- 2 eggs
- 1 tbsp. keto mayonnaise
- ½ tsp. smoked paprika
- 2 tbsp. olive oil

Instructions:

- Turn on your air fryer to 375°F and line the tray with foil or paper.
- Combine all ingredients except olive oil in a large bowl and mix thoroughly with your hands.
- Shape tuna cakes with your hands, aiming for an inch thickness each patty.
- Put the cakes on the lined sheet tray and sprinkle with olive oil.
- Cook cakes for 7 minutes in the air fryer till golden brown.

Nutritional facts per serving: Calories: 313 Kcal; Carbs: 1 g; Fat: 25 g; Protein: 23 g.

7.8 Salmon Cakes

Preparation time: 10 mins

Cooking time: 7 mins

Servings: 8

Level of difficulty: Intermediate

Ingredients:

- 10 oz. canned salmon
- 2 tbsp. olive oil
- 1 cup grated mozzarella cheese
- 4 oz. pork rinds, crushed
- 2 eggs
- 1 tbsp. keto mayonnaise
- 3 tbsp. water
- ½ tsp. smoked paprika

Instructions:

- Turn on your air fryer to 375°F and line the tray with foil or paper.
- Combine all ingredients except olive oil in a large bowl and mix thoroughly with your hands.
- Shape salmon cakes with your hands, aiming for an inch thickness each patty.
- Put the cakes on the lined sheet tray and sprinkle with olive oil.
- Cook cakes for 7 minutes in the air fryer till golden brown.

Nutritional facts per serving: Calories: 378 Kcal; Carbs: 1 g; Fat: 32 g; Protein: 27 g.

7.9 Red Hot Tuna Cakes

Preparation time: 10 mins

Cooking time: 7 mins

Servings: 8

Level of difficulty: Intermediate

Ingredients:

- 10 oz. canned tuna
- 1 tsp. red pepper flakes
- 2 tbsp. olive oil
- 1 cup grated mozzarella cheese
- 4 oz. pork rinds, crushed
- 2 eggs
- 1 tbsp. keto mayonnaise
- ½ tsp. smoked paprika
- 3 tbsp. water

Instructions:

- Turn on your air fryer to 375°F and line the tray with foil or paper.
- Combine all ingredients except olive oil in a large bowl and mix thoroughly with your hands.
- Shape tuna cakes with your hands, aiming for an inch thickness each patty.
- Put the cakes on the lined sheet tray and sprinkle with olive oil.
- Cook cakes for 7 minutes in the air fryer till golden brown.

Nutritional facts per serving: Calories: 318 Kcal; Carbs: 1 g; Fat: 25 g; Protein: 23 g.

7.10 Cajun Tuna Cakes

Preparation time: 10 mins

Cooking time: 7 mins

Servings: 8

Level of difficulty: Intermediate

Ingredients:

- 10 oz. canned tuna
- 1 cup grated mozzarella cheese
- 4 oz. pork rinds, crushed
- 2 eggs
- 1 tbsp. keto mayonnaise
- 3 tbsp. water

- 2 tbsp. olive oil
- 1½ tsp. Cajun seasoning

Instructions:
- Turn on your air fryer to 375°F and line the tray with foil or paper.
- Combine all ingredients except olive oil in a large bowl and mix thoroughly with your hands.
- Shape cakes with your hands, aiming for an inch thickness each patty.
- Put the cakes on the lined sheet tray and sprinkle with olive oil.
- Cook cakes for 7 minutes in the air fryer till golden brown.

Nutritional facts per serving: Calories: 318 Kcal; Carbs: 1 g; Fat: 25 g; Protein: 23 g.

7.11 Lemon Tuna Cakes

Preparation time: 10 mins

Cooking time: 7 mins

Servings: 8

Level of difficulty: Intermediate

Ingredients:
- 10 oz. canned tuna
- 2 tbsp. olive oil
- 1 cup grated mozzarella cheese
- 4 oz. pork rinds, crushed
- 2 eggs
- 1 tbsp. keto mayonnaise
- 3 tbsp. water
- ½ tsp. smoked paprika
- 1 tsp. lemon zest

Instructions:
- Turn on your air fryer to 375°F and line the tray with foil or paper.
- Combine all ingredients except olive oil in a large bowl and mix thoroughly with your hands.
- Shape cakes with your hands, aiming for an inch thickness each patty.
- Put the cakes on the lined sheet tray and sprinkle with olive oil.
- Cook cakes for 7 minutes in the air fryer till golden brown.

Nutritional facts per serving: Calories: 318 Kcal; Carbs: 1 g; Fat: 25 g; Protein: 23 g.

7.12 Cod Fish Sticks

Preparation time: 10 mins

Cooking time: 10 mins

Servings: 4

Level of difficulty: Intermediate

Ingredients:

- 1 lb. cod strips
- 2 tbsp. mustard
- ¼ cup mayonnaise
- 2 tbsp. whole milk
- ½ tsp. ground black pepper
- ½ tsp. salt
- 1½ cups ground pork rinds

Instructions:

- Set your air fryer to 400°F, line the tray with foil, and spray with cooking oil.
- Pat dry cod strips with paper towels.
- Combine mustard, milk and mayonnaise in a small bowl and mix thoroughly.
- In another dish, mix ground pork rinds, pepper and salt.
- Completely coat cod strips by dipping them in the mayonnaise and pork rind mixtures.
- Bake the cod for 10 minutes in air fryer, turning once in between.

Nutritional facts per serving: Calories: 263 Kcal; Carbs: 1 g; Fat: 16 g; Protein: 26 g.

7.13 Tuna Sticks

Preparation time: 10 mins

Cooking time: 10 mins

Servings: 4

Level of difficulty: Intermediate

Ingredients:

- 1 lb. tuna strips
- 2 tbsp. mustard
- ¼ cup mayonnaise
- 2 tbsp. whole milk
- ½ tsp. ground black pepper
- ½ tsp. salt
- 1½ cups ground pork rinds

Instructions:
- Set your air fryer to 400°F, line the tray with foil, and spray with cooking oil.
- Pat dry tuna strips with paper towels.
- Combine mustard, milk and mayonnaise in a small bowl and mix thoroughly.
- In another dish, mix ground pork rinds, pepper and salt.
- Completely coat cod strips by dipping them in the mayonnaise and pork rind mixtures.
- Bake the cod for 10 minutes in air fryer, turning once in between.

Nutritional facts per serving: Calories: 263 Kcal; Carbs: 1 g; Fat: 16 g; Protein: 26 g.

7.14 Crunchy Garlic Salmon

Preparation time: 10 mins
Cooking time: 10 mins
Servings: 4
Level of difficulty: Easy
Ingredients:
- 1 lb. salmon filets
- 2 tsp. fresh minced garlic
- ½ cup fresh grated parmesan
- ½ cup pork rinds, crushed
- ¼ tsp. black pepper
- 2 tbsp. dill, chopped
- ¼ tsp. garlic powder
- ½ tsp. salt
- 2 tbsp. melted butter

Instructions:
- Pre-heat your air fryer to 450°F and line the tray with foil.
- Arrange salmon on the foil-lined tray.
- Combine remaining ingredients in a food processor or small bowl and blend thoroughly.
- Cover the salmon filets with the pork rind mixture, covering the top evenly and filling the crust.
- Bake the filets for 10 minutes in the preheated air fryer. The top crust should be nicely golden.

Nutritional facts per serving: Calories: 352 Kcal; Carbs: 2 g; Fat: 21 g; Protein: 40

7.15 Pistachio Crusted Salmon

Preparation time: 10 mins
Cooking time: 15 mins
Servings: 1

Level of difficulty: Easy

Ingredients:

- 2 pieces of salmon
- 1 tsp. olive oil
- pinch of garlic powder
- 3 tbsp. pistachios
- 1 tsp. mustard
- pinch of sea salt
- 1 tsp. lemon juice
- pinch of black pepper
- 1 tsp. grated Parmesan cheese

Instructions:

- Pre-heat the air fryer to 350 F and mix lemon juice, olive oil and mustard. Season fish with pepper, salt, and garlic powder and apply mustard mixture to fish.
- Mix finely chopped pistachios with Parmesan cheese and sprinkle over salmon. Salmon should be placed skin-side down in the air fryer basket. Cook for 15 minutes or until desired.

Nutritional facts per serving: Calories: 221 Kcal; Carbs: 2 g; Fat: 8 g; Protein: 30 g.

7.16 Creamy Salmon

Preparation time: 10 mins

Cooking time: 10 mins

Servings: 2

Level of difficulty: Easy

Ingredients:

- ¾ lb. salmon, cut into 6 pieces
- 3 tbsp. sour cream
- 1 tbsp. dill, chopped
- ¼ cup yogurt
- Salt to taste
- 1 tbsp. olive oil

Instructions:

- Season fish with salt.
- Pour olive oil over salmon slices in the Air Fryer basket.
- Air-fry fish for 10 minutes at 285°F.
- In the meantime, mix the dill, cream, salt and yogurt.
- Place fish on plate and pour creamy sauce on top.

- Serve hot.

Nutritional facts per serving: Calories: 231 Kcal; Carbs: 2 g; Fat: 5 g; Protein: 30 g.

7.17 Ham Tilapia

Preparation time: 10 mins

Cooking time: 10 mins

Servings: 4

Level of difficulty: Easy

Ingredients:

- 4 ham slices
- 16 oz. tilapia fillet
- ½ tsp. salt
- 1 tsp. sunflower oil
- 1 tsp. dried rosemary

Instructions:

- Cut tilapia in 4 portions. Season each fish portion with dried rosemary, salt, and sunflower oil. Next, gently wrap the fish fillets with ham slices and secure them with toothpicks.
- Preheat the air fryer at 400°F. Place wrapped tilapia in an air fryer basket in one layer and cook for minutes. The fish should be gently flipped after 5 minutes of cooking.

Nutritional facts per serving: Calories: 234 Kcal; Carbs: 11 g; Fat: 5 g; Protein: 32 g.

7.18 Salmon In Garlic Sauce

Preparation time: 10 mins

Cooking time: 15 mins

Servings: 4

Level of difficulty: Easy

Ingredients:

- 4 salmon fillets, boneless
- 3 tbsp. parsley, chopped
- ¼ cup ghee, melted
- 2 garlic cloves, minced
- Salt and black pepper, to taste
- 1 shallot, chopped

Instructions:

- Heat ghee in an air fryer-compatible pan over medium-high heat. Add garlic, salt, pepper, shallots, and parsley, mix, and cook for 5 minutes.
- Gently stir salmon fillets, place pan in air fryer, and cook at 380°F for 15 minutes. Divide and serve.

Nutritional facts per serving: Calories: 176 Kcal; Carbs: 21 g; Fat: 12 g; Protein: 32 g.

7.19 Rice Flour Coated Shrimp

Preparation time: 10 mins

Cooking time: 10 mins

Servings: 3

Level of difficulty: Intermediate

Ingredients:

- 1 tsp. powdered sugar
- 3 tbsp. rice flour
- 2 tbsp. olive oil
- 1 lb. shrimp
- Salt and black pepper, to taste

Instructions:

- Pre-heat the Air fryer to 325°F and oil the basket.
- Mix rice flour, sugar, olive oil, black pepper and salt in a bowl.
- Add shrimp and coat in flour mixture.
- Place breaded shrimp in the Air fryer basket and cook for 10 minutes.

Nutritional facts per serving: Calories: 234 Kcal; Carbs: 10 g; Fat: 11 g; Protein: 24 g.

7.20 Cajun Fish Patties With Cheese

Preparation time: 5 mins

Cooking time: 20 mins

Servings: 4

Level of difficulty: Intermediate

Ingredients:

- 2 catfish fillets
- 1 cup all-purpose flour
- 1 tsp. Cajun seasoning
- 1 tsp. baking powder
- 3 oz. butter
- ½ cup buttermilk
- 1 tsp. baking soda
- 1 cup Swiss cheese, shredded

Instructions:

- Boil salted water. Boil fish fillets for 5 minutes or until opaque. Flake the boiled fish.

- In a bowl, mix the remaining ingredients and flaked fish until completely blended. Form fish mixture into patties.
- Preheat Air Fryer to 375°F and cook patties for 15 minutes. Enjoy!

Nutritional facts per serving: Calories: 213 Kcal; Carbs: 5 g; Fat: 3 g; Protein: 21 g.

7.21 Spicy Shrimps

Preparation time: 15 mins

Cooking time: 8 mins

Servings: 2

Level of difficulty: Easy

Ingredients:

- 1 lb. shrimps, peeled and deveined
- 1 tsp. avocado oil
- 1 tsp. smoked paprika
- Black pepper to taste
- 1 tsp. garlic powder
- ⅛ tsp. cayenne pepper

Instructions:

- For a few minutes, heat the air fryer up to 400°F.
- Put all the spices in a bowl and use it to rub the shrimps.
- Make sure that the shrimps are fully covered with spices.
- Air-fry the shrimps for 8 minutes after putting them in the basket.
- Serve the shrimps hot after they are done cooking.

Nutritional facts per serving: Calories: 214 Kcal; Carbs: 6 g; Fat: 2 g; Protein: 38 g.

7.22 Mustard Salmon

Preparation time: 10 mins

Cooking time: 10 mins

Servings: 4

Level of difficulty: Intermediate

Ingredients:

- 1 lb. salmon filets
- 2 tbsp. mustard
- ¼ cup mayonnaise
- 2 tbsp. whole milk
- ½ tsp. ground black pepper
- ½ tsp. salt

- 1½ cups ground pork rinds

Instructions:

- Set your air fryer to 400°F, line the tray with foil, and spray with cooking oil.
- Pat dry salmon with paper towels.
- Combine mustard, milk and mayonnaise in a small bowl and mix thoroughly.
- In another dish, mix ground pork rinds, pepper and salt.
- Completely coat salmon by dipping them in the mayonnaise and pork rind mixtures.
- Bake the salmon for 10 minutes in air fryer, turning once in between.

Nutritional facts per serving: Calories: 257 Kcal; Carbs: 2 g; Fat: 14 g; Protein: 27 g.

7.23 Creamy Shrimps

Preparation time: 10 mins
Cooking time: 10 mins
Servings: 2
Level of difficulty: Easy
Ingredients:

- ¾ lb. shrimps
- ¼ cup yogurt
- Salt to taste
- 3 tbsp. sour cream
- 1 tbsp. dill, chopped
- 1 tbsp. olive oil

Instructions:

- Season shrimps with salt.
- Pour olive oil over shrimps in the Air Fryer basket.
- Air-fry for 10 minutes at 285°F.
- In the meantime, mix the dill, cream, salt and yogurt.
- Place shrimps on plate and pour creamy sauce on top.
- Serve hot.

Nutritional facts per serving: Calories: 231 Kcal; Carbs: 2 g; Fat: 5 g; Protein: 30 g.

7.24 Lemon Parmesan Tilapia

Preparation time: 12 mins
Cooking time: 15 mins
Servings: 2
Level of difficulty: Intermediate

Ingredients:

- 2 tbsp. olive oil
- 1 lb. tilapia fillet
- 2 garlic cloves, chopped
- ¼ cup parmesan cheese
- Freshly grounded black pepper
- Salt, to taste
- ½ tbsp. lemon juice
- 1 dash of cayenne pepper

Instructions:

- Clean the fish cut and use a paper towel to dry it.
- After that, add salt, black pepper, lemon juice, chili pepper, olive oil, chopped garlic, and pepper to taste.
- Put the fish in the air fryer basket after spraying it with oil.
- At 350°F, cook the fish for 15 minutes.
- Put cheese on top of the fillet to serve and enjoy.

Nutritional facts per serving: Calories: 204 Kcal; Carbs: 12 g; Fat: 16 g; Protein: 14 g.

7.25 Lean And Green Salmon

Preparation time: 15 mins

Cooking time: 16 mins

Servings: 1

Level of difficulty: Easy

Ingredients:

- 1 lb. salmon fillet
- 1 green onion
- ¼ cup ricotta cheese
- ¼ tsp. Red pepper
- 2 garlic cloves, chopped
- 4 oz. baby spinach
- 2 chopped cherry tomatoes
- Oil, as needed
- Salt and black pepper, to taste

Instructions:

- Just put a few drops of oil in the pan and wait for it to heat up.
- Put the tomatoes, onion, red pepper, baby spinach and garlic cloves, in the pan.

- After two more minutes, add the cheese.
- Then Turn off the heat.
- Add oil, black pepper and salt to the fish to season it.
- On top of the cheese mix, put the fish.
- Put the seasoned fish in the basket of the air fryer.
- For 16 to 18 minutes, cook at 390°F.
- When the salmon is done cooking, it's ready to be served with greens.

Nutritional facts per serving: Calories: 179 Kcal; Carbs: 22 g; Fat: 34 g; Protein: 50 g.

7.26 Fish Nuggets

Preparation time: 12 mins

Cooking time: 10 mins

Servings: 2

Level of difficulty: Intermediate

Ingredients:

- 1 lb. salmon fillet
- 1/4 cup honey
- 1 large egg
- 1 cup croutons
- Sea salt, to taste
- ¼ tsp. chipotle pepper
- Cooking oil for greasing

Instructions:

- In a skillet, mix honey and chipotle pepper together. Simmer for 10 minutes.
- Use a small food processor to pulse the croutons.
- In the bowl, beat the egg with a whisk.
- For a few minutes, heat the air fryer up to 390°F.
- Add salt to the salmon now.
- First, dip the salmon in the egg mix, and then in the crouton.
- Spray some oil into the basket of the air fryer.
- Cook fish nuggets for 8 minutes in an air fryer.
- Serve the tasty fish nuggets with sauce when they're done.

Nutritional facts per serving: Calories: 586 Kcal; Carbs: 46 g; Fat: 24 g; Protein: 50 g.

7.27 Mahi Mahi With Brown Butter

Preparation time: 15 mins

Cooking time: 10 mins

Servings: 2

Level of difficulty: Easy

Ingredients:

- 4 Mahi Mahi fillets
- Salt and black pepper, to taste
- Cooking spray
- 1/4 cup butter

Instructions:

- Put salt and pepper in a bowl, and then add the fish.
- Spray cooking spray on the seasoned fish and put it in the air fryer basket and cook for 10 minutes at 390°F.
- Put butter in the pan and cook for five minutes.
- After that, put the fish in the cooked butter and it is ready to be served.

Nutritional facts per serving: Calories: 180 Kcal; Carbs: 0 g; Fat: 4 g; Protein: 34 g.

7.28 Spicy Scallops

Preparation time: 15 mins

Cooking time: 8 mins

Servings: 2

Level of difficulty: Easy

Ingredients:

- 1 lb. scallops
- 1 tsp. avocado oil
- 1 tsp. smoked paprika
- Black pepper to taste
- 1 tsp. garlic powder
- ⅛ tsp. cayenne pepper

Instructions:

- For a few minutes, heat the air fryer up to 400°F.
- Put all the spices in a bowl and use it to rub the scallops.
- Make sure that the scallops are fully covered with spices.
- Air-fry the scallops for 8 minutes after putting them in the basket.
- Serve the scallops hot after they are done cooking.

Nutritional facts per serving: Calories: 210 Kcal; Carbs: 7 g; Fat: 2 g; Protein: 38 g.

7.29 Classic French Mussels

Preparation time: 15 mins

Cooking time: 12 mins

Servings: 2

Level of difficulty: Easy

Ingredients:

- 1 lb. mussels
- 1 tbsp. heavy cream
- 2 tbsp. melted butter
- 2 tbsp. chopped garlic
- 1 tbsp. dry white wine

Instructions:

- Preheat the air fryer to 420°F.
- Put the garlic, white wine, butter, and mussels in a bowl. Be sure to mix everything well. The heavy cream should be whipped before it is added.
- Bake mussels for 5 to 7 minutes in air fryer.
- Give the mussels a shake, and cook for five more minutes.
- Serve and enjoy the mussels once they are done.

Nutritional facts per serving: Calories: 341 Kcal; Carbs: 11 g; Fat: 19 g; Protein: 27 g.

7.30 Cheesy Baked Mussels

Preparation time: 15 mins

Cooking time: 12 mins

Servings: 1

Level of difficulty: Easy

Ingredients:

- 1 lb. mussels
- ½ cup grated cheddar cheese
- 1 tbsp. lemon juice
- ¼ cup butter
- 1 tsp. dried parsley
- 1 tsp. chopped garlic

Instructions:

- Preheat the Air Fryer to 300°F.
- Take the mussels' shells off, clean them, and steam them.

- Put the garlic, lemon juice, butter, and parsley in the bowl and mix them all together well.
- Add cheddar cheese and some of the butter-garlic mix to the mussel.
- Air-fry for 12 to 15 minutes.
- Serve the mussels with hot sauce and lemon wedges after they are done cooking.

Nutritional facts per serving: Calories: 496 Kcal; Carbs: 10 g; Fat: 12 g; Protein: 40 g.

7.31 Herbed Mussels

Preparation time: 15 mins
Cooking time: 10 mins
Servings: 1
Level of difficulty: Easy
Ingredients:

- 1 lb. mussels
- ½ tbsp. thyme
- 2 garlic cloves
- 2 tbsp. lemon juice
- ¼ cup oil
- 2 tsp. dried parsley
- Salt and black pepper, to taste

Instructions:

- Preheat the Air Fryer to 350°F.
- In a bowl, mix all the ingredients together.
- Put the herbed mussels in the basket of the air fryer and cook for 10 minutes.
- Serve and enjoy the mussels once they are done.

Nutritional facts per serving: Calories: 493 Kcal; Carbs: 20 g; Fat: 65 g; Protein: 50 g.

7.32 Crispy Crab Claws

Preparation time: 15 mins
Cooking time: 15 mins
Servings: 2
Level of difficulty: Intermediate
Ingredients:

- 6 Crab claws
- 1/4 cup breadcrumbs
- 1 whole egg
- 1/4 cup all-purpose flour

- Cooking oil spray
- Chili-garlic sauce, as needed
- 1/4 cup Dim Sum shrimp paste

Instructions:

- Clean the crab claws and use a paper towel to soak up any extra water.
- Put the Panko and flour in a bowl and mix them together. In the bowl, beat the egg.
- In a small bowl, add the dim shrimp sauce.
- Put the dim shrimp paste on the crab claws now.
- Cover the crab claw all the way around with the paste.
- One at a time, coat each crab claw in flour. Then dip in the egg that has been beaten. Lastly, coat in bread crumbs.
- Do the same process with the other crab claws as well.
- Preheat the air fryer at 400°F and grease the air fryer pan using cooking spray.
- Cook the crab claws for 15 minutes, or until they turns golden brown.
- Coat the crab claws with the chili-garlic sauce after they are done cooking.

Nutritional facts per serving: Calories: 104 Kcal; Carbs: 21 g; Fat: 11 g; Protein: 23 g.

7.33 Cajun Catfish

Preparation time: 15 mins

Cooking time: 8 mins

Servings: 2

Level of difficulty: Easy

Ingredients:

- 1 lb. catfish fillets
- 2 tsp. Cajun seasoning
- Cooking oil for greasing
- 1/2 cup cornmeal

Instructions:

- Clean the catfish and slice it up.
- Use a paper towel to dry the catfish.
- Put the cornmeal and Cajun seasoning in a Ziploc bag.
- Now add the catfish pieces and give it a good shake to make sure the fish is well covered in the spice.
- Put oil on the air fryer's basket and then arrange the catfish pieces in the air fryer.
- Air fry at 400°F for 8 minutes.
- Flip it over and cook it further 8 to 10 minutes.

Nutritional facts per serving: Calories: 417 Kcal; Carbs: 23 g; Fat: 18 g; Protein: 37 g.

7.34 Spicy Shrimp Patties

Preparation time: 10 mins

Cooking time: 7 mins

Servings: 8

Level of difficulty: Intermediate

Ingredients:

- 10 oz. ground shrimp
- 1 tsp. red pepper flakes
- 2 tbsp. olive oil
- 1 cup grated mozzarella cheese
- 4 oz. pork rinds, crushed
- 2 eggs
- 1 tbsp. keto mayonnaise
- ½ tsp. smoked paprika
- 3 tbsp. water

Instructions:

- Turn on your air fryer to 375°F and line the tray with foil or paper.
- Combine all ingredients except olive oil in a large bowl and mix thoroughly with your hands.
- Shape shrimp patties with your hands, aiming for an inch thickness each patty.
- Put the patties on the lined sheet tray and sprinkle with olive oil.
- Cook them for 7 minutes in the air fryer till golden brown.

Nutritional facts per serving: Calories: 328 Kcal; Carbs: 1 g; Fat: 26 g; Protein: 23 g.

7.35 Fish Burgers

Preparation time: 10 mins

Cooking time: 12 mins

Servings: 4

Level of difficulty: Intermediate

Ingredients:

- 1 lb. white fish, chopped
- Sea salt and black pepper, to taste
- 1 medium onion, chopped
- 4 hamburger buns
- 2 tsp. olive oil
- 1 egg, whisked

- 1/2 cup breadcrumbs
- 2 garlic cloves, minced
- 1 tsp. mustard
- 1 cup Romaine lettuce, torn into pieces
- 1 tomato, sliced

Instructions:

- Preheat Air fryer to 375°F.
- Fish, egg, breadcrumbs, garlic, mustard, onion, olive oil, salt and black pepper should be well combined.
- Make four patties from the mixture and place them in a single layer in the basket of the air fryer.
- The patties should be air-fried for 12 minutes, with a midway flip.
- Put lettuce, tomato and fish patties on hamburger buns and enjoy.

Nutritional facts per serving: Calories: 346 Kcal; Carbs: 4 g; Fat: 6 g; Protein: 6 g.

7.36 Salmon Steaks

Preparation time: 10 mins

Cooking time: 10 mins

Servings: 4

Level of difficulty: Intermediate

Ingredients:

- 1 lb. salmon steaks
- 2 cloves garlic, minced
- 2 tbsp. fresh parsley leaves, chopped
- 2 tbsp. agave nectar
- 2 tbsp. olive oil
- Kosher salt and black pepper, to taste
- 1 tbsp. fresh lemon juice
- 2 tbsp. fresh mint leaves, chopped

Instructions:

- Preheat Air fryer to 400°F.
- In a mixing bowl combine all the ingredients and gently marinate the fish steaks.
- Arrange the marinated steaks on the basket of Air fryer and bake for 10 minutes or until it flakes easily with a fork.

Nutritional facts per serving: Calories: 346 Kcal; Carbs: 4 g; Fat: 6 g; Protein: 6 g.

7.37 Sweet Cod Fillets

Preparation time: 10 mins
Cooking time: 15 mins
Servings: 4
Level of difficulty: Easy
Ingredients:
- 4 cod fillets, boneless
- 1 tbsp. olive oil
- 4 tbsp. light soy sauce
- ¼ cup water
- Salt and black pepper to taste
- 1 tbsp. sugar

Instructions:
- Preheat Air fryer to 400°F.
- Rub some oil over the fish after seasoning it with salt and pepper.
- Place the fish in the basket of air fryer and cook for 12 minutes.
- Over medium heat, add the water to a saucepan; whisk in the sugar and soy sauce; come to a simmer; and then turn off the heat.
- Place a portion of air fried fish on each plate and spread the soy sauce mixture on top, then serve and enjoy!

Nutritional facts per serving: Calories: 270 Kcal; Carbs: 16 g; Fat: 12 g; Protein: 14 g.

7.38 Balsamic Cod

Preparation time: 15 mins
Cooking time: 12 mins
Servings: 2
Level of difficulty: Easy
Ingredients:
- 2 cod fillets, boneless
- ½ tsp. garlic powder
- 1/3 cup balsamic vinegar
- Salt and black pepper to taste
- 2 tbsp. lemon juice
- 1/3 cup water
- 2 tbsp. olive oil

Instructions:

- Preheat Air fryer to 400°F.
- Cod should be well coated in a bowl with the garlic powder, lemon juice, salt, pepper, vinegar, water, and oil.
- Place the fish in the air fryer; turn them halfway through cooking for 12 minutes.

Nutritional facts per serving: Calories: 271 Kcal; Carbs: 16 g; Fat: 12 g; Protein: 20 g.

7.39 Buttery Garlic Shrimps

Preparation time: 5 mins

Cooking time: 10 mins

Servings: 2

Level of difficulty: Intermediate

Ingredients:

- 1 tbsp. butter, melted
- Salt and black pepper, to taste
- 1 tbsp. chives, chopped
- pinch of red pepper flakes
- 1 lb. shrimp
- 1 tbsp. olive oil
- 8 oz. mushrooms, roughly sliced
- ¼ cup heavy cream
- ½ cup beef stock
- 2 garlic cloves, minced
- 1 tbsp. parsley, chopped

Instructions:

- Preheat the Air fryer to 360°F.
- Marinate the shrimps with salt and pepper and put them in your air fryer oven and cook for 7 minutes at 360°F before dividing across plates.
- Over medium heat, melt the butter in a skillet. Add the mushrooms, stir, and cook for 3 to 4 minutes.
- Then, after stirring and a few more minutes of cooking, add the remaining ingredients to the sauce.
- Serve the shrimps with the buttery garlic sauce drizzled over them.

Nutritional facts per serving: Calories: 305 Kcal; Carbs: 14 g; Fat: 13 g; Protein: 11 g.

7.40 Tilapia Nuggets

Preparation time: 10 mins

Cooking time: 10 mins

Servings: 4

Level of difficulty: Intermediate

Ingredients:

- 1 lb. tilapia fillets
- salt and black pepper, to taste
- 1 tsp. cayenne pepper
- 1 tsp. onion powder
- 4 tbsp. cream of onion soup
- 1 tbsp. lemon juice
- 1 tbsp. stone-ground mustard
- 1 large egg, beaten
- 1 tsp. garlic powder
- 1 cup breadcrumbs
- 1 tbsp. olive oil

Instructions:

- Preheat Air fryer to 400°F.
- Cut the fish fillets into bite-sized pieces after patting them dry. Add the fresh lemon juice to the fish and keep them aside.
- Combine the egg, mustard, and onion soup in a small bowl.
- Combine the remaining ingredients in another small dish.
- Tilapia nuggets should be dredged in the egg mixture. Then, coat the snuggest completely with the breadcrumb mixture, brushing off any extra.
- Avoid crowding the nuggets as you arrange them in the basket of Air fryer. The nuggets should be air-fried for 10 minutes, or until completely done. Enjoy!

Nutritional facts per serving: Calories: 223 Kcal; Carbs: 26 g; Fat: 9 g; Protein: 15 g.

7.41 Lemon Pepper Shrimps

Preparation time: 10 mins

Cooking time: 15 mins

Servings: 4

Level of difficulty: Easy

Ingredients:

- 1 lb. shrimps
- 2 tsp. baking powder

- 1 tbsp. lemon pepper seasoning
- ½ tsp. garlic powder
- 4 tbsp. salted butter, melted

Instructions:

- Preheat the Air fryer to 375°F.
- Mix the garlic powder and baking powder together in a small bowl, and then use this mixture to cover the shrimps. Put the shrimps in the air fryer oven.
- At 375°F for 15 minutes, cook the shrimps. Turn them over halfway through and let the other side cook.
- When the shrimps are no longer pink, use a thermometer to make sure it has hit the right temperature, which is 165°F. Take it out of the oven.
- Melt the butter and mix in the lemon pepper spice. Toss the cooked shrimps in the mixture until they are all covered. Serve hot.

Nutritional facts per serving: Calories: 400 Kcal; Carbs: 20 g; Fat: 21 g; Protein: 23 g.

7.42 Shrimp Kabobs

Preparation time: 20 mins

Cooking time: 14 mins

Servings: 3

Level of difficulty: Easy

Ingredients:

- 1 lb. shrimps
- 2 tbsp. chopped ginger and garlic
- 1 tsp. sesame seeds
- 1 tbsp. oil
- ¼ cup pineapple juice
- Salt and black pepper, to taste

Instructions:

- Preheat the Air fryer to 350°F.
- Mix the garlic, sesame seeds, oil, ginger, soy sauce, pineapple juice, and black pepper together in a big baking dish.
- Put shrimps on the wooden skewers that have already been soaked.
- Put the skewers in the Air fryer and spread the marinade all over them.
- Air-fry them for about 5–7 minutes in the air fryer.
- Take the shrimp kabobs out of the Air Fryer and put them on a serving plate.

Nutritional facts per serving: Calories: 302 Kcal; Carbs: 10 g; Fat: 23 g; Protein: 45 g.

7.43 Crab Croquettes

Preparation time: 15 mins
Cooking time: 20 mins
Servings: 4
Level of difficulty: Intermediate
Ingredients:

- 1 lb. crab meat
- 2 tbsp. fresh parsley, chopped
- ¼ cup cream cheese
- 2 large eggs
- Sea salt and black pepper, to taste
- 2 garlic cloves, minced
- 1 small leek, chopped
- 2 tbsp. fresh mint, chopped
- 1 bell pepper, chopped
- 2 tbsp. olive oil
- 1 tsp. red pepper flakes, crushed

Instructions:

- Preheat the Air fryer to 375°F.
- Put a piece of parchment paper in the pan of the air fryer oven.
- Mix all the ingredients together well in a bowl.
- Make croquettes out of the mixture and put them in a single layer in the basket of the air fryer.
- Air-fry the croquettes for 20 minutes and serve.

Nutritional facts per serving: Calories: 360 Kcal; Carbs: 6 g; Fat: 25 g; Protein: 24 g.

7.44 Cajun Cod

Preparation time: 10 mins
Cooking time: 10 mins
Servings: 4
Level of difficulty: Easy
Ingredients:

- 1 lb. cod filets
- 1 tbsp. Cajun seasoning
- ½ cup pork rinds, crushed
- 2 tbsp. melted butter

- 2 tsp. fresh minced garlic

Instructions:

- Preheat the Air fryer to 450°F.
- Mix the rest of the ingredients well in a small bowl or food processor.
- Press the pork rind mixture onto the cod filets, covering the top evenly and pressing the crust into the fish.
- Air-fry the cod for 10 minutes until a nice brown color appears.

Nutritional facts per serving: Calories: 351 Kcal; Carbs: 2 g; Fat: 21 g; Protein: 29 g.

7.45 Italian Fish Sticks

Preparation time: 10 mins

Cooking time: 10 mins

Servings: 4

Level of difficulty: Easy

Ingredients:

- 1 lb. cod
- 1½ cups ground pork rinds
- ½ tsp. ground black pepper
- 2 tbsp. mustard
- ¼ cup mayonnaise
- 1 tsp. Italian seasoning
- ½ tsp. salt
- 2 tbsp. whole milk

Instructions:

- Preheat Air fryer to 400°F.
- With a paper towel, pat the cod filets to dry them. Cut the fish into strips about an inch wide and two inches long.
- Mix the mayonnaise, mustard and milk together well in a small bowl.
- Mix the salt, and Italian seasoning in a separate bowl.
- Dip the fish strips into the mayonnaise mixture and then into the pork rind mixture, making sure the fish is fully covered.
- Bake the fish for 5 minutes in preheated Air fryer and then flip it and bake for another 5 minutes. Serve quickly!

Nutritional facts per serving: Calories: 283 Kcal; Carbs: 2 g; Fat: 16 g; Protein: 26 g.

Chapter 8: Snacks And Appetizers

8.1 Air-Fryer Pickles

Preparation time: 30 mins

Cooking time: 15 mins

Servings: 32

Level of difficulty: Easy

Ingredients:

- 1/2 cup all-purpose flour
- 2 tbsp. chopped fresh dill
- 32 slices dill pickles
- 2 tbsp. dill pickle juice
- ½ tsp. cayenne pepper
- 3 eggs, lightly whisked
- ½ tsp. salt
- 2 cups Panko breadcrumbs
- ½ tsp. garlic powder

Instructions:

- Preheat the air fryer to 400°F. Put the pickles on a paper towel and dry them well. Then, let them sit for 15 minutes.
- In a mixing bowl, mix salt and flour together. Mix the eggs, pickle juice, garlic powder, and the chili pepper in a different bowl.
- In a different bowl, mix the crumbs and dill together.
- Cover the pickles in the flour mixture, and then dip in the egg mixture, and finally the panko mixture. Press the pickles down to make the topping stick together.
- You should spray oil into the air fryer basket and then put the pickles in a single layer in the basket.
- First cook the pickles for 7 to 10 minutes. Then turn them over and cook for another 7 to 10 minutes.
- Cook in groups, and then serve right away with any dressing you like.

Nutritional facts per serving: Calories: 24 Kcal; Carbs: 4 g; Fat: 3 g; Protein: 1 g.

8.2 Siracha Spring Rolls

Preparation time: 35 mins

Cooking time: 25 mins

Servings: 24

Level of difficulty: Intermediate

Ingredients:

- 3 green onions, diced

- 16 oz. softened cream cheese
- 1 tbsp. Soy sauce
- 1 tsp. seasoned salt
- 2 tbsp. siracha chili sauce
- 3 cups Coleslaw mix
- 1 lb. skinless chicken breasts
- 1 tsp. Sesame oil
- 24 Spring roll wrappers

Instructions:

- Preheat the air fryer to 360°F.
- Mix green onions, sesame oil, coleslaw mix and soy sauce.
- Oil After spraying the air fryer basket with frying spray and place the chicken in an even layer and cook for 18-20 minutes or until the internal temperature reaches 165°F.
- Pull the chicken from the pan and let it cool. Sprinkle seasoned salt over chicken and dice it.
- Mix the cream cheese and Siracha sauce in a plate, then add the cabbage and chicken.
- Arrange a roll wrapper on a clean surface, with one corner towards you and 2 tbsp. chicken filling on the other.
- Fold the roll in half and seal the edges with water.
- Cook spring rolls in an oiled air fryer basket for 5–6 minutes.
- After turning and oiling the rolls, cook for 5–6 minutes.
- Add sweet chili sauce and serve immediately.

Nutritional facts per serving: Calories: 127 Kcal; Carbs: 10 g; Fat: 7 g; Protein: 6 g.

8.3 Buffalo Cauliflower Bites

Preparation time: 15 mins

Cooking time: 35 mins

Servings: 4

Level of difficulty: Intermediate

Ingredients:

- 1½ lb. cauliflower florets
- 1 tbsp. crumbled blue cheese
- 2 tbsp. hot sauce
- ¼ cup Sour cream, reduced fat
- 1 egg white
- ¾ cup panko
- ¼ tsp. Black pepper

- 3 tbsp. Ketchup
- 1 clove of garlic, minced
- 1 tsp. Red wine vinegar

Instructions:
- Mix hot sauce, egg white, and ketchup in a bowl until smooth.
- Mix panko in a bowl. Coat cauliflower with ketchup mixture.
- Cover the cauliflower with panko. Grease the cauliflower generously.
- Place only half of the coated cauliflower in an oiled air fryer basket in an even layer.
- Roast 20 minutes at 320°F or until crisp and golden brown.
- Meanwhile, mix sour cream, vinegar, black pepper, garlic, and blue cheese in a bowl. Mix all ingredients in a big bowl and serve over buffalo cauliflower.

Nutritional facts per serving: Calories: 125 Kcal; Carbs: 17 g; Fat: 4 g; Protein: 5 g.

8.4 Calzones

Preparation time: 27 mins

Cooking time: 15 mins

Servings: 2

Level of difficulty: Intermediate

Ingredients:
- 3 cups baby spinach leaves
- 1/3 cup rotisserie chicken breast, shredded
- 6 oz. of prepared pizza dough
- 1 tsp. olive oil
- 6 tbsp. shredded mozzarella cheese
- ¼ cup finely diced red onion
- 1/3 cup marinara sauce

Instructions:
- Heat oil in a cast-iron pan and sauté onion for 2 minutes until tender.
- Now add spinach and cook until spinach wilts. Take the pan off the heat and add the chicken and marinara.
- Cut dough into four equal parts. Roll each piece into a 6-inch round.
- Spread ¼ of the spinach mixture over the ringed dough and ¼ of the cheese on one side.
- Crimp the edges of the remaining half over the filling.
- Coat calzones with oil spray.
- Grease an air fryer basket and place calzones. Bake at 325°F for 12 minutes until the dough turns golden brown. Continue cooking for 8 minutes after turning the calzones.
- Serve and enjoy.

Nutritional facts per serving: Calories: 248 Kcal; Carbs: 12 g; Fat: 44 g; Protein: 21 g.

8.5 Sweet Potato Tots

Preparation time: 45 mins
Cooking time: 35 mins
Servings: 4
Level of difficulty: Easy
Ingredients:

- 1 tbsp. potato starch
- 1¼ tsp. kosher salt, divided
- 1/8 tsp. garlic powder
- 2 sweet potatoes, peeled
- ¾ cup ketchup

Instructions:

- Fill a pot halfway with water and boil on high. Cook potatoes for 15 minutes or until fork tender.
- Let them cool on a plate for 15 minutes.
- Mix grated potatoes, 1 tsp salt, and garlic powder and potato starch in a plate.
- Make 24 tots-like shapes from shredded potato.
- Oil Spray air fryer basket with cooking spray. Spray half of the tots with oil spray and place them in one layer in the basket.
- Flip halfway through baking at 400°F for 12-14 minutes until golden brown. After air-frying, season with 1/8 tsp salt and serve with ketchup.

Nutritional facts per serving: Calories: 78 Kcal; Carbs: 19 g; Fat: 0 g; Protein: 1 g.

8.6 Hot Jalapenos Nachos

Preparation time: 10 mins
Cooking time: 18 mins
Servings: 4
Level of difficulty: Intermediate
Ingredients:

- 1 tbsp. chili powder
- ½ tsp. fresh chopped cilantro
- 1 jalapeno, sliced
- 1 lb. red bell pepper, cut into strips
- 1½ cups grated cheddar cheese
- 1 tsp. salt
- 1 tsp. ground cumin

- 1 tsp. garlic powder
- ½ tsp. ground black pepper
- 1 lb. ground turkey
- 1 tsp. siracha sauce

Instructions:
- Preheat the Air fryer to 400°F.
- In a small bowl, mix the spices together.
- Put the turkey in a pan that fits Air fryer and cook it until it turns brown. Add the spice mix and stir.
- Put the strips of bell pepper in a pan that has been lightly oiled, and then put the cooked turkey and cheese on top.
- Put the pan in the air fryer basket and cook for 8 minutes, or until the cheese is melted and has a light brown color.
- Drizzle siracha on top and serve and enjoy.

Nutritional facts per serving: Calories: 370 Kcal; Carbs: 9 g; Fat: 22 g; Protein: 7 g.

8.7 Sweet Potato Chips

Preparation time: 25 mins
Cooking time: 15 mins
Servings: 4
Level of difficulty: Easy
Ingredients:
- salt and black pepper, to taste
- 1 tsp. ground cinnamon
- ¼ cup extra virgin olive oil
- 2 sweet potatoes, sliced thinly

Instructions:
- Soak potato slices in cold water for 30 minutes.
- Remove the slices from water and dry with paper towels. For crispiness, dry them completely before serving.
- Rub slices with black pepper, olive oil, salt and cinnamon.
- Oil Spray air fryer basket with cooking spray.
- Air-fry the chips at 390°F for 20 minutes, stirring the basket every 7–8 minutes.
- Cook for five more minutes if not crispy.
- Serve with dipping sauce immediately.

Nutritional facts per serving: Calories: 357 Kcal; Carbs: 28 g; Fat: 27 g; Protein: 2 g.

8.8 Rosemary And Garlic Brussels Sprouts

Preparation time: 30 mins

Cooking time: 25 mins

Servings: 4

Level of difficulty: Easy

Ingredients:

- 1½ tsp. chopped fresh rosemary
- ½ cup panko breadcrumbs
- 1/2 tsp. salt
- 3 tbsp. olive oil
- 2 cloves of garlic, minced
- 1 lb. Brussels sprouts, halves
- ¼ tsp. black pepper

Instructions:

- Preheat the air fryer to 350°F.
- Add minced garlic, olive oil, salt and black pepper in a bowl and microwave 30 seconds on high.
- Coated Brussels sprouts with prepared mixture. Coat the air fryer basket using cooking spray, add the Brussels sprouts, and cook for 5 minutes.
- Stir Brussel sprouts. Continue cooking for 8 minutes until tender and crispy.

Nutritional facts per serving: Calories: 164 Kcal; Carbs: 15 g; Fat: 11 g; Protein: 5 g.

8.9 Loaded Potatoes

Preparation time: 25 mins

Cooking time: 2 mins

Servings: 2

Level of difficulty: Easy

Ingredients:

- 2 tbsp. sour cream, reduced fat
- 1 tsp. olive oil
- 8 baby Yukon gold potatoes
- 2 tbsp. chopped fresh chives
- 1/8 tsp. kosher salt
- 2 slices of bacon
- 2 tbsp. shredded cheddar cheese

Instructions:

- Coat potatoes with olive oil. Place potatoes in air fryer basket and cook at 350°F for 25 minutes, stirring after 5-8 minutes.
- Cook bacon in a pan over medium heat for 7 minutes until crispy.
- Crush the cooked bacon.
- Gently crush the potatoes on a dish.
- Pour bacon grease over them. Sprinkle crushed bacon, salt, sour cream, and chives over top.

Nutritional facts per serving: Calories: 199 Kcal; Carbs: 26 g; Fat: 7 g; Protein: 7 g.

8.10 Crispy French Fries

Preparation time: 30 mins

Cooking time: 25 mins

Servings: 4

Level of difficulty: Easy

Ingredients:

- 3 russet potatoes
- Salt, to taste
- 1 tbsp. olive oil
- 2 tbsp. chopped fresh parsley
- 2 tbsp. parmesan cheese

Instructions:

- Slice potatoes for French fries.
- Dry them well with paper towels.
- Mix cheese, olive oil, salt and parsley in a plate. Coat French fries with this spice mix.
- Preheat the air fryer to 360°F. Oil Spray the air fryer basket with cooking spray.
- Cook fries for 10 minutes and then stir the basket after 10 minutes. Cook another 10 minutes.
- Serve with dipping sauce.

Nutritional facts per serving: Calories: 189 Kcal; Carbs: 17 g; Fat: 5 g; Protein: 9 g.

8.11 Corn Dog Bites

Preparation time: 35 mins

Cooking time: 15 mins

Servings: 4

Level of difficulty: Intermediate

Ingredients:

- 2 eggs, lightly whisked
- 1½ cups crushed cornflakes

- 2 beef hot dogs uncured
- ½ cup all-purpose flour

Instructions:
- Slice hot dog to make three equal portions.
- Secure them with bamboo skewers.
- Mix flour with food. Make another egg dish.
- Serve more cornflakes.
- Hot dogs should be coated with flour, then dipped in egg, and finally in crushed corn flakes.
- Spray air fryer basket with oil. Arrange hot dog skewers in a single layer in the basket.
- Cook at 375°F for 10 minutes until crispy and golden, and then serve.

Nutritional facts per serving: Calories: 82 Kcal; Carbs: 8 g; Fat: 3 g; Protein: 5 g.

8.12 Kale Chips

Preparation time: 10 mins
Cooking time: 10 mins
Servings: 2
Level of difficulty: Easy
Ingredients:
- 4 cups loosely packed kale
- 2 tbsp. any seasoning
- Pinch of salt
- 2 tsp. olive oil

Instructions:
- The kale should be covered in salt and olive oil.
- Cook Kale chips at 370°F for 4 to 6 minutes in the Air fryer.
- The basket needs to be stirred twice for equal cooking.
- Add salt to taste, and serve right away.

Nutritional facts per serving: Calories: 84 Kcal; Carbs: 9 g; Fat: 2 g; Protein: 4 g.

8.13 Avocado Fries

Preparation time: 20 mins
Cooking time: 15 mins
Servings: 4
Level of difficulty: Easy
Ingredients:
- 1 avocado, pitted & sliced

- ½ tsp. salt

Instructions:
- Season the fries with salt.
- Preheat Air-fryer to 400°F and cook the fries for 15 minutes.

Nutritional facts per serving: Calories: 178 Kcal; Carbs: 18 g; Fat: 2 g; Protein: 12 g.

8.14 Cheese Sticks

Preparation time: 22 mins
Cooking time: 15 mins
Servings: 6
Level of difficulty: Intermediate
Ingredients:
- 2 whole eggs
- 6 medium-sized cheese sticks
- 1 tsp. Italian seasoning
- ¼ cup grated parmesan cheese
- ¼ tsp. ground rosemary
- ¼ cup whole wheat flour
- 1 tsp. garlic powder

Instructions:
- Whisk the eggs smoothly in a bowl.
- In a different bowl, cheese, flour, and spices should be mixed together.
- To coat the cheese sticks, you should mix eggs and flour together. Give them a full coat.
- Put the coated cheese sticks in the air fryer in a single layer.
- Heat Air fryer to 370°F and cook cheese sticks for 6 to 7 minutes.

Nutritional facts per serving: Calories: 67 Kcal; Carbs: 5 g; Fat: 4 g; Protein: 5 g.

8.15 Apple Chips

Preparation time: 20 mins
Cooking time: 10 mins
Servings: 8
Level of difficulty: Easy
Ingredients:
- 6 apples
- 1 tbsp. avocado oil
- 1 tbsp. cinnamon

Instructions:
- Make thin slices of apple with a mandolin.
- Put cinnamon and avocado oil on the apple slices.
- Place the apple chips in a preheated air fryer at 400°F and bake for 15 minutes.

Nutritional facts per serving: Calories: 178 Kcal; Carbs: 39 g; Fat: 1 g; Protein: 1 g.

8.16 Pumpkin Fries

Preparation time: 15 mins

Cooking time: 25 mins

Servings: 4

Level of difficulty: Easy

Ingredients:
- 1 pie pumpkin
- 2-3 tsp. chipotle peppers in adobo sauce
- ½ cup Greek yogurt
- ¼ tsp. black pepper
- ¼ tsp. garlic powder
- 1/8 tsp. + 1/2 tsp. salt
- 2 tbsp. maple syrup
- ¼ tsp. ground cumin
- ¼ tsp. chili powder

Instructions:
- Mix together chipotle chilies, 1/8 tsp salt, yogurt, and maple syrup. Mix all ingredients and refrigerate in an airtight jar.
- Preheat the air fryer to 400°F.
- Peel and half the pumpkin. Get rid of seeds.
- After slicing into half-inch pieces, place in bowl.
- Coat equally with half a tsp salt, cumin, chili powder, garlic powder and pepper.
- Oil Spray air fryer basket with cooking spray. Pack the basket with pumpkin fries.
- Cook until fries are tender, 6–8 minutes. Continue cooking for 3 to 5 minutes, stirring periodically, until light brown.

Nutritional facts per serving: Calories: 151 Kcal; Carbs: 31 g; Fat: 13 g; Protein: 5 g.

8.17 Pepper Poppers

Preparation time: 35 mins

Cooking time: 20 mins

Servings: 2

Level of difficulty: Easy

Ingredients:

- 1/2 cup dry breadcrumbs
- ¾ cup shredded Monterey jack cheese
- ¼ tsp. chili powder
- ¾ cup cheddar cheese, shredded
- 8 oz. softened cream cheese
- ¼ tsp. garlic powder
- ¼ tsp. salt
- 6 strips of bacon, cooked and crumbled
- 1 lb. jalapenos, halved
- ¼ tsp. smoked paprika

Instructions:

- Preheat the air fryer up to 325°F ahead of time.
- Put the bacon, cheese, and spices in a bowl and mix them together.
- Put about 2 tablespoons of stuffing on each side of the pepper. Make a crust out of bread crumbs.
- First, spray cooking oil into the basket of an air fryer. Then, put the peppers in a single layer.
- Keep cooking for another 15 to 20 minutes, or until the cheese melts.
- Choose your favorite dipping sauce to go with it.

Nutritional facts per serving: Calories: 81 Kcal; Carbs: 18 g; Fat: 6 g; Protein: 3 g.

8.18 Turkey Croquettes

Preparation time: 15 mins

Cooking time: 5 mins

Servings: 2

Level of difficulty: Easy

Ingredients:

- 3 cups cooked turkey, finely chopped
- 2 cups mashed potatoes
- 2 tsp. minced fresh rosemary
- 1/2 cup grated Parmesan cheese

- 1 finely chopped shallot
- 1 tsp. minced fresh sage
- 1/2 cup shredded Swiss cheese
- 1 large egg
- 1/4 tsp. pepper
- Salt to taste
- 1¼ cups Panko bread crumbs
- 2 tbsp. water

Instructions:
- Preheat the air fryer to 400°F.
- Put the cheeses, mashed potatoes, rosemary, shallot, salt, sage, and pepper in a big bowl.
- Mix in the turkey and form croquettes.
- Mix the egg and water together in a small bowl. In a different bowl, put the bread crumbs.
- Dip croquettes first in the egg, and then in the mix of bread crumbs.
- Put the croquettes in the basket of the air fryer and cook for 5 minutes.
- Serve it when it's golden brown.

Nutritional facts per serving: Calories: 187 Kcal; Carbs: 55 g; Fat: 50 g; Protein: 95 g.

8.19 Zucchini Croquettes

Preparation time: 10 mins

Cooking time: 12 mins

Servings: 4

Level of difficulty: Easy

Ingredients:
- Cooking spray
- 3 zucchinis, grated
- 1 egg
- ½ cup dill, chopped
- Salt and black pepper to taste
- ½ cup white flour
- 2 garlic cloves, minced

Instructions:
- Preheat the air fryer to 375°F.
- Stir all the ingredients together in a bowl.
- Make the mixture into medium-sized croquettes and put them in the basket of the air fryer.
- Air-fry them for 12 minutes, turning them over halfway through.

- Serve them right away as a snack.

Nutritional facts per serving: Calories: 120 Kcal; Carbs: 5 g; Fat: 2 g; Protein: 3 g.

8.20 Balsamic Zucchini Slices

Preparation time: 5 mins

Cooking time: 15 mins

Servings: 4

Level of difficulty: Easy

Ingredients:

- 2 tbsp. avocado oil
- Salt and black pepper to taste
- 2 tbsp. balsamic vinegar
- 3 zucchinis, thinly sliced

Instructions:

- Preheat the Air fryer to 220°F.
- Put everything in a bowl and mix it up.
- Put the zucchini slices in basket of Air fryer and cook for 15 minutes.
- As a snack, serve and enjoy!

Nutritional facts per serving: Calories: 40 Kcal; Carbs: 3 g; Fat: 4 g; Protein: 7 g.

8.21 Buttery Corn

Preparation time: 5 mins

Cooking time: 10 mins

Servings: 4

Level of difficulty: Easy

Ingredients:

- 8 tbsp. corn kernels
- 4 tbsp. butter

Instructions:

- Preheat the Air fryer to 350°F.
- Spread butter on corn and put the corn in Air fryer and cook it for 10 minutes.
- As a snack, serve and enjoy!

Nutritional facts per serving: Calories: 70 Kcal; Carbs: 7 g; Fat: 3 g; Protein: 3 g.

8.22 Cheese Sticks

Preparation time: 10 mins
Cooking time: 8 mins
Servings: 4
Level of difficulty: Easy
Ingredients:

- 1 egg, whisked
- ½ cup parmesan cheese, grated
- 4 mozzarella cheese strings, halved
- Salt and black pepper to taste
- ½ tbsp. Italian seasoning

Instructions:

- Preheat the Air fryer to 350°F.
- Stir the salt, pepper, parmesan, and Italian seasoning together in a bowl.
- Put the beaten egg in a different bowl.
- Dip the mozzarella sticks first in the egg mixture, then in the parmesan mixture.
- Dip the sticks again in the egg and Parmesan, and then put them in the basket of your air fryer.
- Cook them at for 8 minutes, turning them over halfway through.
- As a snack, serve.

Nutritional facts per serving: Calories: 200 Kcal; Carbs: 10 g; Fat: 13 g; Protein: 4 g.

8.23 Garlic Bread

Preparation time: 10 mins
Cooking time: 10 mins
Servings: 4
Level of difficulty: Easy
Ingredients:

- 2 stale French rolls
- 1 tbsp. olive oil
- 1 cup mayonnaise
- 4 tbsp. chopped garlic
- 2 tbsp. grated Parmesan

Instructions:

- Preheat the Air fryer to 350°F.
- Mix garlic into the mayo and set it away. Slice the bread, but don't separate the pieces.

- Fill each hole with 1 tbsp. of garlic mayo filling, brush with olive oil, and sprinkle with parmesan cheese. Put in the air fryer's basket and cook for 10 minutes. Serve.

Nutritional facts per serving: Calories: 150 Kcal; Carbs: 20 g; Fat: 7 g; Protein: 4 g.

8.24 Herbed Crackers

Preparation time: 10 mins
Cooking time: 16 mins
Servings: 4
Level of difficulty: Easy
Ingredients:

- ½ tsp. baking powder
- 1 garlic clove, minced
- 4 tbsp. butter, melted
- 1¼ cups flour
- Salt and black pepper to taste
- 2 tbsp. basil, minced
- 2 tbsp. cilantro, minced

Instructions:

- Preheat the Air fryer to 375°F.
- Mix all the ingredients together in a bowl until you get dough.
- Spread this on basket of Air fryer and air-fry for 16 minutes.
- Let it cool, cut it up, and serve.

Nutritional facts per serving: Calories: 170 Kcal; Carbs: 8 g; Fat: 10 g; Protein: 4 g.

8.25 Broccoli Bites

Preparation time: 15 mins
Cooking time: 5 mins
Servings: 4
Level of difficulty: Easy
Ingredients:

- 1 broccoli head, florets separated
- Salt and black pepper to taste
- 2 tsp. garlic powder
- 1 tsp. olive oil
- 1 tsp. butter, melted

Instructions:

- Preheat the Air fryer to 450°F.

- Combine all the ingredients in a mixing bowl and transfer the mixture to Air fryer basket.
- Air Fry for 15 minutes and serve as a snack and enjoy.

Nutritional facts per serving: Calories: 140 Kcal; Carbs: 11 g; Fat: 2 g; Protein: 5 g.

8.26 Turkey Nachos

Preparation time: 10 mins

Cooking time: 18 mins

Servings: 4

Level of difficulty: Intermediate

Ingredients:

- 1 tbsp. chili powder
- ½ tsp. ground black pepper
- 1 lb. ground turkey
- ½ tsp. fresh chopped cilantro
- 1 tsp. salt
- 1 tsp. ground cumin
- 1 tsp. garlic powder
- 1½ cups grated cheddar cheese
- 1 lb. red bell pepper, cut into strips

Instructions:

- Preheat the Air fryer to 400°F.
- In a small bowl, mix the spices together.
- Put the turkey in a pan that fits in your air fryer and cook it until it turns brown. Add the spice mix and stir.
- Put the strips of bell pepper in a pan that has been lightly oiled, and then put the cooked turkey and cheese on top.
- Put the pan in the air fryer basket and cook for 8 minutes, or until the cheese is melted and has a light brown color.
- Serve and enjoy.

Nutritional facts per serving: Calories: 350 Kcal; Carbs: 7 g; Fat: 20 g; Protein: 7 g.

8.27 Cauliflower Tots

Preparation time: 15 mins

Cooking time: 5 mins

Servings: 4

Level of difficulty: Easy

Ingredients:

- 1 cauliflower head, florets separated
- Salt and black pepper to taste
- 2 tsp. garlic powder
- 1 tsp. olive oil
- 1 tsp. butter, melted

Instructions:

- Preheat the Air fryer to 450°F.
- Add all of the ingredients in a mixing bowl and toss.
- Air Fry for 15 minutes and serve as a snack and enjoy.

Nutritional facts per serving: Calories: 130 Kcal; Carbs: 15 g; Fat: 2 g; Protein: 5 g.

8.28 Turmeric Carrots

Preparation time: 5 mins
Cooking time: 25 mins
Servings: 4
Level of difficulty: Easy

Ingredients:

- 4 carrots, thinly sliced
- 1 tsp. olive oil
- ½ tsp. turmeric powder
- Salt and black pepper to taste
- ½ tsp. chaat masala

Instructions:

- Preheat the Air fryer to 350°F.
- Put everything in a bowl and mix it up.
- Put the carrot slices in the basket of your air fryer and cook it for 25 minutes.
- As a snack, serve and enjoy!

Nutritional facts per serving: Calories: 160 Kcal; Carbs: 5 g; Fat: 2 g; Protein: 3 g.

8.29 Eggplant Chips

Preparation time: 5 mins
Cooking time: 10 mins
Servings: 4
Level of difficulty: Easy

Ingredients:
- 2 tbsp. avocado oil
- Salt and black pepper to taste
- 2 eggplants, thinly sliced
- 2 tbsp. balsamic vinegar

Instructions:
- Preheat the Air fryer to 220°F.
- Put everything in a bowl and mix it up.
- Put the eggplant chips in basket of air fryer and cook it for 50 minutes.
- As a snack, serve and enjoy!

Nutritional facts per serving: Calories: 50 Kcal; Carbs: 2 g; Fat: 5 g; Protein: 10 g.

8.30 Cheddar Muffins

Preparation time: 15 mins

Cooking time: 15 mins

Servings: 4

Level of difficulty: Intermediate

Ingredients:
- 1 cup all-purpose flour
- 1 tbsp. sugar
- 1 cup melted cheddar
- ¼ tsp. baking powder
- ¾ cup milk
- 2 tbsp. butter
- ¼ tsp. baking soda
- 1 tsp. vinegar

Instructions:
- Preheat the Air fryer to 375°F.
- Mix everything except for the milk to make a crumbly mixture. Add this milk to the mixture, stir to make a batter, and then pour the batter into the muffin cups.
- Put the muffin cups in Air fryer and cook for 15 minutes. Use a toothpick to see if they are done.

Nutritional facts per serving: Calories: 180 Kcal; Carbs: 14 g; Fat: 4 g; Protein: 3 g.

8.31 Tortilla Chips

Preparation time: 5 mins

Cooking time: 5 mins

Servings: 2

Level of difficulty: Easy

Ingredients:

- 1 tbsp. spice blend
- 2 tbsp. olive oil
- 12 corn tortillas,
- 2 tsp. salt

Instructions:

- Preheat the Air fryer to 350°F.
- Brush both sides of the tortillas with olive oil.
- Season the tortillas on both sides with salt and Spice Mix.
- Each tortilla should be cut into six wedges.
- Add the tortilla wedges to the air fryer and air-fry for 5 minutes, or until golden brown.
- Enjoy.

Nutritional facts per serving: Calories: 240 Kcal; Carbs: 20 g; Fat: 7 g; Protein: 1 g.

8.32 Potato Nuggets

Preparation time: 45 mins

Cooking time: 35 mins

Servings: 4

Level of difficulty: Easy

Ingredients:

- 1 tbsp. potato starch
- 1¼ tsp. kosher salt, divided
- 1/8 tsp. garlic powder
- 2 potatoes, peeled
- ¾ cup ketchup

Instructions:

- Fill a pot halfway with water and boil on high. Cook potatoes for 15 minutes or until fork tender.
- Let them cool on a plate for 15 minutes.
- Mix grated potatoes, 1 tsp salt, and garlic powder and potato starch in a plate.
- Make 24 nuggets from shredded potato.

- Oil Spray air fryer basket with cooking spray. Spray half of the nuggets with oil spray and place them in one layer in the basket.
- Flip halfway through baking at 400°F for 12-14 minutes until golden brown. After air-frying, season with 1/8 tsp salt and serve with ketchup.

Nutritional facts per serving: Calories: 78 Kcal; Carbs: 19 g; Fat: 0 g; Protein: 1 g.

8.33 Cheese Bread

Preparation time: 10 mins

Cooking time: 10 mins

Servings: 4

Level of difficulty: Easy

Ingredients:

- 2 stale French rolls
- 1 tbsp. olive oil
- 1 cup mayonnaise
- 4 tbsp. cheddar cheese
- 2 tbsp. grated Parmesan

Instructions:

- Preheat the Air fryer to 350°F.
- Mix cheddar cheese into the mayo and set it away. Slice the bread, but don't separate the pieces.
- Fill each hole with 1 tbsp. of cheese mayo filling, brush with olive oil, and sprinkle with parmesan cheese. Put in the air fryer's basket and cook for 10 minutes. Serve.

Nutritional facts per serving: Calories: 150 Kcal; Carbs: 20 g; Fat: 7 g; Protein: 4 g.

8.34 Balsamic Eggplant Chips

Preparation time: 5 mins

Cooking time: 15 mins

Servings: 4

Level of difficulty: Easy

Ingredients:

- 2 tbsp. avocado oil
- Salt and black pepper to taste
- 2 tbsp. balsamic vinegar
- 3 eggplants, thinly sliced

Instructions:

- Preheat the Air fryer to 220°F.
- Put everything in a bowl and mix it up.

- Put the eggplant slices in basket of Air fryer and cook for 15 minutes.
- As a snack, serve and enjoy!

Nutritional facts per serving: Calories: 40 Kcal; Carbs: 3 g; Fat: 4 g; Protein: 7 g.

8.35 Zucchini Muffins

Preparation time: 15 mins

Cooking time: 15 mins

Servings: 4

Level of difficulty: Intermediate

Ingredients:

- 1 cup all-purpose flour
- 1 tbsp. sugar
- 1 cup grated zucchini
- ¼ tsp. baking powder
- ¾ cup milk
- 2 tbsp. butter
- ¼ tsp. baking soda
- 1 tsp. vinegar

Instructions:

- Preheat the Air fryer to 375°F.
- Mix everything except for the milk to make a crumbly mixture. Add this milk to the mixture, stir to make a batter, and then pour the batter into the muffin cups.
- Put the muffin cups in Air fryer and cook for 15 minutes. Use a toothpick to see if they are done.

Nutritional facts per serving: Calories: 180 Kcal; Carbs: 14 g; Fat: 4 g; Protein: 3 g.

8.36 Chicken Vegetable Croquettes

Preparation time: 15 mins

Cooking time: 5 mins

Servings: 2

Level of difficulty: Easy

Ingredients:

- 3 cups cooked chicken, finely chopped
- 1 large egg
- 1/4 tsp. pepper
- Salt to taste
- 1¼ cups Panko bread crumbs
- 2 cups mashed potatoes

- 2 tsp. minced fresh rosemary
- 1/2 cup grated Parmesan cheese
- 1 finely chopped shallot
- 1 tsp. minced fresh sage
- 1/2 cup shredded Swiss cheese
- 2 tbsp. water

Instructions:
- Preheat the air fryer to 400°F.
- Put the cheeses, mashed potatoes, rosemary, shallot, salt, sage, and pepper in a big bowl.
- Mix in the chicken and form croquettes.
- Mix the egg and water together in a small bowl. In a different bowl, put the bread crumbs.
- Dip croquettes first in the egg, and then in the mix of bread crumbs.
- Put the croquettes in the basket of the air fryer and cook for 5 minutes.
- Serve it when it's golden brown.

Nutritional facts per serving: Calories: 187 Kcal; Carbs: 55 g; Fat: 50 g; Protein: 95 g.

8.37 Garlic Corn

Preparation time: 5 mins
Cooking time: 10 mins
Servings: 4
Level of difficulty: Easy
Ingredients:
- 8 tbsp. corn kernels
- 4 tbsp. butter
- 2 tbsp. chopped garlic

Instructions:
- Preheat the Air fryer to 350°F.
- Mix the garlic and butter and put this mixture on corn.
- Put the corn in Air fryer and cook it for 10 minutes.
- As a snack, serve and enjoy!

Nutritional facts per serving: Calories: 70 Kcal; Carbs: 7 g; Fat: 3 g; Protein: 3 g.

8.38 Spinach Chips

Preparation time: 10 mins
Cooking time: 10 mins
Servings: 2

Level of difficulty: Easy

Ingredients:

- 4 cups loosely packed spinach
- 2 tbsp. any seasoning
- Pinch of salt
- 2 tsp. olive oil

Instructions:

- The spinach should be covered in salt and olive oil.
- Cook spinach chips at 370°F for 4 to 6 minutes in the Air fryer.
- The basket needs to be stirred twice for equal cooking.
- Add salt to taste, and serve right away.

Nutritional facts per serving: Calories: 84 Kcal; Carbs: 9 g; Fat: 2 g; Protein: 4 g.

8.39 Waffle Cheese Fries

Preparation time: 10 mins

Cooking time: 20 mins

Servings: 4

Level of difficulty: Easy

Ingredients:

- 1 cup Swiss cheese, shredded
- 2 green onions, sliced
- 2 cups frozen waffle fries
- 1 red bell pepper, chopped
- 2 tsp. olive oil
- ½ cup bottled chicken gravy

Instructions:

- Put the waffle fries and olive oil in a bowl and mix them together. Mix well.
- Put the waffle fries in the basket of the air fryer. Put the lid on it and cook for 10 to 12 minutes at 375°F. While it's cooking, shake the basket once.
- Put the fries in a baking dish that is 6 inches by 6 inches by 2 inches. Top with the green onions, cheese, and pepper.
- Place the pan in the air fryer basket and cover the machine. For three minutes, air-fry the veggies until they are soft.
- After taking the pan out of the basket, pour the sauce over the fries. Put the pan back in the basket and air fry for another two minutes, or until the gravy is hot. Let it cool before serving.

Nutritional facts per serving: Calories: 251 Kcal; Carbs: 22 g; Fat: 17 g; Protein: 18 g.

8.40 Jicama Fries

Preparation time: 5 mins

Cooking time: 20 mins

Servings: 4

Level of difficulty: Easy

Ingredients:

- 1 small jicama; peeled
- ¼ tsp. ground black pepper
- ¾ tsp. chili powder
- ¼ tsp. onion powder
- ¼ tsp. garlic powder

Instructions:

- Cut the jicama into fries.
- Put the pieces in a small bowl and top them with the rest of the ingredients. Put the fries in the basket of the air fryer.
- Set the timer for 20 minutes and adjust the temperature to 350°F. Shake the basket around twice or three times while it's cooking.

Nutritional facts per serving: Calories: 37 Kcal; Carbs: 8 g; Fat: 1 g; Protein: 1 g.

8.41 Cornbread

Preparation time: 5 mins

Cooking time: 25 mins

Servings: 8

Level of difficulty: Intermediate

Ingredients:

- ¾ cup almond flour
- 2 eggs, beaten
- 1 tbsp. sweetener
- 1 cup white cornmeal
- ¼ tsp. salt
- 1½ tsp. baking powder
- 6 tbsp. butter, melted
- ½ tsp. baking soda
- 1½ cups buttermilk, low-fat

Instructions:

- Put the frying pan in the air fryer, grease it with olive oil, and then close the lid. Set the temperature to 360°F and let it heat up for 5 minutes.

- Break the egg into a bowl, and then mix in the milk and butter with a whisk.
- In a different bowl, mix the flour with the rest of the ingredients. Then, add the egg mixture and stir until it's fully mixed in.
- Open the fryer and pour the batter into the pan. Cover the fryer with its lid and cook at 360°F for 25 minutes, shaking it every so often, until the food is golden and crispy.
- When the air fryer buzzes, open the door, pull out the fryer pan, and put the bread on a plate to serve. Serve the bread with the butter pieces and enjoy.

Nutritional facts per serving: Calories: 138 Kcal; Carbs: 25 g; Fat: 2 g; Protein: 5 g.

8.42 Tortilla

Preparation time: 5 mins

Cooking time: 10 mins

Servings: 2

Level of difficulty: Easy

Ingredients:

- 2 eggs
- 2 slices of chopped mozzarella
- 2 slices of ham, chopped
- ½ cup chopped parsley
- ½ tsp. oregano
- 1 tbsp. chopped onion
- Salt and black pepper to taste

Instructions:

- Set the air fryer to 400°F and heat it up for 5 minutes. Spread out a refractory that has a high shelf and extra space that fits in the air fryer's basket.
- Make light strokes with a fork over the eggs in a bowl. Fill it up and season it with spices. Be careful not to spill the eggs as you pour them into the refractory container while it is in the air fryer's pan.
- Press the start button and set the time for 10 to 15 minutes. When the tortilla turns golden brown, it's done.

Nutritional facts per serving: Calories: 41 Kcal; Carbs: 6 g; Fat: 1 g; Protein: 1 g.

8.43 Skinny Pumpkin Chips

Preparation time: 5 mins

Cooking time: 13 mins

Servings: 2

Level of difficulty: Easy

Ingredients:

- 1 lb. pumpkin, cut into sticks

- Salt and black pepper, to taste
- ½ tsp. rosemary
- 1 tbsp. coconut oil
- ½ tsp. basil
- Mayonnaise, for serving

Instructions:

- First, heat the Air Fryer up to 395°F. Spread coconut oil on the pumpkin sticks, and then add the spices and mix.
- Toss the basket every five minutes during the 13 minute cooking time. Put mayonnaise on top and serve.

Nutritional facts per serving: Calories: 118 Kcal; Carbs: 2 g; Fat: 14 g; Protein: 6 g.

8.44 Palm Trees Holder

Preparation time: 5 mins

Cooking time: 15 mins

Servings: 2

Level of difficulty: Intermediate

Ingredients:

- 1 sheet of puff pastry
- Sugar

Instructions:

- Puff pastry sheet should be stretched on a flat surface. After adding sugar, fold the puff pastry sheet into half. Top with a thin layer of sugar and fold the puff pastry in halfway again.
- The palm tree is formed by rolling the puff pastry sheet from both ends to the middle. Cut into 5-8 mm sheets.
- Start the Air Fryer at 356°F and place the palm trees in the basket. Air fry for 10 minutes. Serve.

Nutritional facts per serving: Calories: 108 Kcal; Carbs: 29 g; Fat: 12 g; Protein: 4 g.

8.45 Air Fried Ripe Plantains

Preparation time: 10 mins

Cooking time: 10 mins

Servings: 2

Level of difficulty: Easy

Ingredients:

2 ripe plantains, sliced

1 tbsp. coconut butter

Instructions:

- Start the Air Fryer at 350°F. Apply a small amount of coconut butter to all sides of plantain slices.

- Put one uniform layer in the Air Fryer basket, no overlap or touching. Frying plantains takes 10 minutes.
- Get out of basket. Transfer to plates and repeat for all plantains. Serve and enjoy.

Nutritional facts per serving: Calories: 209 Kcal; Carbs: 29 g; Fat: 8 g; Protein: 3 g.

Chapter 9: Vegetables And Sides

9.1 Asparagus And Potatoes

Preparation time: 5 mins

Cooking time: 10 mins

Servings: 4

Level of difficulty: Easy

Ingredients:

- 4 potatoes, sliced
- 2 stalks of scallions, chopped
- 1 lb. asparagus, chopped
- 1 tbsp. salt
- 1 tbsp. dried dill
- 1/2 tbsp. black pepper

Instructions:

- Put onions, asparagus and onions in a bowl and mix them together. Add the oil and mix it in well to coat. It takes 10 minutes to cook the onions in an air fryer set to 350°F.
- Place the asparagus, potatoes onions, and 2 tablespoons of oil in a bowl. Add the salt, dill, and pepper. Mix well, and then serve.

Nutritional facts per serving: Calories: 174 Kcal; Carbs: 40 g; Fat: 1 g; Protein: 5 g.

9.2 Garlic Roasted Carrots

Preparation time: 5 mins

Cooking time: 12 mins

Servings: 4

Level of difficulty: Easy

Ingredients:

- Salt and pepper, to taste
- 1 lb. carrots
- 2 tbsp. garlic powder
- 2 tbsp. olive oil

Instructions:

- Cut the carrots into 2-inch pieces after peeling them. Put them in a small bowl. Salt and pepper should be added. Be sure to cover the carrots well.
- The air fryer should be set to 390°F for 12 minutes after you put the carrots in the basket.

Nutritional facts per serving: Calories: 121 Kcal; Carbs: 14 g; Fat: 7 g; Protein: 2 g.

9.3 Eggplant Cutlets

Preparation time: 10 mins

Cooking time: 9 mins

Servings: 8

Level of difficulty: Easy

Ingredients:

- 1 egg
- 1 eggplant, chopped
- 1 cup Italian breadcrumbs
- 2 tbsp. salt
- 1/4 cup milk

Instructions:

- Spread out the eggplant slices on a flat surface. Season them with salt. And then wait 10 minutes. Add more salt and flip the eggplants over. Take a break.
- Add the breadcrumbs to a bowl while you wait. Add the milk and egg to a different bowl and mix them together.
- First coat the eggplant in the egg mix, then coat it in the bread crumbs. Put the eggplant in the air fryer basket.
- Let it cook for 7 minutes at 320°F. In less than two minutes, flip and cook again. Put the eggplant on a plate and top it with tomato sauce.

Nutritional facts per serving: Calories: 79 Kcal; Carbs: 14 g; Fat: 2 g; Protein: 3 g.

9.4 Roasted Shishito Peppers

Preparation time: 5 mins

Cooking time: 7 mins

Servings: 4

Level of difficulty: Easy

Ingredients:

- Salt and pepper to taste
- 1 oz. shishito peppers
- 2 tbsp. oil

Instructions:

- Put the peppers and olive oil in a bowl and season with pepper and salt. You can cover the peppers well by rubbing them with your hands.
- Spread the peppers out in the basket of the air fryer. Cook for 7 minutes at 380°F.
- Put the peppers on a plate and serve.

Nutritional facts per serving: Calories: 160 Kcal; Carbs: 0 g; Fat: 5 g; Protein: 0 g.

9.5 Roasted Cherry Tomatoes

Preparation time: 5 mins

Cooking time: 5 mins

Servings: 4

Level of difficulty: Easy

Ingredients:

- 1 lb. cherry tomatoes
- 1 tbsp. Italian seasoning
- 1 tbsp. salt
- 2 tbsp. olive oil
- 1/2 tbsp. black pepper

Instructions:

- Put the tomatoes, oil, pepper, salt, and seasonings in a bowl and mix them together. Rub the tomatoes together gently to make sure they are covered.
- Add the tomatoes in the basket of the air fryer. Set it to 300°F and cook for 5 minutes.
- Put the tomatoes on a plate and serve them with vegetables.

Nutritional facts per serving: Calories: 93 Kcal; Carbs: 5 g; Fat: 8 g; Protein: 1 g.

9.5 Creamy Potatoes

Preparation time: 5 mins

Cooking time: 25 mins

Servings: 4

Level of difficulty: Easy

Ingredients:

- 2 lb. baby potatoes, peeled and halved
- 1 tsp. turmeric powder
- salt and black pepper, to taste
- Juice of 1 lime
- 2 garlic cloves, minced
- 1 cup heavy cream
- 2 tbsp. olive oil
- 1 tsp. coriander, ground

Instructions:

- Put the potatoes, cream, turmeric, and other ingredients in a pan that fits your air fryer. Toss the ingredients together, then put the pan in the fryer and cook for 25 minutes at 400°F.

Nutritional facts per serving: Calories: 150 Kcal; Carbs: 6 g; Fat: 3 g; Protein: 6 g.

9.7 Roasted Onions

Preparation time: 5 mins

Cooking time: 5 mins

Servings: 4

Level of difficulty: Easy

Ingredients:

- 1 lb. onions, chopped into wedges
- 1 tbsp. Italian seasoning
- 1 tbsp. salt
- 2 tbsp. olive oil
- 1/2 tbsp. black pepper

Instructions:

- Put the onion wedges, oil, pepper, salt, and seasonings in a bowl and mix them together. Rub the tomatoes together gently to make sure they are covered.
- Add the onion wedges in the basket of the air fryer. Set it to 300°F and cook for 5 minutes.

Nutritional facts per serving: Calories: 95 Kcal; Carbs: 6 g; Fat: 8 g; Protein: 1 g.

9.8 Garlic Roasted Potato Wedges

Preparation time: 5 mins

Cooking time: 12 mins

Servings: 4

Level of difficulty: Easy

Ingredients:

- Salt and pepper, to taste
- 1 lb. potato
- 2 tbsp. garlic powder
- 2 tbsp. olive oil

Instructions:

- Cut the potato into wedges. Put them in a small bowl. Salt and pepper should be added. Be sure to cover the wedges well.
- The air fryer should be set to 390°F for 12 minutes after you put the potato wedges in the basket.

Nutritional facts per serving: Calories: 124 Kcal; Carbs: 15 g; Fat: 8 g; Protein: 2 g.

9.9 Radish Chips

Preparation time: 5 mins

Cooking time: 15 mins

Servings: 2

Level of difficulty: Easy

Ingredients:

- 2 tbsp. olive oil
- 1 lb. radishes
- Salt and pepper to taste

Instructions:

- Take the radishes and wash and dry them. Cut them up into 1-inch slices. Put the radishes in a bowl and season them with salt, pepper, and oil. Toss until everything is covered.
- Turn on the air fryer and set it to 390°F. Cook the radishes for 5 minutes. Cook for 10 more minutes after you toss them.

Nutritional facts per serving: Calories: 150 Kcal; Carbs: 8 g; Fat: 14 g; Protein: 2 g.

9.10 Carrot Chips

Preparation time: 5 mins

Cooking time: 15 mins

Servings: 2

Level of difficulty: Easy

Ingredients:

- 2 tbsp. olive oil
- 1 lb. carrots
- Salt and pepper to taste

Instructions:

- Take the carrots and wash and dry them. Cut them up into 1-inch slices. Put the chips in a bowl and season them with salt, pepper, and oil. Toss until everything is covered.
- Turn on the air fryer and set it to 390°F. Cook the carrot chips for 5 minutes. Cook for 10 more minutes after you toss them.

Nutritional facts per serving: Calories: 145 Kcal; Carbs: 10 g; Fat: 14 g; Protein: 2 g.

9.11 Vegan Pasta Chips

Preparation time: 10 mins

Cooking time: 5 mins

Servings: 2

Level of difficulty: Easy

Ingredients:

- 1 tsp. Italian Seasoning Blend
- 1 cup bow tie pasta, cooked
- 1 tbsp. nutritional yeast
- 1 tbsp. aquafaba

- Salt and black pepper, to taste

Instructions:

- Add yeast, black pepper, salt, and Italian seasoning to the pasta and toss it all together.
- Depending on how much space there is, put the mixes in the air fryer basket.
- At 400°F, cook for 5 minutes.
- In the middle, shake the basket.
- Serve and enjoy it when it's done.

Nutritional facts per serving: Calories: 230 Kcal; Carbs: 45 g; Fat: 2 g; Protein: 10 g.

9.12 Creamy Corns

Preparation time: 5 mins

Cooking time: 5 mins

Servings: 4

Level of difficulty: Easy

Ingredients:

- 2 lb. baby corns
- 1 tsp. turmeric powder
- salt and black pepper, to taste
- Juice of 1 lime
- 2 garlic cloves, minced
- 1 cup heavy cream
- 2 tbsp. olive oil
- 1 tsp. coriander, ground

Instructions:

- Put the corns, cream, turmeric, and other ingredients in a pan that fits your air fryer. Toss the ingredients together, then put the pan in the fryer and cook for 5 minutes at 400°F.

Nutritional facts per serving: Calories: 100 Kcal; Carbs: 6 g; Fat: 3 g; Protein: 7 g.

9.13 Tofu Nuggets

Preparation time: 12 mins

Cooking time: 15 mins

Servings: 2

Level of difficulty: Intermediate

Ingredients:

- 1 block tofu, pressed and drained
- 1 tsp. smoked paprika
- Salt and black pepper, to taste

- 1 cup Panko bread crumbs
- ¼ tsp. garlic powder
- Oil spray

Instructions:
- Tofu should be drained and then cut into small cubes.
- Use a bowl to mix the garlic powder, salt, pepper, and smoked paprika together.
- Cover it in Panko bread crumbs.
- Use oil spray to grease it.
- For 15 minutes, cook it in the air fryer basket at 400°F.
- As soon as the top is brown, serve.

Nutritional facts per serving: Calories: 249 Kcal; Carbs: 41 g; Fat: 7 g; Protein: 14 g.

9.14 Roasted Squash Grits

Preparation time: 20 mins

Cooking time: 23 mins

Servings: 4

Level of difficulty: Expert

Ingredients:
- ½ lb. butternut squash, chopped
- 1 tbsp. fresh chopped rosemary
- 1 tbsp. minced garlic
- 2 tbsp. olive oil
- ½ cup chopped walnuts
- 1 cup heavy cream
- 2 cups cauliflower florets
- 1 cup cheddar cheese, shredded
- ½ cup water
- 1 tsp. salt
- 2 tbsp. butter
- ¼ tsp. ground black pepper

Instructions:
- First, preheat your air fryer to 400°F. Then, put paper on the air fryer tray or bake pan.
- Spread the garlic, walnuts, olive oil, rosemary, and butternut squash out on a baking sheet. Add the rosemary and toss everything around in the olive oil.
- Put the pan in the air fryer and roast for 15 minutes.

- Put the cauliflower in a food processor or blender and pulse it until it looks like rice while the squash is cooking.
- Put the broccoli and water in a pot. Cook for 5 minutes over medium-low heat.
- After you add the heavy cream, cook for three more minutes.
- Add the salt, butter, and pepper, and mix them together to melt the cheese.
- Put some in each bowl, and then add the roasted mushrooms on top. Serve.

Nutritional facts per serving: Calories: 485 Kcal; Carbs: 18 g; Fat: 37 g; Protein: 13 g.

9.15 Zucchini Boats

Preparation time: 5 mins

Cooking time: 7 mins

Servings: 4

Level of difficulty: Easy

Ingredients:

- ¼ cup mozzarella cheese, shredded
- 2 zucchinis
- ½ cup pizza sauce

Instructions:

- Preheat the Air fryer to 350°F.
- Half the zucchini and scoop out the inside flesh. Fill the zucchini with pizza sauce, and then top with cheese.
- Air Fry the zucchini for 7 minutes. Serve, and enjoy.

Nutritional facts per serving: Calories: 31 Kcal; Carbs: 6 g; Fat: 1 g; Protein: 2 g.

9.16 Mexican Style Corn On The Cob

Preparation time: 20 mins

Cooking time: 22 mins

Servings: 4

Level of difficulty: Easy

Ingredients:

- 4 ears fresh corn, shucked
- 2 tbsp. fresh cilantro, chopped
- 2 tsp. garlic minced
- Oil spray, for greasing
- 1 tsp. lime zest
- 2 tbsp. vegan butter
- Salt and black pepper, to taste

- 1 tsp. lemon juice

Instructions:
- Spray oil on all sides of the corn.
- Put it in the air fryer basket and cook it at 400°F for 20 minutes, turning it over once.
- In a bowl, mix together green onion, lime zest, lemon juice, vegan butter, pepper, salt, and cilantro.
- Place these mixes in the microwave and heat them for one minute.
- Cover the cooked corn with this mix after that.
- Serve right away.

Nutritional facts per serving: Calories: 296 Kcal; Carbs: 50 g; Fat: 8 g; Protein: 10 g.

9.17 Onion Rings

Preparation time: 5 mins

Cooking time: 12 mins

Servings: 4

Level of difficulty: Easy

Ingredients:

1 packet of onion rings

Instructions:
- Preheat the air fryer for 5 minutes at 330°F. Put the onion rings in the air fryer basket in a single layer.
- For seven minutes, air fry the onion rings while shaking it every now and then. Put the onions on a plate and serve.

Nutritional facts per serving: Calories: 114 Kcal; Carbs: 18 g; Fat: 1 g; Protein: 5 g.

9.18 Roasted Pineapple

Preparation time: 5 mins

Cooking time: 15 mins

Servings: 2

Level of difficulty: Easy

Ingredients:
- 1 pineapple, fresh

Instructions:
- Preheat the air fryer to 375°F. Use parchment paper to line the air fryer basket.
- Cut the pineapple into rings after taking out the core. Put the rings in the air fryer basket that has been lined.
- After 10 minutes, flip the food over and air fry for another 5 minutes. Serve and enjoy.

Nutritional facts per serving: Calories: 341 Kcal; Carbs: 89 g; Fat: 1 g; Protein: 4 g.

9.19 Potato Wedges

Preparation time: 10 mins

Cooking time: 15 mins

Servings: 4

Level of difficulty: Easy

Ingredients:

- 2 russet potatoes, cut into wedges
- ½ tbsp. sea salt
- ½ tbsp. paprika
- 1½ tbsp. olive oil
- ½ tbsp. chili powder
- ½ tbsp. parsley flakes
- 1/8 tsp. black pepper, ground

Instructions:

- Preheat the air fryer to 400°F. Mix the oil, paprika, chili powder, parsley, pepper and salt with the potato wedges in a bowl until everything is well mixed.
- In an air fryer basket, put the potato wedges. Cook for 15 minutes, making sure to flip them over every 10 minutes.
- Put the potato wedges on a plate to serve. Serve and enjoy.

Nutritional facts per serving: Calories: 129 Kcal; Carbs: 19 g; Fat: 5 g; Protein: 2 g.

9.20 Herbed Potatoes

Preparation time: 10 mins

Cooking time: 20 mins

Servings: 4

Ingredients:

- 1 lb. potatoes cut into wedges
- 2 tbsp. olive oil
- 1 tbsp. oregano, chopped
- 2 tbsp. chives, chopped
- 1 tbsp. Italian seasoning
- 1 tbsp. balsamic vinegar
- A pinch of salt and black pepper

Instructions:

- Preheat the Air fryer to 350°F.
- Mix the vinegar, potatoes, chives and the other ingredients in the pan of your air fryer oven and air-fry for 20 minutes.

Nutritional facts per serving: Calories: 89 Kcal; Carbs: 4 g; Fat: 7 g; Protein: 2 g.

9.21 Acorn Squash

Preparation time: 5 mins

Cooking time: 20 mins

Servings: 4

Level of difficulty: Easy

Ingredients:

- 1 acorn squash
- 2 tbsp. brown sugar
- 3 tbsp. melted butter
- 1/2 tbsp. kosher salt

Instructions:

- Preheat the air fryer to 375°F. Cut your squash in half lengthwise after trimming the top and bottom. Get rid of the seeds and then cut them into half rings that are ½ inch thick.
- In a bowl, mix the sugar, butter, pepper and salt together until they are well mixed. Toss the squash in the butter mixed together to cover them.
- Make sure to flip the acorn squash every 10 minutes while it's cooking for 20 minutes. Move the squash to a plate for serving. Serve and enjoy.

Nutritional facts per serving: Calories: 126 Kcal; Carbs: 13 g; Fat: 9 g; Protein: 1 g.

9.22 Creamy Beets

Preparation time: 5 mins

Cooking time: 25 mins

Servings: 4

Level of difficulty: Easy

Ingredients:

- 2 lb. baby beets, peeled and halved
- 1 tsp. turmeric powder
- 1 cup heavy cream
- 2 tbsp. olive oil
- salt and black pepper, to taste
- Juice of 1 lime
- 2 garlic cloves, minced
- 1 tsp. coriander, ground

Instructions:

- Put the beet, cream, turmeric, and other ingredients in a pan that fits your air fryer. Toss the ingredients together, then put the pan in the fryer and cook for 25 minutes at 400°F.

Nutritional facts per serving: Calories: 135 Kcal; Carbs: 4 g; Fat: 3 g; Protein: 6 g.

9.23 Salsa Zucchini

Preparation time: 10 mins

Cooking time: 15 mins

Servings: 4

Level of difficulty: Easy

Ingredients:

- 1 lb. zucchinis, roughly sliced
- 1 tsp. coriander, ground
- 1 red onion, chopped
- 1 cup mild salsa
- 2 tbsp. lime juice
- Salt and black pepper, to taste
- 2 tbsp. olive oil

Instructions:

- Toss the zucchini with the salsa and the other ingredients in a pan that fits your air fryer. Put the pan in the fryer and cook at 390°F for 15 minutes.

Nutritional facts per serving: Calories: 150 Kcal; Carbs: 4 g; Fat: 4 g; Protein: 5 g.

9.24 Spicy Avocado Mix

Preparation time: 5 mins

Cooking time: 15 mins

Servings: 4

Level of difficulty: Easy

Ingredients:

- 2 small avocados, cut into wedges
- Zest of 1 lime, grated
- 1 tsp. sweet paprika
- 1 tbsp. olive oil
- 1 tsp. avocado oil
- Juice of 1 lime
- salt and black pepper, to taste

Instructions:

- Place the lime juice, avocado, and other ingredients in an air fryer-safe pan. Mix the ingredients. Place the pan in the air fryer and cook for 15 minutes at 350°F.

Nutritional facts per serving: Calories: 153 Kcal; Carbs: 4 g; Fat: 3 g; Protein: 6 g.

9.25 Spicy Black Beans

Preparation time: 5 mins

Cooking time: 20 mins

Servings: 4

Level of difficulty: Easy

Ingredients:

- 2 cups canned black beans, drained
- 1 tsp. chili powder
- 1 tbsp. olive oil
- salt and black pepper, to taste
- 2 red chilies, minced
- 1 cup tomato sauce

Instructions:

Put the oil, beans, and other ingredients in an air fryer-safe pan. Toss the beans around, then put the pan in the air fryer and cook for 20 minutes at 375°F.

Nutritional facts per serving: Calories: 160 Kcal; Carbs: 5 g; Fat: 4 g; Protein: 4 g.

9.26 Cajun Tomatoes And Peppers

Preparation time: 5 mins

Cooking time: 20 mins

Servings: 4

Level of difficulty: Easy

Ingredients:

- 1 tbsp. avocado oil
- 1 tbsp. Cajun seasoning
- 1 lb. cherry tomatoes, halved
- 1 lb. mixed bell peppers, sliced
- salt and black pepper, to taste
- 1 red onion, chopped
- 1 tsp. sweet paprika

Instructions:

- Add the tomatoes, peppers, and other ingredients to a pan that fits in your air fryer. Place the pan in the air fryer and cook for 20 minutes at 390°F.

Nutritional facts per serving: Calories: 151 Kcal; Carbs: 4 g; Fat: 3 g; Protein: 5 g.

9.27 Herbed Tomatoes

Preparation time: 10 mins

Cooking time: 20 mins

Servings: 4

Ingredients:

- 1 lb. tomatoes cut into wedges
- 2 tbsp. olive oil
- 1 tbsp. oregano, chopped
- 2 tbsp. chives, chopped
- 1 tbsp. Italian seasoning
- 1 tbsp. balsamic vinegar
- A pinch of salt and black pepper

Instructions:

- Preheat the Air fryer to 350°F.
- Mix the vinegar, tomatoes, chives and the other ingredients in the pan of your air fryer oven and air-fry for 20 minutes.

Nutritional facts per serving: Calories: 89 Kcal; Carbs: 4 g; Fat: 7 g; Protein: 2 g.

9.28 Lemon Tomatoes

Preparation time: 5 mins

Cooking time: 15 mins

Servings: 4

Level of difficulty: Easy

Ingredients:

- 2 lb. cherry tomatoes, halved
- 1 tsp. coriander, ground
- 1 tsp. sweet paprika
- handful parsley, chopped
- 2 tbsp. olive oil
- 2 tsp. lemon zest, grated
- 2 tbsp. lemon juice

Instructions:

- To cook in an air fryer, put the tomatoes, paprika, and other ingredients in the pan. Toss the ingredients around and cook at 370°F for 15 minutes.

Nutritional facts per serving: Calories: 151 Kcal; Carbs: 5 g; Fat: 2 g; Protein: 5 g.

9.29 Zucchini Sauté

Preparation time: 10 mins

Cooking time: 20 mins

Servings: 4

Level of difficulty: Easy

Ingredients:

- 1 lb. zucchinis, roughly cubed
- ½ cup heavy cream
- 1 tsp. sweet paprika
- 1 tbsp. olive oil
- 3 garlic cloves, minced
- 2 tbsp. dill, chopped
- Salt and black pepper, to taste

Instructions:

- Put the zucchini, garlic, and other ingredients in your air fryer. Give it a quick stir, and cook at 370°F for 20 minutes.

Nutritional facts per serving: Calories: 109 Kcal; Carbs: 1 g; Fat: 4 g; Protein: g.

9.30 Cumin Eggplant Mix

Preparation time: 10 mins

Cooking time: 20 mins

Servings: 4

Level of difficulty: Easy

Ingredients:

- 1 lb. eggplant, cubed
- 1 cup cherry tomatoes, halved
- 1 red onion, chopped
- Salt and black pepper, to taste
- 2 tbsp. olive oil
- ½ tsp. chili powder
- ½ tsp. cumin, ground
- 1 tbsp. chives, chopped

Instructions:

- Combine eggplants and the rest of the ingredients and put them in air fryer basket. Toss them gently and cook for 20 minutes at 370°F.

Nutritional facts per serving: Calories: 110 Kcal; Carbs: 13 g; Fat: 5 g; Protein: 9 g.

Chapter 10: Vegetarian Mains

10.1 Mixed Veggies Pancakes

Preparation time: 20 mins

Cooking time: 15 mins

Servings: 2

Level of difficulty: Intermediate

Ingredients:
- 4 tbsp. ground flaxseed
- 3 russet potatoes, shredded
- ½ cup water
- Salt and black pepper, to taste
- 1/4 cup fresh cilantro, finely chopped
- 1 small onion, shredded
- ½ cup peas
- ½ cup carrots, chopped
- ½ cup peas
- ¼ cup corn, drained
- 1/2 cup all-purpose flour
- Oil spray for greasing

Instructions:
- Add carrots, potatoes, onions, corn and peas to a big bowl. Then mix flaxseed with water.
- Really mix it.
- Season with salt and black pepper, and then add the flour and parsley.
- Mix together to form pancake batter.
- Make burgers out of this mixture and put them in a basket that has been lined with parchment paper.
- After 15 minutes, turn the heat down to 400°F and cook in batches.
- Serve the pancakes hot when they're all done.

Nutritional facts per serving: Calories: 514 Kcal; Carbs: 98 g; Fat: 6 g; Protein: 16 g.

10.2 Vegan Coconut French Toasts

Preparation time: 10 mins

Cooking time: 4 mins

Servings: 1

Level of difficulty: Easy

Ingredients:

- 2 slices of gluten-free bread
- 2 tbsp. maple syrup
- ½ tsp. baking powder
- 1 cup coconut milk
- 1 cup coconut, shredded

Instructions:

- In a bowl, mix the coconut milk and baking powder together.
- Put coconut flakes on a flat surface.
- Soak a piece of bread in coconut milk and then roll it in coconut shreds.
- The bread should be put in the air fryer and closed. It should then be cooked at 400°F for 4 minutes, flipping the bread over halfway through.
- Take it out of the oven and drizzle the maple syrup over it.

Nutritional facts per serving: Calories: 947 Kcal; Carbs: 50 g; Fat: 80 g; Protein: 8 g.

10.3 Delicious Lemon Tofu

Preparation time: 15 mins

Cooking time: 22 mins

Servings: 2

Level of difficulty: Intermediate

Ingredients:

- 1 lb. super-firm tofu, drained and pressed
- 4 tsp. arrowroot powder, divided
- 2 tsp. tamari
- ¼ cup lemon juice
- 1 tsp. lemon zest
- 3 tbsp. organic sugar
- ½ cup water

Instructions:

- To begin, cut the tofu into cubes and put them in a zip lock bag. Add the soy sauce and shake the bag really well.
- Put in 2 tsp arrowroot powder and give it another good shake.
- Wait twenty minutes.
- Once the basket is ready, grease it and put the tofu in it.
- At 400°F cook for 15 minutes.
- In the meantime, put lemon juice, lemon zest, water, organic sugar and 2 tsp of arrowroot powder in a pan and cook for 5 minutes.

- When the tofu is done, put it and the sauce in a pan.
- After that, serve hot.

Nutritional facts per serving: Calories: 238 Kcal; Carbs: 9 g; Fat: 23 g; Protein: 20 g.

10.4 Crispy Potato Nuggets

Preparation time: 15 mins

Cooking time: 25 mins

Servings: 4

Level of difficulty: Intermediate

Ingredients:

- 4 cups cooked kale, coarsely chopped
- 2 cups potatoes, chopped
- 1 clove garlic, minced
- 1 tsp. canola oil
- 1/6 cup almond milk
- Salt and black pepper, to taste
- Oil spray, for greasing

Instructions:

- Put the water in pot and boil it.
- Now add the potatoes and cook for 30 minutes.
- After that, drain the potatoes and pat them dry.
- Put garlic into a pan with hot oil. After that, add the kale and cook for two minutes.
- Put the potatoes in a bowl and season them with black pepper, salt, and milk.
- Make sure the potatoes are well mashed.
- Afterwards, add the green mix and mix it well.
- For 5 minutes, heat the air fryer up to 400°F.
- Form nugget-shaped balls out of the kale and potato mix.
- Spray oil on the air fryer basket and put the nuggets in the air fryer and shake it every five minutes for fifteen minutes.
- Serve hot.

Nutritional facts per serving: Calories: 88 Kcal; Carbs: 4 g; Fat: 13 g; Protein: 2 g.

10.5 Herbed and Spiced Baked Tofu Fries

Preparation time: 12 mins

Cooking time: 15 mins

Servings: 4

Level of difficulty: Intermediate

Ingredients:
- 16 oz. tofu, drained and pressed
- ¼ tsp. garlic powder
- ¼ tsp. basil
- 2 tbsp. olive oil
- ¼ tsp. paprika
- ¼ tsp. oregano
- 1/3 tsp. onion powder
- 1/3 tsp. cayenne pepper
- Salt and black pepper, to taste

Instructions:
- Preheat the Air fryer to 400°F.
- Put the above herbs and spices in a bowl and mix them together.
- For the tofu, cut it up and then cover it with the sauce.
- Set it on the air fryer basket that has been lined with foil.
- For 15 minutes, cook at 400°F. When it's done, serve hot.

Nutritional facts per serving: Calories: 423 Kcal; Carbs: 1 g; Fat: 25 g; Protein: 44 g.

10.6 Mushroom Pizza

Preparation time: 15 mins

Cooking time: 8 mins

Servings: 2

Level of difficulty: Expert

Ingredients:
- 6 large Portobello mushrooms
- Salt and black pepper, to taste
- 2 olives Kalamata olives, sliced
- ½ tbsp. Balsamic vinegar
- 2 cloves of garlic, minced
- 4 tbsp. pasta sauce
- 3 tbsp. sweet red pepper diced
- 4 oz. zucchini, julienned
- ½ tsp. dried basil

Instructions:
- Preheat the air fryer to 400°F.
- Cut the mushroom stems off and press them down with a spoon.

- Mix in the balsamic vinegar and add salt and pepper to taste.
- It will take 4 minutes to cook the mushrooms in the air fryer.
- Garlic, pepper, olives, salt, basil, and zucchini should all be mixed together in a bowl.
- After that, put the same amount of mixture on top of each mushroom.
- Put it back in the air fryer and cook for another 4 minutes.

Nutritional facts per serving: Calories: 234 Kcal; Carbs: 26 g; Fat: 10 g; Protein: 16 g.

10.7 Vegan Air Fryer Cold Soup

Preparation time: 15 mins

Cooking time: 8 mins

Servings: 2

Level of difficulty: Intermediate

Ingredients:

- 1 cup raw peanuts
- 1½ cups broccoli
- 2 cups coconut milk
- Salt and black pepper, to taste
- ½ cup of leeks, sliced
- ½ cup spinach
- ½ tsp. ginger, grated
- 2 tbsp. lemon juice
- 2 garlic cloves, chopped

Instructions:

- Grease the inside of an air fryer basket. Then add spinach, broccoli, garlic, leeks, salt, ginger, and pepper.
- At 400°F, cook for 8 minutes.
- Once it's cool enough, take it out and put it in the blender.
- Then add the rest of the ingredients and pulse until the mixture is soupy.

Nutritional facts per serving: Calories: 1029 Kcal; Carbs: 100 g; Fat: 40 g; Protein: 30 g.

10.8 Rosemary And Garlic Sweet Potatoes Wedges

Preparation time: 15 mins

Cooking time: 22 mins

Servings: 2

Level of difficulty: Intermediate

Ingredients:

- ½ tsp. rosemary

- 2 medium sweet potatoes, wedges
- 2 cloves Garlic, minced
- 2 tbsp. avocado oil
- Salt and black pepper, to taste

Instructions:
- For 5 minutes, heat the air fryer up to 400°F.
- Add the garlic cloves, rosemary, salt and pepper to a bowl and mix them together.
- Add potato wedges and toss it well.
- In an air fryer set to 400°F, cook it for 22 minutes after putting it in the basket.
- In the middle, flip or shake the wedges.
- Serve hot when it's done.

Nutritional facts per serving: Calories: 201 Kcal; Carbs: 40 g; Fat: 3 g; Protein: 3 g.

10.9 Vegetable Fries

Preparation time: 12 mins

Cooking time: 15 mins

Servings: 2

Level of difficulty: Easy

Ingredients:
- 2 large eggplants, very thin sliced
- ½ cup water, or more
- ½ tsp. coriander
- ¼ tsp. red chilies
- ¼ tsp. dry pomegranate seeds
- ¼ tsp. baking powder
- Salt, to taste
- 1 cup chickpea flour

Instructions:
- Put salt, dry pomegranate seeds, baking powder, water, chickpea flour, and red chilies in a bowl. Mix the ingredients until you get a smooth paste.
- The batter needs to be thin.
- Cover the eggplant slices with the batter and arrange them in a baking sheet that has been lined with parchment paper.
- Put it in the fridge for one hour.
- For 15 minutes at 400°F, flip it over and cook for another five minutes in an air fryer basket.
- Put yogurt on top after it's done cooking.

Nutritional facts per serving: Calories: 514 Kcal; Carbs: 96 g; Fat: 7 g; Protein: 2 g.

10.10 Easy Rocket Pancakes

Preparation time: 10 mins

Cooking time: 5 mins

Servings: 4

Level of difficulty: Intermediate

Ingredients:

- 2 cups of all-purpose flour
- 2 cups water
- 2 handfuls of rocket
- 2 tbsp. olive oil
- 1 cup red peppers, sliced
- ½ cup pitted olives, roughly sliced
- ¼ cup parsley, chopped
- Salt, to taste
- Oil spray, for greasing

Instructions:

- Add flour, salt and water in a big bowl.
- After you mix it well, add the olives, red pepper, parsley, rockets, and olive oil.
- Pour this pancake mix into a basket that has been greased with oil.
- At 400°F, cook for 5 minutes.
- When the pancakes are done and all the batter has been used up, serve and enjoy.

Nutritional facts per serving: Calories: 361 Kcal; Carbs: 60 g; Fat: 10 g; Protein: 8 g.

10.11 Classic Falafel

Preparation time: 12 mins

Cooking time: 10 mins

Servings: 4

Level of difficulty: Intermediate

Ingredients:

- 1½ cup dry garbanzo beans
- ½ cup cilantro, chopped
- ½ cup parsley, chopped
- 1/6 tsp. ground cardamom
- 6 cloves garlic

- ½ cup onion, chopped
- Salt, to taste
- 1 tsp. ground coriander
- 2 tbsp. purpose flour
- 1 tsp. ground cumin
- Pinch of cayenne pepper

Instructions:
- Put the soaked beans in a bowl and drain them.
- In a pot with about 2 inches of water, bring it to a boil.
- As soon as it starts to boil, take it off the heat and set it away.
- Make a paste with the garlic, parsley, onion and cilantro.
- Give it a good pulse.
- Then pulse in the flour, pepper, cumin, coriander, and cardamom, along with the beans.
- Put the mixture in a bowl and put it in the fridge for one to two hours.
- Form it into 1½-inch balls, and then press it out to make burgers.
- For 10 minutes at 400°F, flip it over and cook the other side.
- Once it's done, serve.

Nutritional facts per serving: Calories: 204 Kcal; Carbs: 34 g; Fat: 3 g; Protein: 10 g.

10.12 Vegan Peanut Noodles

Preparation time: 15 mins

Cooking time: 25 mins

Servings: 2

Level of difficulty: Intermediate

Ingredients:

For Peanut sauce:
- ½ cup peanut butter
- 2 tbsp. agave syrup
- 4 tbsp. coconut amino
- ¼ cup water
- 1 inch of ginger, peeled and minced
- 2 tbsp. lemon juice
- 2 cloves garlic, minced
- 1 tsp. sesame oil

For Noodles:
- 2 green onions, chopped

- 6 oz. vegan rice noodles
- 2 carrots, peeled and sliced
- 1 red bell pepper, chopped

Instructions:
- Put everything for the peanut sauce in a bowl and mix it together really well.
- Follow the steps on the package to cook the noodles, and then drain them.
- Then put it aside until you need it again.
- Fill an air fryer basket with oil and add the carrots, bell pepper, and onions. Cook for 15 minutes at 400°F.
- Add it to noodles after its done cooking and serve with peanut sauce on the side.

Nutritional facts per serving: Calories: 214 Kcal; Carbs: 25 g; Fat: 6 g; Protein: 5 g.

10.13 Mustard Cabbage Rolls

Preparation time: 10 mins
Cooking time: 12 mins
Servings: 2
Level of difficulty: Intermediate
Ingredients:
- 10 egg roll wrappers
- 4 tbsp. spicy Mustard
- 1 cup cabbage, thinly sliced
- ½ cup cooked pasta, drained
- ¼ cup peas, cooked
- Salt and black pepper, to taste
- ¼ tsp. red chili flakes
- 2 tsp. lemon juice
- Oil spray, for greasing

Instructions:
- Start by putting oil in a pan.
- After you add the cabbage, cook for about 10 minutes, until it's soft.
- When the pasta is done, add the cooked peas, pepper, salt, and spicy mustard.
- Mix in the lemon juice and red pepper flakes, and then set the bowl aside to cool.
- After that, put the egg rolls on an even surface.
- Add the cabbage mixture to each roll in similar amounts, starting from one side.
- Start rolling from the sides and bind the ends shut.
- Spray oil on the rolls from all sides.

- Flip the food over halfway through the 12 minutes of cooking in the air fryer at 400°F.
- Serve it after it's done.

Nutritional facts per serving: Calories: 146 Kcal; Carbs: 20 g; Fat: 7 g; Protein: 38 g.

10.14 Vegetable Fried Rice

Preparation time: 20 mins

Cooking time: 25 mins

Servings: 2

Level of difficulty: Expert

Ingredients:
- 2 tbsp. vegetable oil
- 1 cup celery, chopped
- ½ cup green onions, chopped
- 2 cups rice, boiled
- ½ cup carrot, thinly sliced
- 1 cup tofu, cubed
- 1 cup green peas,
- ½ tsp. garlic
- 4 tbsp. lemon juice
- ½ tsp. ginger, grated
- Pinch of black pepper
- Salt, to taste
- 2 tbsp. coconut amino

Instructions:
- Heat oil in the pan and cook onion in it.
- In a pan, cook the ginger and garlic.
- Set the timer for two minutes and cook.
- Put oil spray on a pan and add the tofu, celery, peas, carrots, salt, pepper, coconut amino acids and lemon juice.
- Put it in an air fryer and cook at 400°F for 7 to 16 minutes.
- Take the pan out of the oven and add the green peas, rice, and tofu.
- Set a five-minute timer.
- Serve it after it's done.

Nutritional facts per serving: Calories: 280 Kcal; Carbs: 20 g; Fat: 67 g; Protein: 30 g.

10.15 Cauliflower Poppers

Preparation time: 12 mins

Cooking time: 15 mins

Servings: 2

Level of difficulty: Easy

Ingredients:

- ½ tsp. onion powder
- 1½ cup cauliflower florets
- Black pepper, to taste
- Salt, to taste
- ¼ tsp. paprika
- 1/3 cup flour
- ½ cup water

Instructions:

- In a bowl, mix together the water, paprika, almond flour, salt, onion powder, and black pepper.
- It should be well mixed so that it becomes runny.
- The cauliflower pieces should be dipped in it and then put in the foil-lined basket of air fryer.
- At 350°F, cook it for 15 minutes.
- When the top is golden, serve and enjoy.

Nutritional facts per serving: Calories: 19 Kcal; Carbs: 1 g; Fat: 2 g; Protein: 3 g.

10.16 Vegetable Cheesy Pizza

Preparation time: 25 mins

Cooking time: 18 mins

Servings: 2

Level of difficulty: Intermediate

Ingredients:

- Oil spray, for greasing
- 1 Pizza Dough

Topping

- 6 slice White Onion
- 6 cremini mushrooms
- 1 cup vegan cheese
- 4 tbsp. vegan Pesto
- ½ cup baby spinach
- 1 green pepper, chopped

- 2 large Tomatoes, sliced

Instructions:

- Spray oil on an air fryer basket.
- Make the pizza dough as big as the air fryer basket by rolling it out.
- Use oil spray to cover both sides of the dough.
- Put the bread on the basket.
- For 10 minutes, cook at 400°F.
- Once the time is up, flip the dough over.
- After the cooking processes are over, take the dough out and add the toppings.
- Once more, cook for 8 minutes.
- Serve it when it's done.

Nutritional facts per serving: Calories: 656 Kcal; Carbs: 60 g; Fat: 41 g; Protein: 13 g.

10.17 Spinach Casserole

Preparation time: 10 mins

Cooking time: 30 mins

Servings: 4

Level of difficulty: Expert

Ingredients:

- 4 eggs
- ¼ cup grated parmesan cheese
- ½ tsp. minced garlic
- ¼ tsp. ground black pepper
- 2 tbsp. chopped white onion
- 4 oz. artichokes, drained
- 2 tbsp. whole milk
- ¼ cup cheddar cheese, grated
- 4 oz. spinach
- ¼ cup whole milk ricotta
- ¼ tsp. dried thyme
- ¼ tsp. sea salt

Instructions:

- Preheat Air fryer to 400°F.
- Grease a baking dish; make sure it will fit in your air fryer basket.
- In a big bowl, whisk the milk and eggs together.
- Artichokes and spinach should be added to the egg mixture.

- Stir well and add the rest of the ingredients, except for the ricotta.
- Pour the eggs and vegetables into the tray that has been prepared.
- Spread the ricotta around the pan in small dollops.
- Bake for 30 minutes or until the eggs are fully set in the air fryer.

Nutritional facts per serving: Calories: 230 Kcal; Carbs: 4 g; Fat: 16 g; Protein: 16 g.

10.18 Vegetable Egg Casserole

Preparation time: 10 mins
Cooking time: 30 mins
Servings: 4
Level of difficulty: Expert
Ingredients:

- 4 eggs
- ½ tsp. minced garlic
- ¼ tsp. ground black pepper
- 2 tbsp. chopped white onion
- ¼ tsp. dried thyme
- 2 tbsp. whole milk
- ¼ cup cheddar cheese, grated
- 8 oz. spinach
- ¼ cup whole milk ricotta
- ¼ cup grated parmesan cheese
- ¼ tsp. sea salt

Instructions:

- Preheat the Air fryer to 400°F.
- Grease a baking dish; make sure it will fit in your air fryer.
- In a big bowl, whisk the milk and eggs together.
- Artichokes and spinach should be added to the egg mixture.
- Stir well and add the rest of the ingredients, except for the ricotta.
- Pour the eggs and vegetables into the tray that has been prepared.
- Spread the ricotta around the pan in small dollops.
- Bake for 30 minutes or until the eggs are fully set in the air fryer.

Nutritional facts per serving: Calories: 236 Kcal; Carbs: 16 g; Fat: 4 g; Protein: 16 g.

10.19 Cheesy Broccoli Fritters

Preparation time: 10 mins

Cooking time: 10 mins

Servings: 4

Level of difficulty: Intermediate

Ingredients:

- ¾ cup almond flour
- 4 oz. grated mozzarella cheese
- 1 tsp. salt
- 2 tsp. baking powder
- 1 cup broccoli, fresh
- 7 tbsp. ground flaxseeds
- 1 tbsp. olive oil
- 2 eggs
- ¼ tsp ground black pepper

Instructions:

- Preheat your Air fryer to 400°F.
- Put the broccoli, 4 tablespoons of the flaxseeds, almond flour, mozzarella, and baking powder in a food processor. Pulse the ingredients until they become crumbly.
- Add the eggs, pepper and salt and pulse the mixture until it makes dough.
- Make bite-sized balls by scooping out the mixture and rolling it between your hands.
- Roll the balls in the rest of the flaxseeds and put them in the basket of Air fryer.
- Drizzle the olive oil over the balls and bake for 10 minutes, or until nicely golden brown. Enjoy hot.

Nutritional facts per serving: Calories: 237 Kcal; Carbs: 7 g; Fat: 19 g; Protein: 15 g.

10.20 Cheesy Carrot Fritters

Preparation time: 10 mins

Cooking time: 10 mins

Servings: 4

Level of difficulty: Intermediate

Ingredients:

- ¾ cup almond flour
- 4 oz. grated mozzarella cheese
- 1 tsp. salt
- 2 tsp. baking powder
- 1½ cup chopped carrots

- 7 tbsp. ground flaxseeds
- 1 tbsp. olive oil
- 2 eggs
- ¼ tsp ground black pepper

Instructions:

- Preheat the Air fryer to 400°F.
- Put the chopped carrots, baking powder, almond flour, mozzarella and 4 tablespoons of the flaxseeds in a food processor. Pulse the ingredients until they become crumbly.
- Add the eggs, pepper and salt and pulse the mixture until it makes dough.
- Make bite-sized balls by scooping out the mixture and rolling it between your hands.
- Roll the balls in the rest of the flaxseeds and put them in the basket of air fryer.
- Drizzle the olive oil over the balls and bake for 10 minutes, or until nicely golden brown. Enjoy hot.

Nutritional facts per serving: Calories: 290 Kcal; Carbs: 10 g; Fat: 19 g; Protein: 15 g.

10.21 Stromboli

Preparation time: 10 mins

Cooking time: 15 mins

Servings: 4

Level of difficulty: Intermediate

Ingredients:

- 1¼ cups mozzarella cheese, grated
- 4 tbsp. almond flour
- 1 tsp. dried basil
- 1 egg
- ½ cup grated cheddar cheese
- 3 tbsp. coconut flour
- ¼ cup sliced mozzarella cheese

Instructions:

- Preheat the Air fryer to 400°F.
- Melt the shredded mozzarella in the microwave, stirring it every so often, in a big bowl.
- Add the coconut and almond flour and dried basil with the mozzarella in the bowl and mix until a nice dough forms after adding the egg.
- Put the dough on a piece of parchment paper and roll it into a square about 4 inches wide.
- Place the mozzarella slices and cheese pieces in the middle of the dough.
- Cover the mozzarella and cheese slices with the dough, making a hole in the middle for the filling.
- Put the Stromboli in the basket of air fryer and bake for 20 minutes. Cut it up and serve!

Nutritional facts per serving: Calories: 400 Kcal; Carbs: 8 g; Fat: 22 g; Protein: 21 g.

10.22 Potato Fritters

Preparation time: 15 mins

Cooking time: 7 mins

Servings: 4

Level of difficulty: Intermediate

Ingredients:

- ¼ cup all-purpose flour
- 7 oz. Halloumi cheese
- 10½ oz. potatoes, grated and squeezed
- 1 tsp. fresh dill, minced
- 2 eggs
- salt and black pepper, to taste

Instructions:

- Preheat the Air fryer to 360°F.
- In a big bowl, combine all the ingredients.
- From this mixture, form little fritters and arrange them on the basket of air fryer.
- Bake for 7 minutes.

Nutritional facts per serving: Calories: 250 Kcal; Carbs: 10 g; Fat: 17 g; Protein: 5 g.

10.23 Zucchini Lasagna

Preparation time: 5 mins

Cooking time: 15 mins

Servings: 2

Level of difficulty: Easy

Ingredients:

- 1 large zucchini, sliced thinly
- ½ cup fresh chopped mozzarella
- 6 tbsp. keto marinara sauce
- 1 cup sliced cherry tomatoes
- 4 tbsp. ricotta, whole milk

Instructions:

- Preheat the Air fryer to 400°F.
- Get a pan that be adjusted in air fryer.
- Put a few slices of zucchini in the bottom of the pan and a few pieces of tomato on top.

- On top of the zucchini and tomatoes, spread about 1 tablespoon of the marinara sauce and then 1 tablespoon of the ricotta.
- Layer more tomatoes and zucchini on top of the marinara, and keep doing this until all of the tomatoes, zucchini, ricotta, and marinara sauce have been used.
- The mozzarella should go on top.
- Put the lasagna in the air fryer basket and bake for 15 minutes, or until the mozzarella is melted and bubbly. Enjoy hot

Nutritional facts per serving: Calories: 250 Kcal; Carbs: 10 g; Fat: 25 g; Protein: 20 g.

10.24 Extra Cheese Pizza

Preparation time: 20 mins

Cooking time: 20 mins

Servings: 3

Level of difficulty: Intermediate

Ingredients:

- 1 cup almond flour
- 1 tsp. minced garlic
- ½ cup mozzarella, fresh diced
- 3 tbsp. water
- 1 egg
- 1 tbsp. fresh basil, chopped
- ¼ cup cheddar cheese, shredded
- ¼ cup keto tomato sauce
- ½ cup shaved parmesan
- 4 tbsp. parmesan, grated

Instructions:

- First, Preheat heat your air fryer to 375°F. Then, put paper on the air fryer basket.
- Mix the water and almond flour together in a medium-sized bowl.
- Add the flour and cheese together in the almond flour mix and knead until you get soft dough.
- Before you put the dough on the pan, make a flat circle about ¼ inch thick out of it. If you need to, wet your hands to make it easier to press the dough down.
- Spread the tomato sauce on top of the dough. Then add the shaved parmesan, fresh basil, mozzarella and cheddar.
- Put it in an air fryer that has already been heated up and bake for 18 minutes, or until the cheese melts and bubbles.
- Cut and serve.

Nutritional facts per serving: Calories: 400 Kcal; Carbs: 13 g; Fat: 36 g; Protein: 19 g.

10.25 Broccoli And Grits

Preparation time: 20 mins

Cooking time: 23 mins

Servings: 4

Level of difficulty: Expert

Ingredients:

- ½ lb. chopped broccoli florets
- ¼ tsp. ground black pepper
- 1 tbsp. fresh rosemary, chopped
- 1 tbsp. minced garlic
- 2 tbsp. olive oil
- ½ cup chopped pecans
- 1 cup heavy cream
- 2 cups chopped cauliflower florets
- 1 cup shredded cheddar cheese
- ½ cup water
- 1 tsp. salt
- 2 tbsp. butter

Instructions:

- First, preheat your air fryer to 400°F. Then, put paper on the air fryer tray or bake pan.
- On a tray, mix the garlic, broccoli, olive oil, rosemary, and pecans. Toss everything around to cover it with the oil.
- Put the pan in the air fryer and roast for 15 minutes.
- Put the cauliflower in a food processor or blender and pulse it until it looks like rice while the broccoli is cooking.
- Put the broccoli and water in a pot. Cook for 5 minutes over medium-low heat.
- After you add the heavy cream, cook for three more minutes.
- Add the salt, butter, and pepper, and mix them together to melt the cheese.
- Put some in each bowl, and then add the roasted mushrooms on top. Serve.

Nutritional facts per serving: Calories: 450 Kcal; Carbs: 17 g; Fat: 36 g; Protein: 16 g.

Chapter 11: Dessert Recipes

11.1 Carrot brownies

Preparation time: 10 mins

Cooking time: 25 mins

Servings: 8

Level of difficulty: Easy

Ingredients:

- 1 tsp. almond extract
- 2 cups almond flour
- ½ cup butter, melted
- 2 eggs, whisked
- 4 tbsp. sugar
- ½ cup grated carrot

Instructions:

Whisk butter, eggs, and other ingredients in a bowl, then transfer the mixture to an air fryer-compatible pan. Bake the brownies for 25 minutes at 340°F.

Nutritional facts per serving: Calories: 230 Kcal; Carbs: 12 g; Fat: 12 g; Protein: 5 g.

11.2 Yogurt cake

Preparation time: 10 mins

Cooking time: 30 mins

Servings: 8

Level of difficulty: Easy

Ingredients:

- 6 eggs, whisked
- 1 tsp. baking soda
- 1 tsp. vanilla extract
- 4 tbsp. sugar
- 9 oz. almond flour
- 2 cups yogurt

Instructions:

- To make the cake, whisk eggs, vanilla, and other ingredients, then transfer into a parchment-lined pan and air fry at 330°F for 30 minutes.
- Slice and serve the cake after cooling.

Nutritional facts per serving: Calories: 231 Kcal; Carbs: 11 g; Fat: 13 g; Protein: 5 g.

11.3 Chocolate ramekins

Preparation time: 10 mins

Cooking time: 20 mins

Servings: 4

Level of difficulty: Easy

Ingredients:

- 2 cups cream cheese, room temperature
- 4 eggs, whisked
- 3 tbsp. sugar
- ½ cup heavy cream
- 1 tsp. vanilla extract
- 2 cups melted white chocolate

Instructions:

- Whisk the cream cheese, sugar, and other ingredients in a dish, divide into 4 ramekins, and air fry at 370°F for 20 minutes.

Nutritional facts per serving: Calories: 261 Kcal; Carbs: 12 g; Fat: 12 g; Protein: 6 g.

11.4 Grapes cake

Preparation time: 10 mins

Cooking time: 25 mins

Servings: 8

Level of difficulty: Easy

Ingredients:

- 1 cup coconut flour
- 1 cup heavy cream
- ¾ tsp. almond extract
- 1 tsp. baking powder
- 1 egg, whisked
- ¾ cup sugar
- 2 cup grapes, halved
- Cooking spray

Instructions:

- Mix flour, baking powder, and other ingredients except cooking spray in a bowl and stir thoroughly.
- Grease a cake pan using cooking spray, pour batter in and air fry at 330°F for 25 minutes.

Nutritional facts per serving: Calories: 214 Kcal; Carbs: 14 g; Fat: 9 g; Protein: 8 g.

11.5 Pear pudding

Preparation time: 10 mins

Cooking time: 20 mins

Servings: 6

Level of difficulty: Easy

Ingredients:

- 2 pears, peeled and chopped
- 3 tbsp. sugar
- 2 eggs, whisked
- ½ cup heavy cream
- ½ cup melted butter
- 1/3 cup almond milk

Instructions:

- Combine butter, sugar, and other ingredients in a bowl, mix well, and transfer into a pudding pan.
- Bake the pudding in air fryer for 20 minutes at 340°F.

Nutritional facts per serving: Calories: 211 Kcal; Carbs: 14 g; Fat: 4 g; Protein: 6 g.

11.6 Lime Cake

Preparation time: 10 mins

Cooking time: 30 mins

Servings: 4

Level of difficulty: Easy

Ingredients:

- 1 egg, whisked
- 2 tbsp. butter, melted
- 2 tbsp. sugar
- 2 tbsp. lime juice
- ½ cup almond milk
- 1 cup heavy cream
- 1 tbsp. lime zest, grated
- ½ tsp. baking powder

Instructions:

- Combine egg, butter, sugar, and other ingredients in a bowl, mix well, and transfer to a parchment-lined cake pan.
- Bake the cake in air fryer for 30 minutes at 320°F.

Nutritional facts per serving: Calories: 213 Kcal; Carbs: 15 g; Fat: 5 g; Protein: 6 g.

11.7 Pear stew

Preparation time: 10 mins

Cooking time: 20 mins

Servings: 4

Level of difficulty: Easy

Ingredients:

- 2 tsp. cinnamon powder
- 2 tbsp. sugar
- 1 cup water
- 4 pears, cut into wedges

Instructions:

- Combine pears, water, and other ingredients in an air fryer pan. Cook at 300°F for 20 minutes, divide into cups, and serve cold.

Nutritional facts per serving: Calories: 200 Kcal; Carbs: 16 g; Fat: 3 g; Protein: 4 g.

11.8 Carrot Coffee Cake

Preparation time: 15 mins

Cooking time: 30 mins

Servings: 2

Level of difficulty: Expert

Ingredients:

- 1 egg
- 1/3 cup + 2 tbsp. sugar, divided
- ½ cup buttermilk
- 2 tbsp. dark brown sugar
- 3 tbsp. canola oil
- 1 tsp. grated orange zest
- 2/3 cup all-purpose flour
- 1 tsp. vanilla extract
- 1/4 cup dried cranberries
- 1 tsp. baking powder
- 1 cup shredded carrots
- 1 tsp. pumpkin pie spice, divided
- 1/3 cup white whole wheat flour
- ¼ tsp. baking soda
- ¼ tsp. salt

- 1/3 cup chopped walnuts, toasted

Instructions:

- Preheat the air fryer to about 350°F.
- A 6-inch round baking pan should be greased and floured. Mix the egg, sugar, buttermilk, brown sugar, oil, vanilla and orange zest in a bowl using a whisk.
- Mix the flour, baking soda, salt, baking powder, and one teaspoon of pumpkin pie spice together in a different bowl.
- Add this flour mix to the egg mix you already made.
- Put it in the pan that has been greased after adding the carrots and cherries.
- In a small bowl, mix together the walnuts, one teaspoon of pumpkin spice and two tablespoons of sugar.
- Sprinkle it all over the batter, and then carefully put the pan in the air fryer.
- Put it in the oven for 30 minutes.
- If the top gets too dark, quickly cover it with foil. Let it cool for 10 minutes on a wire rack in the pan before taking it out. Serve.

Nutritional facts per serving: Calories: 679 Kcal; Carbs: 70 g; Fat: 40 g; Protein: 17 g.

11.9 Strawberry Shortcake

Preparation time: 25 mins

Cooking time: 15 mins

Servings: 4

Level of difficulty: Expert

Ingredients:

- 2 cups fresh strawberries, sliced
- 1 cup all-purpose flour
- 3 tbsp. granulated sugar
- ½ cup low-fat buttermilk
- pinch of baking soda
- 1 tbsp. baking powder
- 3 tbsp. cold unsalted butter, diced
- ¼ tbsp. kosher salt
- Whipped cream, for serving

Instructions:

- First, put the sugar and strawberries in a bowl and mix them together. Set this bowl away.
- Turn on the air fryer and heat it up to 350°F. Spray a non-stick spray on the baking pan to keep it from sticking. In a bowl, mix the sugar, flour, baking soda, baking powder, and salt with a whisk.
- Add some butter and use a pastry cutter to break it up into smaller pieces.
- Add the buttermilk slowly and mix until the dough forms together and gets sticky.

- Put the mix into the baking pan and spread it out. Then, press it down to make a flat layer.
- Air fry it for about 15 minutes, the top should be golden brown.
- Serve it whipped cream and with strawberries.

Nutritional facts per serving: Calories: 291 Kcal; Carbs: 29 g; Fat: 50 g; Protein: 21 g.

11.10 Chocolate brownies

Preparation time: 10 mins

Cooking time: 25 mins

Servings: 8

Level of difficulty: Easy

Ingredients:

- 1 tsp. almond extract
- 2 cups almond flour
- ½ cup butter, melted
- 2 eggs, whisked
- 4 tbsp. sugar
- ½ cup cocoa powder

Instructions:

Whisk butter, eggs, and other ingredients in a bowl, then transfer the mixture to an air fryer-compatible pan. Bake the brownies for 25 minutes at 340°F.

Nutritional facts per serving: Calories: 250 Kcal; Carbs: 11 g; Fat: 12 g; Protein: 5 g.

11.11 Orange Cake

Preparation time: 10 mins

Cooking time: 30 mins

Servings: 4

Level of difficulty: Easy

Ingredients:

- 1 egg, whisked
- 2 tbsp. butter, melted
- 2 tbsp. sugar
- ½ cup orange juice
- ½ cup almond milk
- 1 cup heavy cream
- 1 tbsp. orange zest, grated
- ½ tsp. baking powder

Instructions:
- Combine egg, butter, sugar, and other ingredients in a bowl, mix well, and transfer to a parchment-lined cake pan.
- Bake the cake in air fryer for 30 minutes at 320°F.

Nutritional facts per serving: Calories: 215 Kcal; Carbs: 16 g; Fat: 5 g; Protein: 6 g.

11.12 Peanut Butter Cupcake

Preparation time: 10 mins
Cooking time: 16 mins
Servings: 3
Level of difficulty: Intermediate
Ingredients:
- 1½ cup all-purpose flour
- ½ tsp. baking powder
- 1/2 cup almond milk
- 1/3 cup peanut butter
- Salt, to taste
- 1/2 tsp. baking soda
- ½ cup brown sugar
- 3 eggs
- 1 tsp. pure vanilla extract

Instructions:
- In a big bowl, mix the eggs, peanut butter and brown sugar together.
- Add the vanilla extract and almond milk to the egg mixture after it is fully mixed.
- Put the dry ingredients in a bowl and mix them well.
- Grease the muffin tins and fill them up with the batter.
- At 350°F, cook the muffin cups for 14 to 16 minutes in the air fryer.
- Take the cupcakes out and enjoy them.

Nutritional facts per serving: Calories: 146 Kcal; Carbs: 10 g; Fat: 12 g; Protein: 23 g.

11.13 Orange Cornmeal Cake

Preparation time: 10 mins
Cooking time: 25 mins
Servings: 3
Level of difficulty: Intermediate
Ingredients:
- 2 cups all-purpose flour

- 1 cup white sugar
- 1 cup yellow cornmeal
- ½ cup powdered sugar
- ½ cup olive oil
- 1 tsp. baking soda
- 1 tsp. vanilla
- 1 cup orange juice
- Cooking spray

Instructions:
- Grease the baking pan using cooking spray.
- Put all the dry ingredients in a bowl and whisk them.
- In another bowl combine all the wet ingredients. Now combine dry and wet ingredients and put the batter in the prepared baking pan.
- For 25 minutes, cook the cake in the air fryer at 350°F.
- Serve and enjoy the cake once it's cool enough.

Nutritional facts per serving: Calories: 109 Kcal; Carbs: 21 g; Fat: 11 g; Protein: 23 g.

11.14 Chocolate Cupcake

Preparation time: 10 mins

Cooking time: 16 mins

Servings: 3

Level of difficulty: Intermediate

Ingredients:
- 1½ cup all-purpose flour
- ½ tsp. baking powder
- 1/2 cup almond milk
- 1/3 cup cocoa powder
- Salt, to taste
- 1/2 tsp. baking soda
- ½ cup brown sugar
- 3 eggs
- 1 tsp. pure vanilla extract
- ½ cup butter

Instructions:
- In a big bowl, mix the butter, eggs and brown sugar together.
- Add the vanilla extract and almond milk to the egg mixture after it is fully mixed.

- Put the dry ingredients in a bowl and mix them well.
- Grease the muffin tins and fill them up with the batter.
- At 350°F, cook the muffin cups for 14 to 16 minutes in the air fryer.
- Take the cupcakes out and enjoy them.

Nutritional facts per serving: Calories: 146 Kcal; Carbs: 10 g; Fat: 12 g; Protein: 23 g.

11.15 Cinnamon Puffs

Preparation time: 10 mins

Cooking time: 5 mins

Servings: 4

Level of difficulty: Easy

Ingredients:

- 1 tsp. ground cinnamon
- 1 sheet puff pastry
- ¼ cup granulated sugar

Instructions:

- Preheat the Air Fryer to 375°F.
- Cut puff pastry into strips and carefully twist each strip to make a coil.
- Put the puffs in the tray and cook for 3–5 minutes, or until golden brown.
- While the puffs are cooking, combine the cinnamon and sugar.
- Take the puffs out of the oil and toss them in the cinnamon sugar mixture. Let them cool for 5 minutes on a wire rack before you serve them.

Nutritional facts per serving: Calories: 200 Kcal; Carbs: 12 g; Fat: 5 g; Protein: 1 g.

11.16 Apple Cupcakes

Preparation time: 10 mins

Cooking time: 20 mins

Servings: 4

Level of difficulty: Intermediate

Ingredients:

- 2 tsp. cinnamon powder
- ½ cup pure applesauce
- 1 apple, cored and chopped
- 1 tsp. vanilla extract
- 4 tbsp. vegetable oil
- 3 tbsp. water
- 3 tbsp. flax meal

- ¾ cup whole wheat flour
- 4 tsp. maple syrup
- ½ tsp. baking powder

Instructions:

- Preheat the Air fryer to 350°F.
- Over medium heat, heat the oil in a pan. Add the applesauce, water, sugar, flax meal, and maple syrup. Stir, then take the pan off the heat and let it cool.
- Mix together the, baking powder, cinnamon, flour, and apples. Pour the mixture into a cupcake pan, put it in your air fryer and bake for 20 minutes.
- Place the cupcakes on a plate and serve them hot. Enjoy!

Nutritional facts per serving: Calories: 214 Kcal; Carbs: 12 g; Fat: 1 g; Protein: 4 g.

11.17 Orange Cake

Preparation time: 0 mins

Cooking time: 0 mins

Servings: 2

Level of difficulty: Intermediate

Ingredients:

- 1 tbsp. flax meal
- 4 tbsp. almond milk
- ½ tsp. baking powder
- 1 tbsp. cocoa powder
- 2 tbsp. water
- 2 tbsp. olive oil
- 4 tbsp. coconut sugar
- 4 tbsp. whole wheat flour
- ½ tsp. orange zest, grated

Instructions:

- Preheat the Air fryer to 350°F.
- Mix the flax meal, oil, baking powder, sugar, flour, milk, cocoa powder, and orange zest in a bowl. Stir very well, and then pour the mixture into greased ramekins that fits in your air fryer oven.
- Cook the cake for 20 minutes and serve it warm.

Nutritional facts per serving: Calories: 191 Kcal; Carbs: 13 g; Fat: 7 g; Protein: 4 g.

11.18 Egg Pudding

Preparation time: 10 mins

Cooking time: 25 mins

Servings: 4

Level of difficulty: Intermediate

Ingredients:

- 4 eggs, whisked
- ¾ cup sugar
- ½ cup heavy cream
- 1 cup almond milk
- 1 tsp. cinnamon powder
- ½ tsp. ginger powder

Instructions:

- Whisk the almond milk, eggs and the other ingredients together in a bowl. Pour the mixture into a pudding mold, put it in the air fryer, and cook it for 25 minutes at 340°F.
- Cool the pudding and serve it.

Nutritional facts per serving: Calories: 161 Kcal; Carbs: 14 g; Fat: 3 g; Protein: 4 g.

11.19 Pear Pudding

Preparation time: 10 mins

Cooking time: 20 mins

Servings: 4

Level of difficulty: Intermediate

Ingredients:

- 3 tbsp. sugar
- 2 pears, peeled and chopped
- 2 eggs, whisked
- ½ cup butter, melted
- 1/3 cup almond milk
- ½ cup heavy cream

Instructions:

- Mix the butter, sugar, and other ingredients well in a bowl with a whisk, and then pour the mixture into a pudding pan.
- Put the pan in the air fryer and cook it for 20 minutes at 340°F.
- Put the pudding in bowls, let it cool, and serve.

Nutritional facts per serving: Calories: 211 Kcal; Carbs: 14 g; Fat: 4 g; Protein: 6 g.

11.20 Lemon Shortbread

Preparation time: 15 mins

Cooking time: 15 mins

Servings: 4

Level of difficulty: Intermediate

Ingredients:

- ¼ cup butter
- ½ cup almond flour
- ½ tsp. vanilla extract
- ¼ cup swerve sweetener
- ½ tsp. salt
- 1 tsp. lemon zest

Instructions:

- Preheat the Air fryer to 300°F.
- Put the swerve and butter in a bowl and beat with a mixer until the mixture is soft and fluffy.
- Add the lemon zest and vanilla extract and then beat again to mix everything together.
- Slowly add the almond flour and mix it in a little at a time until you have smooth dough.
- Put it in an air fryer that has already been heated up.
- Bake the shortbread for 15 minutes, or until the sides are golden brown.
- Let the shortbread cool for 10 minutes, then flip it out of the pan, cut it, and eat it while it's still warm.

Nutritional facts per serving: Calories: 189 Kcal; Carbs: 3 g; Fat: 19 g; Protein: 7 g.

11.21 Chocolate Walnuts Brownies

Preparation time: 15 mins

Cooking time: 20 mins

Servings: 4

Level of difficulty: Hard

Ingredients:

- ¼ cup melted butter
- ¼ tsp. salt
- 2 tbsp. water
- ½ tbsp. plain, gelatin
- 2 tbsp. cocoa powder
- ¼ tsp. baking powder
- ¼ tsp. vanilla extract

- ¼ cup swerve
- ¼ cup almond flour
- 1 room temperature egg
- ¼ cup chopped walnuts

Instructions:

- Preheat the Air fryer to 325°F.
- In a bowl, mix the vanilla extract, melted butter, eggs and swerve together well with a whisk.
- Mix again until smooth. Add the cocoa powder, almond flour, gelatin, baking powder and salt.
- Stir again after adding the water.
- Add the chopped walnuts and stir.
- Pour the batter into the greased baking dish and put it in an air fryer that has already been heated up. Bake for 15 minutes.
- Let the brownies cool and serve them.

Nutritional facts per serving: Calories: 178 Kcal; Carbs: 8 g; Fat: 19 g; Protein: 3 g.

11.22 Fudge Brownies

Preparation time: 15 mins

Cooking time: 20 mins

Servings: 4

Level of difficulty: Intermediate

Ingredients:

- ¼ cup melted butter
- 1 room temperature egg
- ½ tbsp. gelatin
- 2 tbsp. cocoa powder
- ¼ tsp. baking powder
- ¼ tsp. vanilla extract
- ¼ cup swerve
- ¼ cup almond flour
- ¼ tsp. salt
- 2 tbsp. water

Instructions:

- Preheat the Air fryer to 325°F.
- In a bowl, mix the vanilla extract, egg, melted butter and swerve together well with a whisk.
- Mix again until smooth. Add the almond flour, cocoa powder, gelatin, baking powder and salt.
- Stir again after adding the water.

- Pour the batter into the prepared baking dish and put it in an air fryer that has already been heated up. Bake for 15 minutes.
- Let the brownies cool in the pan for a while before you cut them and serve them.

Nutritional facts per serving: Calories: 110 Kcal; Carbs: 4 g; Fat: 10 g; Protein: 3 g.

11.23 Strawberry And Cream Mug Cake

Preparation time: 25 mins

Cooking time: 12 mins

Servings: 2

Level of difficulty: Intermediate

Ingredients:

- 4 tbsp. all-purpose flour
- 2 tbsp. milk
- ½ tsp. baking powder
- 1½ tbsp. sugar
- 2 tbsp. heavy cream
- 2 strawberries, diced

Instructions:

- Combine heavy cream, strawberries, sugar, milk, and baking powder.
- Use cooking spray on the mug or dish.
- Put the cake batter into the cup or dish.
- Set the timer for 12 minutes at 350°F and put it in the air fryer.
- Serve and savor the goodness.

Nutritional facts per serving: Calories: 150 Kcal; Carbs: 23 g; Fat: 4 g; Protein: 3 g.

11.24 Quick Brownies

Preparation time: 20 mins

Cooking time: 15 mins

Servings: 2

Level of difficulty: Easy

Ingredients:

- ½ cup all-purpose flour
- A pinch of salt
- ¾ cup sugar
- 6 tbsp. unsweetened cocoa powder
- 2 large eggs
- ¼ cup melted butter, unsalted

- ½ tbsp. vanilla extract
- 1 tbsp. vegetable oil
- ¼ tbsp. baking powder

Instructions:

- Put some butter on the air pan to grease it.
- Preheat the Air Fryer to 350°F while you make the brownie batter.
- Put the cacao powder, butter, sugar, vegetable oil, eggs, vanilla extract, flour, salt, and baking powder into a big bowl. Then, stir the ingredients together until they are well blended.
- Make sure the top of the batter is smooth after you pour it into the pan.
- In a hot Air Fryer, put the food in and bake for 15 minutes, or until a knife stuck in the middle comes out mostly clean.
- Take it out of the pan and let it cool down before taking it out and cutting it.

Nutritional facts per serving: Calories: 287Kcal; Carbs: 50 g; Fat: 7 g; Protein: 7 g.

11.25 Coffee Cake

Preparation time: 25 mins

Cooking time: 25 mins

Servings: 4

Level of difficulty: Easy

Ingredients:

Cake:

- ¾ cup sugar
- 2 cups of flour
- ½ tsp. salt
- 1 tsp. vanilla
- 2 tsp. baking powder
- ¾ cup of milk+2 tbsp. of coffee (mixed)
- ½ cup melted butter
- 1 egg

Topping:

- 2 tsp. ground cinnamon
- 2/3 cup sugar
- ¼ cup melted butter
- ¼ cup flour

Instructions:

- Mix the wet and dry ingredients together to make the cake batter.

- Coat air fryer pan using cooking spray.
- Put the mix in the pan.
- Next, make the filling. In a small bowl, mix it all. Add it to the cake after mixing it well.
- Set the air fryer to 350°F and put the pan in it. Leave it there for 25 to 35 minutes.
- Watch out for the time because it depends on how thick the batter is. To make sure it's done, poke a toothpick in it and make sure it comes out clean.
- Let it cool down before you serve it.

Nutritional facts per serving: Calories: 275 Kcal; Carbs: 83 g; Fat: 54 g; Protein: 17 g.

11.26 Apricot And Raisin Cake

Preparation time: 20 mins

Cooking time: 12 mins

Servings: 3

Level of difficulty: Easy

Ingredients:

- ½ cup self-rising flour
- 1/3 cup dried apricots
- 4 tbsp. orange juice
- 1 egg
- 4 tbsp. sugar
- 2 tbsp. raisins

Instructions:

- Preheat the air fryer to 400°F.
- Put the dried apricots and juice in a food processor or blender and blend them until they are smooth.
- Put the flour and sugar in a different bowl and mix them together.
- Get the egg ready. It should be added to the flour and sugar and mixed in more.
- Mix in the apricot sauce and raisins.
- You can use an air fryer. Spray a baking pan with some oil. Move the batter and make the top smooth.
- Air fry for 12 minutes, and check on it after 10 minutes. Check with a stick to see if it's done. Put the cake back in the air fryer if you think it needs more time to brown.
- Leave to cool.

Nutritional facts per serving: Calories: 289 Kcal; Carbs: 61 g; Fat: 3 g; Protein: 7 g.

11.27 Pineapple Cake

Preparation time: 20 mins

Cooking time: 40 mins

Servings: 2

Level of difficulty: Intermediate

Ingredients:

- 1¼ cup self-rising flour
- ½ cup caster sugar
- 2 tbsp. whole milk
- ½ cup butter
- ¼ cup pineapple juice
- 2 cups chopped pineapple
- 1 medium egg
- ¼ cup grated dark chocolate

Instructions:

- Preheat the air fryer to 400°F and grease the pan.
- It will look like breadcrumbs if you mix the butter and flour together.
- Put the sugar, juice, pineapple chunks, and dark chocolate in a bowl and mix them together.
- In a jug, mix the milk and egg together.
- Add the liquid to the bread pieces and mix until you get a soft cake batter.
- Bake the cake in the air fryer for 40 minutes.
- Wait for it to cool down before serving.

Nutritional facts per serving: Calories: 91 Kcal; Carbs: 15 g; Fat: 5 g; Protein: 12 g.

11.28 Three Ingredient Cake

Preparation time: 20 mins

Cooking time: 25 mins

Servings: 3

Level of difficulty: Easy

Ingredients:

- 2½ cups iced coffee
- 6 cups mixed dried fruit
- 2 cups self-rising flour

Instructions:

- Put all of the dried fruits together in a very big bowl.
- Mix the iced coffee well with any other drink you want to use.

- Put it in the fridge overnight and cover it with plastic wrap.
- Preheat the air fryer to 350°F.
- Set the cake pan away after greasing it and lining it with baking paper.
- Prepare the cake box and pour the fruit mixture into it. Then mix the self-rising flour with it.
- Put it in the air fryer and bake it for about 25 minutes, or until the cake is hard in the middle and a toothpick put into it comes out with a few wet crumbs on it.

Nutritional facts per serving: Calories: 193 Kcal; Carbs: 84 g; Fat: 2 g; Protein: 15 g.

11.29 Eggless Cake

Preparation time: 20 mins

Cooking time: 12 mins

Servings: 4

Level of difficulty: Easy

Ingredients:

- 2/3 cup all-purpose flour
- 2 tsp. warm water
- 3 tsp. vanilla extract
- 5 tbsp. white sugar
- 3/8 tsp. baking soda
- 3 tbsp. cocoa powder
- 3 tbsp. olive oil
- 5 tbsp. coconut milk
- Oil spray

Instructions:

- Preheat the air fryer to 350°F.
- Mix dry ingredients. Blend the egg and the rest of the wet ingredients together.
- Assemble the dry and wet ingredients together.
- Put the mix into a pan that has already been greased.
- In the air fryer, put the cake pan and cook it on air fry mode for 12 minutes.
- Put a toothpick in and see if it comes out clean to see if it's done.
- Let it cool down before you serve it.

Nutritional facts per serving: Calories: 283 Kcal; Carbs: 34 g; Fat: 15 g; Protein: 4 g.

11.30 Chocolate Oatmeal Cookies

Preparation time: 20 mins

Cooking time: 12 mins

Servings: 3

Level of difficulty: Expert

Ingredients:

- 3 cups quick-cooking oatmeal
- 2/3 cup cocoa powder
- 2 cups chocolate chips
- 2 cups all-purpose flour
- 2 tsp. baking soda
- 7 oz. instant chocolate pudding mix
- 1 cup brown sugar
- 2 cups softened butter
- 2 tsp. vanilla extract
- 3 eggs
- Non-stick cooking spray

Instructions:

- Preheat the air fryer to 350°F.
- Spray nonstick cooking spray on the air fryer sheet.
- In a bowl, mix the cocoa powder, brown sugar, salt, baking soda, flour, and oats.
- Use a hand mixer to mix the brown sugar and cream butter in a different bowl.
- Put in the eggs and vanilla extract.
- In a big bowl, mix the oats with the other ingredients.
- Toss in the chocolate chips and mix everything together well.
- Make cookie scoop shapes out of dough and drop them on a baking sheet.
- In the air fryer, bake the cookies for 12 minutes or until it turns light brown.
- Cool on a wire rack, and then serve.

Nutritional facts per serving: Calories: 203 Kcal; Carbs: 92 g; Fat: 40 g; Protein: 30 g.

Chapter 12: Guide To Cleaning And Maintenance Of Air Fryer

In recent years, air fryers have grown to be one of the most often used kitchen equipment. They let you indulge in your favorite fried dishes without putting on extra fat or calories. To guarantee their durability and peak performance, air fryers need to be cleaned and maintained on a regular basis, just like any other kitchen equipment. We'll guide you through the process of cleaning and maintaining your air fryer for years to come in this chapter.

12.1 The Importance of Cleaning and Maintaining Your Air Fryer

Cooking oil, grease, and food residue can build up in air fryers, reducing their lifespan and functionality. Frequent cleaning keeps these materials from accumulating and guarantees that your air fryer is operating at its best.

12.2 Cleaning Tips for Your Air Fryer

- Cleaning the Pan and Basket: Take the pan and basket out of the air fryer and give them a good cleaning in warm, soapy water. To remove any food residue, you may alternatively use a sponge or brush without any abrasives. Before putting them back in the air fryer, give them a thorough rinse and drying.

- Heating Element Cleaning: Wipe the heating element off with a moist cloth or sponge. Avoid scratching or damaging the component since this may impair its operation.

- Cleaning the Outside: Use a moist cloth or sponge to clean the air fryer's outside. Steer clear of using strong chemicals or abrasive materials, as this might cause harm to the air fryer's surface.

12.3 Maintenance of Air Fryer

- Preheat Your Air Fryer: A few minutes of preheating your air fryer before cooking can assist to enhance cooking results and reduce sticking.

- Using the Appropriate Cooking Time and Temperature: Make sure you always cook your food according to the appropriate temperature and time. Your air fryer may get damaged by overcooking or undercooking, which can also change the flavor and texture of your food.

- Inspecting and Replacing the Air Fryer Filter: A few air fryers contain filters that require routine inspection and cleaning. Your air fryer's performance may suffer from poor air circulation caused by a dirty or clogged filter.

To ensure the durability and best functioning of your air fryer, it is imperative that you clean and maintain it. You can make sure your air fryer lasts for many years and continues to provide tasty and healthful meals by adhering to these easy measures. For precise cleaning and maintenance recommendations, never forget to consult the manufacturer's instructions.

Chapter 13: Weekly Cooking Plan

13.1 Week 1

Monday

Breakfast: Fluffy Cheesy Omelet

Lunch: Chicken Ham Casserole

Dinner: Pork Chops with Broccoli

Calorie intake: 216 Kcal+ 320 Kcal+ 310 Kcal.

Tuesday

Breakfast: Crust-Less Quiche

Lunch: Saucy Garam Masala Fish

Dinner: Teriyaki Beef

Calorie intake: 348 Kcal+ 190 Kcal+ 377 Kcal.

Wednesday

Breakfast: Milky Scrambled Eggs

Lunch: Glazed Pork Belly

Dinner: Pork Tenderloin

Calorie intake: 351 Kcal+ 184 Kcal+ 543 Kcal.

Thursday

Breakfast: Toasties and Sausage in Egg Pond

Lunch: Alfredo Chicken

Dinner: Sweet Pork Barbecue

Calorie intake: 261 Kcal+ 458 Kcal+ 170 Kcal.

Friday

Breakfast: Banana Bread

Lunch: Thanksgiving Turkey

Dinner: Teriyaki Lamb Chops

Calorie intake: 295 Kcal+ 393Kcal + 377 Kcal.

Saturday

Breakfast: Bacon Cups

Lunch: Orange and Maple Glazed Chicken

Dinner: Milky Lamb

Calorie intake: 260 Kcal+ 672 Kcal+ 281 Kcal.

Sunday

Breakfast: Ham Omelet

Lunch: Tandoori Chicken Legs

Dinner: Black Pepper Parmesan Salmon

Calorie intake: 255 Kcal+ 588 Kcal+ 354 Kcal.

13.2 Week 2

Monday

Breakfast: Banana Bread

Lunch: Thanksgiving Turkey

Dinner: Teriyaki Lamb Chops

Calorie intake: 295 Kcal+ 393Kcal + 377 Kcal.

Tuesday

Breakfast: Milky Scrambled Eggs

Lunch: Glazed Pork Belly

Dinner: Pork Tenderloin

Calorie intake: 351 Kcal+ 184 Kcal+ 543 Kcal.

Wednesday

Breakfast: Fluffy Cheesy Omelet

Lunch: Chicken Ham Casserole

Dinner: Pork Chops with Broccoli

Calorie intake: 216 Kcal+ 320 Kcal+ 310 Kcal.

Thursday

Breakfast: Crust-Less Quiche

Lunch: Saucy Garam Masala Fish

Dinner: Teriyaki Beef

Calorie intake: 348 Kcal+ 190 Kcal+ 377 Kcal.

Friday

Breakfast: Toasties and Sausage in Egg Pond

Lunch: Alfredo Chicken

Dinner: Sweet Pork Barbecue

Calorie intake: 261 Kcal+ 458 Kcal+ 170 Kcal.

Saturday

Breakfast: Ham Omelet

Lunch: Tandoori Chicken Legs

Dinner: Black Pepper Parmesan Salmon

Calorie intake: 255 Kcal+ 588 Kcal+ 354 Kcal.

Sunday

Breakfast: Bacon Cups

Lunch: Orange and Maple Glazed Chicken

Dinner: Milky Lamb

Calorie intake: 260 Kcal+ 672 Kcal+ 281 Kcal.

13.3 Week 3

Monday

Breakfast: English Muffins Pizza

Lunch: Herbed Fried Chicken

Dinner: Spicy Crunchy Salmon

Calorie intake: 255 Kcal+ 344 Kcal+ 301 Kcal.

Tuesday

Breakfast: Blueberries Oats Muffin

Lunch: BBQ Fried Chicken

Dinner: Pork Meat and Cabbage Rolls

Calorie intake: 426 Kcal+ 412 Kcal+ 620 Kcal.

Wednesday

Breakfast: Savory Breakfast Muffins

Lunch: Greek Garlic Chicken

Dinner: Rubbed Steaks

Calorie intake: 342 Kcal+ 244 Kcal+ 290 Kcal.

Thursday

Breakfast: Breakfast Omelet

Lunch: Black Pepper Chicken Thighs

Dinner: Asian Flavored Pork Chops

Calorie intake: 163 Kcal+ 206 Kcal+ 90 Kcal.

Friday

Breakfast: Breakfast Potatoes

Lunch: Cheesy Chicken Sausage Rolls

Dinner: Thai Style Beef

Calorie intake: 281 Kcal+ 212 Kcal+ 433 Kcal.

Saturday

Breakfast: English Style Breakfast

Lunch: Japanese Chicken Tenders

Dinner: Gingery Pork Meatballs

Calorie intake: 617 Kcal+ 260 Kcal+ 620 Kcal.

Sunday

Breakfast: Baked Cheesy Eggs

Lunch: Chicken Enchiladas

Dinner: Juicy Pork Chops

Calorie intake: 215 Kcal+ 817 Kcal+ 569 Kcal.

13.4 Week 4

Monday

Breakfast: Breakfast Omelet

Lunch: Black Pepper Chicken Thighs

Dinner: Asian Flavored Pork Chops

Calorie intake: 163 Kcal+ 206 Kcal+ 90 Kcal.

Tuesday

Breakfast: Breakfast Potatoes

Lunch: Cheesy Chicken Sausage Rolls

Dinner: Thai Style Beef

Calorie intake: 281 Kcal+ 212 Kcal+ 433 Kcal.

Wednesday

Breakfast: English Muffins Pizza

Lunch: Herbed Fried Chicken

Dinner: Spicy Crunchy Salmon

Calorie intake: 255 Kcal+ 344 Kcal+ 301 Kcal.

Thursday

Breakfast: Blueberries Oats Muffin

Lunch: BBQ Fried Chicken

Dinner: Pork Meat and Cabbage Rolls

Calorie intake: 426 Kcal+ 412 Kcal+ 620 Kcal.

Friday

Breakfast: Savory Breakfast Muffins

Lunch: Greek Garlic Chicken

Dinner: Rubbed Steaks

Calorie intake: 342 Kcal+ 244 Kcal+ 290 Kcal.

Saturday

Breakfast: Blueberries Oats Muffin

Lunch: BBQ Fried Chicken

Dinner: Pork Meat and Cabbage Rolls

Calorie intake: 426 Kcal+ 412 Kcal+ 620 Kcal.

Sunday

Breakfast: Crust-Less Quiche

Lunch: Saucy Garam Masala Fish

Dinner: Teriyaki Beef
Calorie intake: 348 Kcal+ 190 Kcal+ 377 Kcal.

Chapter 14: Food Storage

Every day in the kitchen, people store food to avoid wastage. You know you need to do certain things to keep your food safe to eat again and avoid getting sick from it, especially if it's rice.

But are you keeping your cooked food in the right way? Soups and stews are easy to keep fresh. Put it in a dry jar and put it in the fridge. It's harder to store hot food, though. This is because if you take a bite out of cooked food, it will get mushy, soft, and not very tasty. It stops being crunchy and crispy on the outside.

14.1 Containers And Packaging Recommendations:

The main goal of packaging is to keep food from drying out and to keep its color, taste, texture, and nutritional value. There will be labels on the bags that say if the food can be frozen. The following traits should be present in good packaging material:

- Made of food-grade materials, which means they are made to be used with food.
- Moisture-proof or at least moisture resistant.
- It's strong and won't leak and it doesn't get weak and crack when it gets cold.
- Can handle water, oil, and grease.
- Keep foods from getting bad smells and tastes.
- It's simple to fill and seal.
- Simple to store and mark.

14.2 Cooling Procedure Before Storage

Food is best kept when it is cool, no matter how you store it. Putting this in your fridge will not only make its job easier, but it will also keep food from making condensation.

Condensation is when heat changes the water atoms in the air back into liquids. In the event that your hot food is stuck in a container, this can happen instead of cooling down. The steam from your newly fried food causes condensation, which means that water will form in the container. You can taste this water in your fried food now that it has been kept. To avoid this, let the food cool down before putting it in a container.

Not sure if your food has all the oil it can lose or is as cool as it needs to be to keep it from condensation while it's being stored? Putting a napkin or paper towel at the base of the container under the food will soak up any extra oil. The paper will also soak up some of the water that forms from condensation, not the food.

14.3 Refrigerator Storage

Food that has already been cooked should be kept in the fridge at 40 F or less and eaten within 3 to 4 days. The USDA says that putting food in the fridge slows the growth of germs but does not stop it.

After the food is cooked and cooled, put it in the fridge within two hours of letting it sit out at room temperature. Put any leftover food in a jar that won't let air in and put it in the fridge (at 40 F or less). Make sure to write the date and what's inside on the container.

14.4 Freezer Storage

The best method to store food is to freeze it. Making plans ahead of time will help you save money. Putting food in the freezer before it goes bad will also help you waste less of it.

If you freeze food the right way, it will stay safe to eat forever, but its flavour and texture may reduce over time.

The rules for good freezing are the same whether you have a chest freezer or a standing freezer.

How long should you keep food in the freezer, and at what temperature?

When you can store frozen items, it depends on the type of food and the fridge you have. The number of stars on a freezer tells you how long the food can be kept safely. You should look at both the number of stars and the directions on frozen food that comes in a package. This will help you figure out how long the frozen food in packages can stay in the freezer. Also, keep in mind that coolers should be kept at -18°C.

Let the food cool down before putting it in the freezer.

When you freeze hot food, the freezer temperature will rise, which could make other foods start to melt. Cutting the food into smaller pieces can help it cool down faster.

Make sure the food is properly wrapped or put it in cases with lids.

Food can get "freezer-burn" if you don't seal it. What this means is that water leaves the food and goes to the freezer's coolest part, drying out the food. Even though this makes the food less good, it is still safe to eat.

Freeze food in amounts that are reasonable

You don't want to have to thaw a pot that's meant to feed eight people when your family of three is only there.

Put a label on everything you freeze

Without clear labels, you might not even remember what the foods or ingredients are or when you froze them. Get a red marker for foods that are cooked and a blue marker for foods that are raw. Always write down the date it was frozen.

Look at the "use-by" date

After the "use-by" date, don't freeze any food because it won't be safe to eat.

Don't let ice form

Ice in the freezer makes it less useful, so thaw it if it starts to build up. The food won't go bad; most of it will stay frozen in the fridge for a few hours while the freezer defrosts.

If you're not sure, throw it away

Bacteria can still live after being frozen. Don't take any chances with something that you don't know how long it has been frozen or that you are wary of once it has thawed.

14.5 Labelling And Dating

Labelling the food helps you keep track of what's in the fridge. When you put the labels on the food, you can see what's in the fridge. On the sticker, it should say when the food was stored and when it goes bad. This makes it easier to use up the oldest items first.

14.6 Reheating And Annealing

Are you tired of being let down every time you reheat leftovers and they turn out sloppy, sad, and bland?

If you know how to use an air fryer to reheat food, you can turn those boring leftovers into meals that taste as good as they did the day they were made.

Reheating food in an air fryer is so quick and easy that you won't want to do it any other way! This is true whether the food was cooked in the air fryer or another way.

The same steps are used to cook food for the first time and to heat up leftovers. The main change is that you will cook at a lower temperature to keep the food from drying out too much.

Your food will always be properly heated and taste great, which will amaze you!

Chapter 15: Sauce Recipes

15.1 Jelly Chili Li'l Smokies

Preparation time: 5 mins

Cooking time: 10 mins

Servings: 4

Level of difficulty: Easy

Ingredients:

- ½ cup grape jelly
- smoked sausages
- ½ cup chili sauce

Instructions:

- Put the smoked sausages in the basket and set the timer for 5 minutes at 350°F.
- To get to a dish, remove.
- Add grape juice and chili sauce and mix well.

Nutritional facts per serving: Calories: 436 Kcal; Carbs: 28 g; Fat: 12 g; Protein: 20 g.

15.2 S'mores Dip

Preparation time: 3 mins

Cooking time: 5 mins

Servings: 10

Level of difficulty: Easy

Ingredients:

- 10 oz. semi-sweet chocolate chips
- Graham crackers
- 30 marshmallows large

Instructions:

- The first step is to heat up your air fryer. Set the temperature to 350°F for about 3 minutes.
- Before you move on, make sure that the chocolate chips are spread out properly in the cake pan.
- Use just thirty marshmallows.
- Air-fry for 4 to 5 minutes at 350°F to get a golden-brown top and a marshmallow that jiggles.
- Serve s'mores dip with graham crackers.

Nutritional facts per serving: Calories: 236 Kcal; Carbs: 93 g; Fat: 2 g; Protein: 1 g.

15.3 Fry Sauce

Preparation time: 5 mins

Cooking time: 2 mins

Servings: 24

Level of difficulty: Easy

Ingredients:

- 3 cups Mayonnaise Real
- 1 tbsp. Franks Buffalo Sauce
- ½ cup Ketchup
- 2 tsp. Worcestershire sauce
- 1 tbsp. bread and butter pickle juice
- ¼ tsp. paprika
- ¼ tsp. ancho powder chili
- ½ tsp. seasoned salt

Instructions:

- Put everything in a medium bowl and whisk it together until it's smooth.
- Set your air fryer to 225°F and cook for three to four minutes.

Nutritional facts per serving: Calories: 149 Kcal; Carbs: 2 g; Fat: 16 g; Protein: 1 g.

15.4 Bolognese Sauce

Preparation time: 5 mins

Cooking time: 35 mins

Servings: 2

Level of difficulty: Intermediate

Ingredients:

- 8 oz. lean beef ground
- 1 oz. carrot
- 3 oz. onion
- 1 clove garlic, minced
- 1 oz. celery
- 15 oz. tomatoes crushed
- 1 tbsp. olive oil
- ½ tbsp. oregano dried
- 2 tbsp. basil leaves fresh
- ½ tbsp. parsley dried

- salt and pepper, to taste
- ½ tbsp. basil dried
- 2 tbsp. Parmesan cheese, grated

Instructions:

- Cut the onion and garlic into small pieces. Dice the carrots and celery into pieces that are no bigger than ¼ inch. To cook faster, the carrots and celery need to be cut up very small.
- It will take five minutes to heat up your air fryer to 375°F.
- Place the ground beef on top of half of a hot air fryer tray. Place the celery, onions, carrots, and garlic on the other side of the tray. Add the olive oil to the veggies and toss them around to coat them. The tray should go on the top rack of the air fryer oven.
- Air-fried for five minutes at 375°F. If you need to, use a meat tool to break up the beef until it is crumbly. The sauce won't make the carrots and celery too soft. If you need to, keep cooking them in the air fryer for a few more minutes.
- Cover an 8-inch-by-8-inch aluminum pan with parchment paper. Put the meat and vegetables in the pan. Taste and add salt and pepper to your liking. Then add the dried basil, oregano, crushed tomatoes, and parsley. Put foil around the pan to keep air out. For about 35 to 45 minutes, air fry on the rack inside the air fryer at 375°F. Wait five minutes and let the sauce cool down.

Nutritional facts per serving: Calories: 256 Kcal; Carbs: 19 g; Fat: 15 g; Protein: 23 g.

15.5 Roasted Hot Sauce

Preparation time: 2 mins

Cooking time: 10 mins

Servings: 4

Level of difficulty: Easy

Ingredients:

- 3 Roma tomatoes
- 2 jalapeños
- 1 yellow onion
- 2 tbsp. garlic
- 2 tbsp. cilantro
- 2 tbsp. salt

Instructions:

- Put everything except for the parsley and garlic in the air fryer basket.
- Put the basket back into the air fryer and cook at 385°F for the time given at that temperature.
- Once the timer goes off, blend what's in the basket. Serve it with chopped cilantro and a sprinkle of salt.

Nutritional facts per serving: Calories: 25 Kcal; Carbs: 5 g; Fat: 0 g; Protein: 1 g.

Chapter 16: Allergen Free Recipes

16.1 Buffalo Broccoli Bites

Preparation time: 20 mins

Cooking time: 20 mins

Servings: 1

Level of difficulty: Easy

Ingredients:

- 2 tsp. seasoning
- ¼ head of cauliflower, florets
- 1/6 cup cayenne pepper sauce
- 2 tbsp. melted butter
- 1 cup almond flour
- ¼ cup ranch dressing, for dipping

Instructions:

- Turn off the air fryer after heating it up to the lowest setting. Change it to the "keep warm" setting instead.
- Bundles of broccoli should be put in a big bowl.
- Melt the butter and mix it with the cayenne pepper sauce in a small bowl. Then, pour the sauce over the cauliflower. Well mix everything together.
- In a different big bowl or large plastic bag that can be closed again and again, mix the almond flour and spices. Add the broccoli to the bag or bowl that has the breading in it.
- You don't want to add too much sauce, so use tongs or a forked spoon. Shake the broccoli in the breading to cover it.
- Use both the bottom and top racks to keep the broccoli from getting too crowded as you move half of the covered broccoli to the air fryer.
- The air fryer should be set to 350°F. Cook the broccoli for 12 to 15 minutes, or until it is light brown and cooked all the way through but not mushy.
- Put the broccoli that has been cooked on a sheet pan and put it in the air fryer to keep it warm. Keep using the air fryer to cook the rest of the broccoli.
- Add as much cayenne pepper as you like to the ranch dressing to make the buffalo ranch dipping sauce. Enjoy the buffalo broccoli with sauce.

Nutritional facts per serving: Calories: 695 Kcal; Carbs: 89 g; Fat: 31 g; Protein: 17 g.

16.2 Bacon Avocado Fries

Preparation time: 12 mins

Cooking time: 8 mins

Servings: 1

Level of difficulty: Easy

Ingredients:

- 1/4 cup ranch dressing
- 1 avocado
- 8 slices of bacon

Instructions:

- Cut each avocado into 8 wedges of the same size. Cut the bacon into strips if you need to. Wrap each piece in a bacon strip. Put them in the air fryer basket in a single layer and cook for 8 minutes, at 400°F until it is crispy and cooked all the way through.
- Serve with ranch dressing.

Nutritional facts per serving: Calories: 228 Kcal; Carbs: 20 g; Fat: 11 g; Protein: 36 g.

16.3 Cajun Cod

Preparation time: 10 mins

Cooking time: 10 mins

Servings: 4

Level of difficulty: Easy

Ingredients:

- 1 lb. cod filets
- 2 tbsp. melted butter
- 1 tbsp. Cajun seasoning
- ½ cup pork rinds, crushed
- 2 tsp. fresh minced garlic

Instructions:

- Preheat Air fryer to 450°F.
- Mix all the ingredients except for fish well in a small bowl or food processor.
- Press the pork rind mixture onto the cod filets, covering the top evenly and pressing the crust into the fish.
- The filets need 10 minutes in air fryer that has already been preheated. The crust on top should have a nice brown color.
- Serve while it's still hot.

Nutritional facts per serving: Calories: 350 Kcal; Carbs: 2 g; Fat: 20 g; Protein: 40 g.

16.4 Lemon Pepper Cod

Preparation time: 10 mins

Cooking time: 10 mins

Servings: 4

Level of difficulty: Intermediate

Ingredients:

- 1 lb. cod
- 1½ cups ground pork rinds
- ½ tsp. ground black pepper
- 2 tbsp. mustard
- ¼ cup mayonnaise
- 1 tsp. lemon pepper seasoning
- ½ tsp. salt
- 2 tbsp. almond milk

Instructions:

- Preheat your air fryer to 400°F. With a paper towel, pat the cod filets to dry them. Cut the fish into strips about an inch wide and two inches long.
- Mix the mustard, mayonnaise, and milk together well in a small bowl.
- Mix the salt, and lemon pepper seasoning in a separate bowl.
- Dip the fish strips into the mayonnaise mixture and then into the pork rind mixture, making sure the fish is fully covered. Put it on the basket of air fryer and cook the fish for 5 minutes, then flip it and cook for another 5 minutes. Serve quickly!

Nutritional facts per serving: Calories: 250 Kcal; Carbs: 1 g; Fat: 15 g; Protein: 30 g.

16.5 Chicken Fajitas

Preparation time: 10 mins

Cooking time: 15 mins

Servings: 4

Level of difficulty: Easy

Ingredients:

- 1 lb. boneless, chicken breasts, cut into strips
- 1 red onion, cut into wedges
- 1 tsp. ground cumin
- 1 tsp. chili powder
- 1 tsp. Dijon mustard
- 2 tbsp. olive oil
- 2 garlic cloves, sliced

- 2 bell peppers, seeded and sliced
- salt and black pepper, to taste
- 4 whole-wheat tortillas

Instructions:

- Preheat the Air fryer to 375°F.
- Olive oil, black pepper, salt, bell peppers, mustard, cumin, garlic, and chili powder should be mixed with the chicken strips to marinate them.
- In a small baking pan, put the peppers and chicken.
- For 15 minutes, or until the chicken registers 165°F on a meat thermometer, roast the peppers and chicken in the preheated air fryer.
- With tortillas and onion wedges, assemble your fajitas. Enjoy!

Nutritional facts per serving: Calories: 400 Kcal; Carbs: 25 g; Fat: 20 g; Protein: 30 g.

Conclusion

After reading this guide and trying some of the recipes, you should have a good idea of how versatile and useful your air fryer is.

It doesn't matter how good you are at cooking. This book can be used by anyone.
No matter how much you know about cooking tools, this cookbook has all that you need to know about this hot trend. You now know everything you need to know about the Air Fryer and how easy it is to make a tasty meal with just a few easy steps.

A lot of people are crazy about the Air Fryer right now, and for good reason. It's better for you, easier, and cleaner to cook with. Getting the whole family involved in making dinner is a great way to make cooking fun! You can make your favourite foods healthy without giving up any taste with the help of the Air Fryer Cookbook. It is possible to make sure your family eats healthy foods that taste great. No longer do you have to feel bad about what you feed your family. That's right; you don't have to feel bad after eating healthy things you love.

Food that is deep-fried no longer needs all the extra calories and fat it adds. If you cook in an air fryer, you can get the same great taste without the extra calories and fat. No longer do you have to feel bad about eating tasty food. You learned how to make delicious meals in an air fryer that are just as good as those made in a deep fryer, but with less calories and fat. Now you know that the food you eat is good for you and tastes good. There will be a place on your counter for the Air Fryer Cookbook for many years to come. Let go of all the unhealthy foods you used to eat and start living a better life. It's time to enjoy cooking again.

Not only should you not limit yourself to the recipes in this guide, you should try new things, too! Try out some new recipes! Try out different spices, ingredients, and cooking ways! Keep your mind open and come up with some new ideas. This is what you should do to get the most out of your air fryer.

Printed in Great Britain
by Amazon